THE
HOSPICE
HANDBOOK

THE

HOSPICE

HANDBOOK

**NURSE DEBBIE'S COMPASSIONATE GUIDE
TO NAVIGATING END-OF-LIFE CARE**

Debbie J. Johnston R.N.

Advantage.

Published by Advantage, Charleston, South Carolina.
Member of Advantage Media Group.

ADVANTAGE is a registered trademark, and the Advantage colophon is a trademark of Advantage Media Group, Inc.

Printed in the United States of America.

10 9 8 7 6 5 4 3 2 1

ISBN: 978-1-64225-305-4
LCCN: 2022902423

Cover design by David Taylor.
Layout design by Wesley Strickland.

This publication is designed to provide accurate and authoritative information in regard to the subject matter covered. It is sold with the understanding that the publisher is not engaged in rendering legal, accounting, or other professional services. If legal advice or other expert assistance is required, the services of a competent professional person should be sought.

 Advantage Media Group is proud to be a part of the Tree Neutral® program. Tree Neutral offsets the number of trees consumed in the production and printing of this book by taking proactive steps such as planting trees in direct proportion to the number of trees used to print books. To learn more about Tree Neutral, please visit **www.treeneutral.com**.

Advantage Media Group is a publisher of business, self-improvement, and professional development books and online learning. We help entrepreneurs, business leaders, and professionals share their Stories, Passion, and Knowledge to help others Learn & Grow. Do you have a manuscript or book idea that you would like us to consider for publishing? Please visit **advantagefamily.com**.

To my parents, Eunice and Richard (Pappy) Johnston, who were my greatest cheerleaders, mentors, and teachers and who loved me enough to adopt me at age three. They are the reason I've gotten where I am. I am so lucky to have had both of them as parents, and I love them to the moon and back!

Contents

Navigating Hospice Care with Nurse Debbie

If there comes a day we can't be together, keep
me in your heart. I'll stay there forever.
—WINNIE THE POOH

When we say, "Keep me in your heart," to someone special to us, it's not just a cozy platitude. We're saying love is more powerful than time and space. Love binds us together when we're separated from each other by an ocean or a mountain or even by the veil that separates this world from eternity. "Keep me in your heart" says we *know* we are more than these bodies we live in and that death isn't the end. But our passing is still a daunting prospect, the greatest mystery each of us will ever face. So who wouldn't want support as we approach death, either our own or our loved ones'?

Welcome to my book about hospice care and how it takes that beautiful sentiment, "Keep me in your heart," seriously. I'm Nurse Debbie, your compassionate, cheerful—and always opinionated—guide. When I get talking about my passion for hospice and what it can do for my patients and their families, I have a lot to say, and I do so with gladness in my heart. I look forward to spending some quality time together. You're here to learn more about how to navigate end-of-life situations, and I'm here to help.

Thanks to my being brought up by loving parents in a supportive, happy home, I have a huge heart and a friendly ear. I know beyond a doubt that I was meant to become a nurse. Very ill patients and their family and friends need to be seen and heard. Do they ever! So I listen. And I hug. And I love on my patients as much as they'll let me. It makes everyone's suffering a little bit more bearable to know other people care.

I care. I care so much I've spent the majority of my adult life as a nurse helping others up close and personal, and now I want to help you. We might never meet face-to-face in a hospital room or in your home, where your sick loved one might be in hospice care. But that's okay. We can get a lot done together here.

Before I get into the nitty-gritty of what my book is about—which is helping you feel more comfortable navigating the last phase of life for someone you love or even preparing for your own final days—I want to assure you that when it comes to seriously ill folks and how they and their families cope, I've seen it all. Not everyone has had experience dealing with the stress that comes with witnessing the hospitalization of a loved one and their eventual transition to hospice care. But someday that scenario will likely happen to almost all of us. It's a good idea to know how to prepare, whether that time is near or still far away and whether it's your loved one in that hospital bed or you.

And please don't feel guilty, embarrassed, or nervous if you're totally unfamiliar with hospice and what it entails. Plenty of people have no idea what it really is, even though they've lost family members, friends, or colleagues. When death nears, many people close their circle entirely or make it smaller, which means only a very few people know what's going on. So it's not uncommon to witness another person's passing from the sidelines, where you're not privy to information.

Or it could be you've never lost an immediate family member or someone close to you at all. Inevitably, though, you'll find yourself in that place. The cycle of life affects us all at some point. So I'll say it again because this is so important: it's a good idea to know in advance what hospice is and what it can provide.

Of course I understand that you, my reader friends, have different schedules and your own preferred way to take in new information, so please feel free to read this straight through, or a page at a time, or even start from back to front. Just know that you'll feel better afterward, however you dig in to these pages. I promise!

Hospice Care Is a True Gift

Believe it or not, hospice helps us find joy in a trying time. It allows us to celebrate a person's unique life. Everyone deserves an acknowledgment of their birthday each year, don't you think? A cake, a hug, a heartfelt card? Once a person's perspective shifts to realizing that *each day* they live is precious—and claiming each day becomes a genuine physical, emotional, and spiritual accomplishment—that person deserves to be shown love, respect, and appreciation even more.

And on the flip side, in addition to enjoying extra attention, patients faced with their own mortality want normalcy. They want to laugh. They want to forget the big issues and relax into the everyday rituals of life they might have had for many decades. No matter what their individual preferences for care, patients in hospice long to be comforted and feel that they matter. Hospice gives us that opportunity. It is a true gift.

We're Stronger Than We Realize

You may be afraid that reading about hospice will bring you down right when you need to be strong. You've likely received scary news about either yourself or someone you love receiving a diagnosis of a terminal illness. But I want you to take a second to think back to when you were a kid. Remember how the best campfire stories and fairy tales scared the heck out of us and kept us on the edge of our seats worried about our favorite characters? A prince couldn't ride his horse up an iced-over mountain. Snow White ate a poisoned apple. Hansel and Gretel were almost roasted alive by a witch. But by the end, the bad guys were vanquished, and the good people lived happily ever after. Thank goodness!

These stories taught us that life ain't easy, but it's doable. Not only that, when we handle it with grit and grace, it can be downright glorious. As impressionable young children, we learned that the key is to listen to your gut and follow your heart, especially when you're dealing with the hard questions and the big challenges you'll inevitably face.

I want to remind the stressed-out adult version of you (who's probably left that wondrous campfire mentality far behind) that those old stories we listened to as kids told a rock-solid truth that you'll also find in this book about end-of-life care: our bodies are vulnerable. We *will* die eventually. But the human spirit is invincible. Knock it down repeatedly, and it comes back up fighting.

Let me give you one more very recent real-life example of why reading about hospice care is something you can definitely handle. If there's anything good that came from the COVID-19 era, it was the millions of extraordinary displays, both on a grand scale and small, of our resilience. The clapping for hospital workers. Chalk drawings on sidewalks to cheer up the neighbors. Wistful, encouraging hugs through panes of glass.

And I say all this not as a mere onlooker to the phenomenon of our hardiness but as a full-fledged participant in the battle to survive the pandemic, to protect what I love and what we all love: our family, friends, and communities. I lost friends, employees, and patients. I know plenty of people who lost family. And who doesn't know someone who lost a job? Who had to move because an income stream dried up? Who didn't see at least one of their favorite restaurants or shops close permanently, places we had deep personal connections to?

God bless us all. Not one person on this planet was able to call time-out from the ongoing anxiety the COVID-19 era brought to the planet. Pockets of darkness, despair, and wretched grief brought us low. If we think hard enough, we can get right back to that hollow, scared feeling we carried in the pit of our stomach for months on end with no letup. Just seeing a UPS box on the front porch and trying to figure out how to bring it indoors was a trial. Going to the grocery store was a true challenge. Figuring out how to cancel a wedding, hold a funeral, or celebrate a holiday when no one could be there came near to breaking us.

Yet here we are, still standing, and here *you* are, opening this book, afraid maybe, but hoping for knowledge, inspiration, a way forward. And I'm here to assure you, you will find it. You, the same person who made it through COVID-19, will find your way through the many questions you have about end-of-life care. We will find our way together.

Being brave when death looms is an anxiety-provoking prospect. But with courage to act in alignment with your principles comes peace of mind, a sense that it was hard, but you did the right thing. You did your duty, and you're proud of yourself. You might be aggrieved, you might be mad at the world, but you can lay your head on your pillow at night and have no regrets. You can sleep the peaceful sleep of the wise warrior who protected their loved ones to their very last breaths or faced your own future, the inevitable end, with self-compassion and courage.

We Can Walk This Path Together

Y'all, I'm a lot of things to a lot of people: a hand-holder at the bedside of a vulnerable human about to leave this world, a caregiver to thousands of ailing patients over decades of my life as a registered nurse, an entrepreneur who knows the home healthcare industry inside and out, and a philanthropist who's won numerous good citizenship awards. I'm a nurturing boss to hundreds of employees and a nonprofit creator and state leader in adoption advocacy. I'm also a gosh-darned reality TV star! Above all, I pride myself on being a loving daughter, sister, aunt, and friend.

But all those identities aside, at my very essence, I'm simply a child of God like you. Sometimes when we are stripped down to that core of who we are, we can feel the opposite of comforted; we can feel alone, frail, lost. And the unfortunate thing is that when we're at our most vulnerable, that's often when our biggest challenges come. We grapple with universal questions about life and death, and too often it feels like we're facing them by ourselves: How do I take care of the people I love in their last days? How do I want my own story to conclude in its final moments?

It was this sense of aloneness in a time of challenge in my own life that inspired me to write this book. Having lost my dear mother and with my beloved father currently in hospice, as knowledgeable as I am about hospital settings and illness, I still have had many moments of feeling small, scared, and confused. Before I felt confident navigating this bumpy road about end-of-life care, I faltered. I took a few wrong turns. My professional experience was at loggerheads with my very strong personal wishes, which were human and natural—to keep my loved one alive, to avoid the realities that death brings.

I had only to think about the millions of people in the world dealing with similar trials—good people who want to do the right thing but don't have the professional expertise and hard-won personal wisdom I now have—to be inspired to write this book. I'm talking about healthy or already ill people confronting their own mortality. And I'm also addressing their loving families and friends. That group, in particular the witnesses to end-of-life scenarios, I hear asking for guidance, and I will gladly give it. There's nothing worse than watching helplessly while someone you love suffers. Seriously. I've been there.

And I want to be there for you. If I can give you one more night's decent sleep than you would have had without reading this, I'll be happy. But I'd like to do far more than that. I'd like you to feel so prepared and at peace about your loved one's situation you can go to bed each night and dream the dreams people do who have done their best and given their all. I want you to be proud you lived life to the fullest by embracing not only the fun stuff, which makes life so worth living, but also the difficult, sometimes frightening challenges that remind us how strong we can be, how strong we *are* here and now.

We only need reminding.

No One Should Leave This World
Feeling Abandoned or Alone

If there is any basic human right I want to protect, it is your and your loved ones' right to have a peaceable, dignified death. This book is my attempt to fight fiercely for that. And I want you to as well. You must.

We must. We must cry out as a nation to make it so that no one *ever* dies feeling abandoned or alone.

We all saw the stories about COVID-19 patients dying alone. We might have been witness to this tragedy ourselves within our own circles. It's hard to write about, and I'm truly sorry if it pains you. It does me, so deeply that I have to speak out about it. I feel I have no choice. We need to face this problem as a country and *solve* it so that it never happens again. I offer this book as a platform to start the much-needed conversation.

There were countless heartbreaking deaths of good people denied basic human rights at the time they most needed them. I feel profound sorrow as I recall those individuals and the sense of confusion, pain, loss, and abandonment they surely felt. Many of their stories will slip unheard into history. We will never know the true depth of suffering those people endured.

This appalling situation simply can't happen anymore.

Yes, some people might actually choose to die alone, and that's their right. But during the pandemic, the overwhelmingly vast majority of dying COVID-19 patients would have preferred to have a loved one by their side—or, quite frankly, anyone. A human making eye contact. Holding their hand. Murmuring words of comfort and assurance.

Thousands of medical teams and hospice care workers—God love them—did their best to provide comfort when they could. Their noble efforts should be praised. We should shower them with gratitude. Maybe you're one of those heroes yourself, and if you are, thank you for the role you played in bringing ease to the ailing.

But let's face it. As hard as overworked medical teams tried to help, it wasn't enough. Those suffering patients needed hospice care during the pandemic, and so, so many of them didn't receive it.

This is unacceptable. We don't want this happening again. Who knows when the next pandemic will arrive? It will, at some point. And unless we change how we handle pandemics, the same nightmare scenario could happen to you. To me. To our loved ones.

I say no, and no, and no again!

I want you to read this book and be inspired to fight along with me to change current practices so that every person is afforded the comforting presence of another human being as their life candle burns low and is finally extinguished.

By reading this book, you are walking with me on the road of honoring those people who died feeling abandoned and alone. Together let's make sure it never happens to another soul again. One way you can do that is to understand what hospice is and spread the word about its necessity. Everyone deserves to leave this world in dignity and feeling comforted to their very last breath.

This Book Will Help You on Several Levels

In addition to that important message—that we all deserve compassion and respect to the end—there's so much more I want to share with you. Too often I've seen families attempt to navigate end-of-life situations with no mentors to guide them. I'd be honored to help illuminate this sometimes winding, unpredictable road for you. With that goal always at the forefront of my mind, I wrote this book to help you gain the following:

1. *Knowledge.* It's a game changer. It makes all the difference in the world when you're trying to understand end-of-life matters: What is hospice care exactly? What needs to be done, and why? In what order should these decisions take place? Which decision is more urgent? Which one is more necessary?

Focus is called for. But y'all, it's impossible to focus if you're not feeling confident and at the top of your game. You need to anchor yourself with good information, which frees you up to zero in on whatever scenario presents itself in your particular situation on any given day or moment. Only then can you make the best decisions for your loved one and know that you have done so from a strong, assured place.

Some of that information you'll need to make decisions is not obvious to people who've never gone through a hospice care experience before. I'm here to make it readily available to you.

2. *Options.* Instead of feeling in a corner with no way out, you're going to look around and see that you can exert some control over what's going on. You'll see several ways forward, and you'll choose the one that works best for you or for you and the patient you love who needs compassionate attention.

3. *Hope.* This may be the understatement of the century, but it's a downer working with the cold, hard reality of end-of-life situations. This book will give you hope. Believe me, I am so on board with not wanting to see silver linings when I'm sad and depressed and maybe even angry. I want to feel all the feels and get through them as best I can. Denying our emotions is unhealthy. However, there's a point where you'll likely need support as those feelings grow in intensity. You'll get tired. You'll lose track of your motivation. It won't seem logical to look for hope. But whatever stage your loved one is in, hope is essential to protecting your spirit and theirs most of all. Think of it this way: hope is not a disavowal of reality. It's simply your lifeboat through it.

4. *Comfort.* You're not alone. If there is anything I want you to get from this book, it's this: we are all in this together. It may not look like it from inside the vortex of the crisis, some of which can last not only months but also years. You may be scared about what to do, crying about how sad it all is and trying to be cheerful for your ill loved one. But you are not the first or the last person to struggle, to worry, to suffer as an end-of-life plan advances. This is an obvious point, you'd think, but we forget that death is a common, everyday occurrence. And it's normal to forget. We couldn't function if we were consumed with end-of-life matters all day every day.

But until your own personal life is affected, you just don't see how big a part of the human experience end-of-life situations are. This book will remind you that beneath our daily "busy work," the cycle of life is ever present, a natural part of who we are and how we function as human beings. This book will remind you that, like your own, other people's end-of-life dramas are generally played out behind closed doors, at hospitals and at home. And like everyone else who goes through the stressful, life-altering experience of overseeing a loved one's end-of-life care, you *will* come out the other side. Grief will likely occupy you for as long as you need to grieve. But I promise you that you'll still be able to live and love. *You will.* And you'll be able to do so without remorse over how you handled yourself and the decisions you made in your loved one's final days.

How the Book Works

Sure, we're grown-ups now, but stories are still the best way to learn how to deal with life. Stories make it easier to absorb hard realities. They offer key strategies for coping. And they keep our distractible adult minds, which are often filled with useless mental chatter, focused on vital lessons and useful information, enabling us to easily recall those details later, at crucial times we need them the most. So in almost every chapter, you'll read about someone else's experience with hospice, including my own.

I'll talk about my own life, both personal and professional, and how I came to see hospice care as my ultimate calling. My professional story will reassure you that I am an expert in the field and worthy of your trust. I also hope the personal side of my story, which focuses a lot on my father, Pappy, and his time in and out of hospice, will inspire you to become the best advocate you can possibly be for your loved one entering hospice care or for yourself if you're preparing your own future options.

I'll also provide some surprising advice for the families of hospice patients, along with interviews with hospice caregivers. My patients and their families find it helpful to have a general impression of what the hospice experience is like from the perspective of the caregiver. We'll hear from a doctor, a bereavement counselor, a registered nurse, a social worker, a music therapist, and a hospice aide. They observe the families and the patients and have a lot to say about what they see and hear that could be beneficial to you.

I'll give you the best counsel I can about hospice without actually knowing your personal story. I'll focus on common issues I see crop up all the time among families.

And having been brought up to speak my mind when there's need for improvement or outright change, I'll also address the state of the hospice care industry right now.

Finally I'll wrap up the biggest points I make in the book and provide a call to action for you, my fellow travelers on the hospice care road. Never fear. You'll learn so many good things about yourself and humanity in general from involving yourself in hospice care, starting with what you absorb from this book.

PART 1:

The Basics of Hospice Care

Educated patients and families have better hospice care experiences. So my mission in this section is to provide you all the information and support you'll need to carry you through the highly personal hospice journey either you or your loved one is facing. You'll find invaluable advice here, which I offer to all my readers with love and compassion, along with facts about the many facets of hospice that will not only enlighten you but also bolster your confidence and hope. My aim is for you to discover that this challenging road you're walking is not only doable but also filled with many meaningful opportunities to celebrate life and love to the very end.

CHAPTER 1:

Pappy and Me

Why would anyone—especially someone who's been on ABC's *The Secret Millionaire* and never needs to work another day in her life— start a hospice care center, of all things, when she can hit the links or bask on a beach instead? Isn't it like going into the funeral home business? Isn't everyone involved in hospice care depressed? How the heck can you stay your happy, go-get-'em self in that environment, Nurse Debbie?

I get asked these sorts of questions all the time. And honestly I don't mind them. People have lots of flawed, preconceived notions about hospice care, which I assure you I'll clear up shortly. But let me first give you a better picture of who I am. I'll tell you why my calling in life is to help ease people out of this world with grace and tender loving care. I grew up in the country in Virginia with hardworking parents who loved me and taught me and my brother and four sisters how to be good people. And being a good person means you look at your life with gratitude and try to figure out how to give back for all the blessings you've received. I've done that since I was a little girl and as an adult too, first as a nurse then as an owner of an enormously successful home healthcare company. And I'm still doing it.

Good people don't ever stop counting their blessings and contributing something positive to the world. They take nothing for granted. They see loss and pain and suffering like everyone else. But like the Energizer Bunny, we keep going and going, seeing opportunity in the storm, holding on to hope. We're fueled by the peace we get by being brave enough to truly participate in life, with all its ups and downs, and taking chances. Because when your heart is in the right place, good things will follow.

A Lifetime of Love and Learning Led Me to Open Serenity First

That's what excellent parents give you—the courage and drive to use your gifts and make a positive difference in the world, even when you're sore, exhausted, sad, or confused. As I get older and see the cycle of life so clearly—when I see how I've entered and exited both dark and light times and am still here breathing and standing tall—I know deep in my bones that all that strength and love in me is there for a reason. What better way to show it than by caring for and pro-

tecting the most vulnerable among us, those who are nearing the end of their lives, like my own father?

When I look at Pappy's smiling face and the trust and love in his eyes, I am determined to be the best hospice caregiver in the United States. And the world too. Why not? As God is my witness, I believe I can be that person.

I don't mind saying I completely owe my belief in myself

and my success to Pappy and my dear late mother. They took me in at age three to be their very own daughter when my birth mother, Momma's sister, couldn't care for me anymore. Pappy was a mere twenty-one-year-old when they adopted me! Can you imagine? And then my gorgeous mother went on to have many other babies too. Our house was always filled with laughter and lessons and the sense that no one could slide by thinking only of themselves.

As I grew up, occasionally I'd hear from someone at school that I was different because I was adopted. My own family never treated me that way, but cruel attempts to stigmatize me by ignorant classmates was one reason I worked extra hard to be the best I could be. I wanted to make Pappy and Momma proud.

When I was a little girl, Momma and Pappy gave me a toy nursing kit. As far back as I can remember, Pappy would tell me I'd make a wonderful nurse someday. I'd always planned on being a secretary like my mother, but I took Pappy's advice to heart and began vocational training in high school to become a nurse. I truly loved it, so after high school, I completed the licensed practical nurse (LPN) program. Pappy had been right—nursing suited me as a career path. I thought I'd stop there and get right to work with my LPN certificate, but Pappy had bigger dreams for me. He knew I could be an RN, a registered nurse.

I appreciated how much faith Pappy had in me, but I wasn't sure I would do well in the advanced nursing program. But my parents *and* my vocational teachers told me I could do it, so with their encouragement, I enrolled. And wow, did I ever learn about discipline and adhering to excellent standards of care during my three years' training to be an RN! I grew to love the camaraderie between me and my fellow nurses. We knew our patients did better when we were a wonderful team. It was never easy work, but it was so rewarding being there for people. My life has had such a strong purpose. That feeling still sustains me each morning when I wake up with a determination to make a difference for the better that day.

Eventually I worked as an RN in the discharge area of the hospital and saw patients being sent home before they were ready, thanks to new insurance company rules that encouraged hospitals to turn over those hospital beds as fast as possible. As a consequence people left the hospital "sicker and quicker." I could see in some patients' eyes that they were scared and confused.

It was wrong and bothered my conscience, so I wanted to do something about it. My simple ambition to help those poor patients who were suffering led me to leave my nursing job at the hospital and enter the home healthcare business. At first I worked for a company to learn the ropes, but when I realized how much they relied on me and my ideas without paying me what my efforts were worth, I took myself back to the hospital setting and made a huge impact there by introducing the bigwigs to the concept of home healthcare. But once again, as the hospital ran with my ideas, I was pushed aside.

Finally, with the help of my lawyer and good friend, I decided to believe in myself and start my own company in Virginia. It was not easy. It took every ounce of courage and know-how I had to make it work, but I was determined to. And it did. It grew and grew, and my faith in myself and my gift for helping patients in their time of need did too. Over twenty years my business, Care Advantage, flourished with fifteen offices and hundreds of employees. We helped ease the suffering of thousands of patients, Virginians like Momma and Pappy, at home.

I was still going strong in that business when my sweet mother passed away. I'll never forget how many tests I made the doctors run—anything I could do to keep her alive. But then one day she told me she was going to a wedding. She saw it in her mind's eye. That was her way of telling me she was ready to go, no matter how hard I was trying to save her.

It broke my heart to lose Momma, and it was emotionally gut-wrenching to make those funeral arrangements for her, as it would be for anyone who loses a cherished parent. But ultimately I was able to handle all the responsibilities involved. The big lesson I learned from Momma's passing was that I wished I'd listened a lot better to what she was saying about her own needs instead of panicking and blindly seeking treatment for her at all costs. I don't want you to have those sorts of regrets. Listening to your loved one is so important … recognizing what they're trying to say when they don't necessarily come right out and say it, either because they don't want to upset you or they don't want to upset themselves.

To this day, when I think about sweet Momma, I ask her how that wedding in heaven is going. I know she's dancing and having as much cake as she wants, and I hope she's telling the angels her daughter has learned a lot about recognizing how much she can control and not control when it comes to end-of-life situations.

Fifteen years after Momma left us, life took an unexpected turn again when my precious pappy got sick, and we had the worst time getting him help. This was during the COVID-19 pandemic. For millions of people, navigating the healthcare system when it was in upheaval because of the pandemic was a true trial. Pappy was going to doctor visits four times a week and

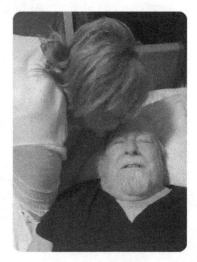

felt like he was on an endless hamster wheel. We couldn't find him a hospital bed and some other medical equipment he needed.

One day he said to me, "I quit." Thankfully I had learned my lesson from Momma. I needed to hear what my father was saying to me rather than try to run the show myself. So I said, "Okay, Pappy." But seeing how lost and depressed he felt, to the point that he wanted to stop trying to get better and let himself die, I realized there was a huge gap in the home healthcare field that I had never taken on— helping patients burdened with end-of-life problems they didn't know how to handle. I began to think it would be a worthwhile goal to move into that field. It would be so fulfilling to make seriously ill patients' lives better. Instead of dealing with stressful medical issues on their own, they could find the comfort and peace they deserve with my help.

Meanwhile, after Pappy told me he couldn't take any more, we went to see his primary care doctor, and he told us that yes, it was time to call in hospice. I appreciated that Pappy's doctor took the weight off me with that decision. I was more willing to listen to expert advice this time around. And voilà! On the very first day that we called hospice, the much-needed hospital bed that Pappy couldn't find on his own appeared. All kinds of equipment showed up: a walker, a cane, a bath chair. A home healthcare aide, a social worker, and all the people we needed to help Pappy came through right away too.

Wow. Once again I had the thought that hospice is truly an amazing service. Because we'd called hospice, the confusion surrounding Pappy's care got sorted out. His stress levels plummeted, he stopped declining, and eventually my dear dad was discharged from hospice. Yes, that can happen! When patients start feeling secure, their bodies tend to focus on restoring balance, which sometimes can lead to a renewed vigor for life, like Pappy had.

I'm so thankful my father got the care he needed. But once again I started thinking about all the people in similar situations who didn't have support. So it was because of that eye-opening experience with Pappy that I decided it was time to change my professional trajectory again. I would sell my wildly successful home healthcare company and start a new one focusing only on assisting patients nearing the ends of their lives, like my father. These patients need a guiding hand, someone they can trust to help them when they are at their most defenseless and scared.

I wanted to be that person, and that's who I am now.

So that's my short answer to why I started Serenity First Hospice Care. I love my parents to the moon and back, and I can't think of any more loving way to honor Pappy's and Momma's lives than by making it my mission to bring comfort to the dying. Helping others is what my parents taught me life is about.

The Loving Mission of Hospice

And now for all those preconceived notions about what hospice is. It is not, contrary to what most people think, a dismal, dreary business to be in. It's a calling, the same way teachers and doctors have callings. It's something that speaks to your heart. I witness such love every single day I work in the hospice care field, love so powerful and deep it makes me gasp even as it breaks my heart, and I also get to experience a soft, sunshiny love that fills my heart right back up again. People need laughter and friendship at every stage of life. Hospice patients and their caregivers have a unique rapport. When you know there isn't a lot of time left, the silly pressures of life fall away. You can indulge yourself. You make true friends fast. Pappy did. He loved his hospice nurse so much, he told me one day, "Debbie, I feel alive again."

How wonderful! My dear Pappy who'd wanted to quit this earth was feeling like his old vibrant self again. Gone was that man who was so exhausted by traveling all over town to his medical appointments that he wanted to up and die. It was a moment to celebrate.

It may not look like it at first glance, but that's what hospice is, really, a celebration of one particular patient as they near their final days. It's an acknowledgment that they matter. It's a way for the rest of the world to say, "We see you" to that person. Our attention gives them dignity and appreciation when they need it the most.

There's really nothing more special in this world to do than to witness miracles happen through loving actions. Hospice is one loving action after another. I'm blessed to have this calling laid on my heart. And while it took me decades to get here, what's that old saying? *You're never too late for your own destiny.* From the time I was a little girl, I set my sights on being of service to the world, and now I'm reaping the rewards of keeping that intention alive. I own a business that truly makes a difference in people's lives and enriches my own beyond measure.

> **Hospice is, really, a celebration of one particular patient as they near their final days.**

It turned out that Pappy had to go back to hospice care eventually. He is in it now. God bless him. And more than ever, I'm grateful for the services he receives. My favorite one is music therapy. Pappy's short-term memory isn't the greatest, but boy, can he remember songs from his youth! The joy I see on his face when he's singing a song with his music therapist makes me so happy.

It's possible to find happiness, love, and a sense of community to your very last days through hospice. It's truly a blessing. I think about the old days, before hospice was a thing, and I feel sorry for the people who left this world without it. And I realize that even now millions of people around the world could possibly die alone or unappreciated, either because they don't know about hospice or because there might be no hospice where they live. Instead of letting that terrible thought depress me and freeze me into inaction, it actually drives me to get up each morning and go to work to make sure that doesn't happen to people in my community. The more patients I can help, the more families learn about hospice. And hopefully those families will spread the word to other families and to individuals with no family support at all. Those people especially need to know about hospice. No one should feel alone at such a crucial stage of their life.

Honestly my hope, my dream, is that when people hear the word *hospice*, they won't feel scared or nervous. They will immediately smile instead. The burdens hospice lifts from patients and their loved ones improve the quality of their lives immeasurably during a very challenging time.

Love and care are what hospice care is about. Let's lift it up as a calling for more people. And let's share the good news with our communities that providing readily available hospice care is one of the most effective ways to care for its citizens. Every stage of life matters. We need to put more energy toward supporting the needs of our families, friends, and neighbors entering the last stage of their lives.

Someday we will be that person. Someday we will want to hold the hand of a caring individual who truly sees us, who recognizes our worth as a human being. Someday you and I will crave a loving presence to bring ease and grace to our final days.

Everyone rates such kindness. Everyone who needs hospice deserves to experience its compassionate mission.

CHAPTER 2:

Nurse Debbie Answers Your Questions about Hospice

Nurse Debbie, exactly what is hospice?

Okay, first I'm going to start with what hospice is *not*. It is not about death. Nor is it a surrender or admission of defeat.

Y'all, hospice is about *life*. Hospice is the patient saying, "I am going to live my best life for as long as I can *toward* the end."

Toward, not *at* the end.

Toward is a long time, not just a patient's final week or last few days! Of course it's wonderful to have hospice involved at the end. It's a huge comfort and support. But there is so much more to hospice that patients and families can appreciate and take advantage of over a much longer period of time.

Patients can call in hospice for six whole months, and then who knows? They might be discharged because they're getting better. Or if they need hospice for more than six months, as long as the doctor can provide evidence the patient is going into further decline, they can be reenrolled in the program.

Whatever each patient's story, imagine how many victories you can rack up in six months' time! Think about all the joy you can squeeze out of life, no matter what stage of it you're in, when you prioritize dignity and comfort.

So please spread the word to everyone you know. We have to stop thinking of hospice as a death sentence and a sign of surrender and a rushed means of support. We need to see it as *an amazing opportunity to live until the end—and to live your best life—without stress and with a sense of peace.*

Okey dokey, back to our regularly scheduled programming. Now that we understand that hospice is a positive experience that's *not* limited to a patient's final few days, let's look at some additional important facts that define the experience.

Plain and simple, hospice is receiving medical care when a patient has been given a terminal diagnosis. I hate the word *terminal*. Heck, we're *all* terminal, right? It's a dreary word, but for the sake of being as accurate as possible here, only people who've been told there's a chance they have less than six months to live are eligible for hospice. The most important thing to know about this particular medical care is this: *it's meant to increase both the quantity and quality of life for the patient.*

But there's more!

Hospice provides *all* medications, equipment, and services the patient needs. Not just a few essentials. *All of them.* Hospice also treats patients where they live. This comes as a surprise to many people who think they have to *go* to hospice. On the contrary hospice comes to *them.* Most patients receive hospice in the place they call home. This could be your house. Or if you're in a nursing home or an assisted-living facility, hospice will go there.

To map out someone's hospice journey requires an interdisciplinary team of professionals who will review all aspects of the patient's life. They'll make a plan based on that patient's unique diagnosis to ensure that they are receiving the physical, psychological, and spiritual care they need to be as happy and comfortable as possible.

The team will also address the family's needs. Many people don't realize that the patient's loved ones are also able to get support. It's a truly helpful bonus part of the hospice experience that validates the entire family's journey.

Hospice caregivers work together as a unit to tweak the plan whenever they feel it needs adjusting based on their primary mission of maximizing the patient's quality and quantity of life. This means the team is on the ball. They talk to each other. They talk to the patient and the family. They consider all aspects of the patient's life when they carry out the hospice mission.

In other words hospice is a flexible, ongoing care experience that is never the same for anyone. Every patient has different needs, so the goal of hospice is to be of the utmost service to each individual patient and their loved ones.

Wait a minute, Nurse Debbie. Just to clarify, hospice is not a *place*?

Right. Hospice is a *service*. The majority of patients want to receive end-of-life care at home. Hospice brings physical, emotional, and spiritual care and support to patients at home or wherever it is that they call home, such as a long-term care facility. Hospice also shows up at hospitals.

Hospice is a flexible, ongoing care experience that is never the same for anyone.

I'm one of those folks who needs to know every little thing about everything because someday I want to go on *Jeopardy!* So how did hospice ever even start, Nurse Debbie? And don't make me yawn, please!

Don't you worry. This country-born-and-bred Virginia gal learned from a young age not to tell boring stories! And as for *Jeopardy!*? More power to you, my trivia-loving friend. I'm a *Wheel of Fortune* girl myself. But I do love telling this story because two stubborn, visionary women—in an age when women's opinions weren't as valued as men's—are responsible for the wonderful worldwide change in how we approach end-of-life situations.

Let's not forget that *my* stubbornness and *my* vision are exactly why I am in the hospice care field today!

Another reason I like sharing this story with my clients and their families is because when you hear it, you're just so grateful that times have changed and that options for patient and family support, like Serenity First, exist.

This historic struggle to right a wrong also reminds us we should never stop advocating for our most vulnerable patients! We do *not* want to go back to the old days.

So here we go: hospice is about *hospitality*. Hospice has been around as a compassionate concept since 2500 BCE, begun in India and Egypt. Throughout history, from ancient times to the Middle Ages to the Victorian era, there have been organized attempts to provide comfort to weary travelers, who were often on pilgrimage, and comfort of both body and soul to the sick. Religious orders often provided this service.

But it wasn't until the mid-twentieth century that what we call *modern* hospice was founded. And it happened because that whole idea of taking care of people passing through your community on the way to somewhere else or sick people with no family to help them fell out of favor. We were so darned busy fighting world wars and trying to recover from those. We developed thick skins after all that trauma. We also got very excited about scientific advances making us more self-sufficient.

We lost a sense of community, to some extent. We might have lost track of our essential compassion too. One fallout of this was that people with serious medical diagnoses weren't given much attention by the medical community *if they couldn't be cured.*

Imagine two puppies in a basket, both sick. One's going to get better, and one won't. They're both snuggly and sweet. Can you envision turning your back on either one of those precious furballs? No! Neither can I!

So why would anyone do that to a human being?

Sounds cruel and almost hard to believe, but doctors in the mid-twentieth century actually thought they didn't have any role to play when a patient wasn't anticipated to get well again. Those physicians checked out of the whole situation. And no one felt that was weird or wrong.

Except for the late Dame Cicely Saunders (1918–2005). She felt it was *very* wrong. She's a true medical hero, a woman who's inspired me in my own quest to bring comfort to patients with life-limiting diagnoses. She's so famous now she's often compared with Florence Nightingale because she was that much of a leader among caregivers. She truly changed everything when it came to end-of-life medical care. A social worker, a nurse, *and* a physician, she turned the whole medical community on its head in 1958 with her radical ideas about how to treat patients who couldn't be cured.

Here's her radical idea: keep patients with a terminal diagnosis *happy*. Imagine that! That's our number one priority here at Serenity

First. We consider keeping our patients happy our sacred duty. It makes so much sense, right? In both our heads and our hearts!

But back in the '50s, a lot of medical people weren't ready to jump on Dame Cicely's bandwagon. Why? Because she was essentially saying that doctors and a team of support are still needed when cures can't be found and that patients deserve to have attentive care, *no matter what their prognosis.*

Dame Cicely said no excuse is good enough to deny an uncurable patient all the comforts we'd give patients who can get better. In fact she actually said, "You matter because of who you are. You matter to the last moment of your life, and we will do all we can, not only to help you die peacefully, but also to live until you die."

Live until you die! I tear up even thinking about that. It's what we all need and deserve to do.

Anyway, because of the dame, the medical world slowly started to rethink what it meant to take care of the seriously ill. Dame Cicely wouldn't stop insisting that until their dying breath, patients merit being noticed, to be given dignity and comfort, even if no medicine can cure their illness.

Here's one of the practices she started up that blew people's minds: she was a wonderful listener and would spend a lot of time encouraging her patients to tell their stories. People couldn't believe that a doctor, a highly educated professional with a lot of heavy responsibilities, would stop everything and listen to patients with no hope of a cure.

Why did she do it? Well, as we all know, companionship lifts people's spirits, especially when they're ill. The dame simply listened to her heart. Yet ever the scientist, she knew that the heart, soul, and body are connected, so she intuited that *if the heart is happy, the body will be better off.*

Convinced that happy patients have a better chance of improving all around, she told her staff, to heck with visiting hours! Let patients nearing the end of life see their loved ones whenever they wanted to.

Nowadays, except during horrible situations like the COVID-19 pandemic, where no one knew what to do, we don't discount dying patients' wishes to see their loved ones. *In fact the patient's personal wishes drive the hospice mission.*

But back to Dame Cicely ... beyond her modeling how important it is to listen to her patients and her insistence on relaxing visiting hours, she is best known for establishing the crucial notion of "pain control," which we take for granted now. But in the 1950s and before that, if you were in a grave condition with no hope of a cure and your pain meds wore off, the medical staff would still wait the proper amount of time to give you your next dose, leaving the patient often suffering.

How awful!

Dame Cicely Saunders hated this practice. She couldn't understand why someone who couldn't be cured had to deal with such strict dosage rules and suffer needlessly. She said, "Constant pain needs constant control." She noticed that when she tamped down her patients' pain, their mental anguish was alleviated too, and a calm mind, in turn, would help them feel better physically. She didn't even worry about opiate dependence because what mattered the most was making the patient comfortable until their last breath.

She also studied Elisabeth Kübler-Ross's groundbreaking research on death and dying. You've probably heard of Kübler-Ross. She's the woman who taught us about the five stages of grief (denial, anger, bargaining, depression, and acceptance). It was a good thing her ideas took such a strong hold on the public. People discussed her theory about the stages of grief around the water cooler and in churches and counseling centers. Kübler-Ross also specifically spoke up about the worldwide problem of terminally ill people being neglected. She shared Dame Cicely's passion to correct this terrible wrong.

The growing grassroots awareness about the stages of grief and end-of-life concerns helped back up Dame Cecily's message that we need to start talking about death and not simply ignore it—or our fellow humans in the final cycle of life.

It was a historic moment when Dame Cicely built the first hospice care center in the world. After years of trying to get enough money to fund it, it finally opened in London in 1967 with almost sixty beds for people with life-limiting illnesses. It's still operating to this day.

Talk about hospice equaling hospitality. Taking in people who need comfort at such a vulnerable time is the greatest kind of hospitality there is. And people have known this for thousands of years! But it took Dame Cicely and Elisabeth Kübler-Ross to remind us. I'm grateful they got the world to see again that patients expected to die without a cure shouldn't be overlooked by the society in which they live, especially the medical community. It's so sad, but thank goodness modern hospice came into being.

I feel the same calling as these two wonderful women and intend to carry on the noble mission of spreading hospice care to all in need of it.

Nurse Debbie, this all makes sense, and it's *really* inspiring, but I'm still nervous about the reality of hospice. I need another way to look at it that's simple to understand and helps me *feel* what hospice is truly like.

Nurse Debbie to the rescue. I get it. It always helps to walk into a room knowing the *mood* before you get there so you're not blindsided. And sometimes tough subjects require a little fun injected so we don't all collapse from nerves and worry.

I want you to *feel good* about hospice. So let me tell you about my personal go-to formerly top secret but now declassified (wink) explanation of hospice that I came up with to keep me energized and excited as I started up my hospice care business. I want you to feel comfortable and happy that you're making the right decision to look into hospice care.

So plop down on a cozy couch with your favorite beverage and some fuzzy socks on your feet and get ready for Nurse Debbie's true confession.

You may think this is pretty corny, but sometimes I think of my dream to inspire everyone to learn about hospice and feel good about it as Operation HOSPICE. Uh-huh. I do. I love the idea of being on a very important mission! Don't you?

When you break down the word hospice into an acronym—HOSPICE—it's easy to remember, and it tells the absolute truth about this amazing service, *truths that most people do not know*. Some may even call them secrets!

Well, let's let those secrets out of the bag, shall we? It'll clear up all the misconceptions floating around about hospice that need to be nipped in the bud. Knowing the truth will relieve your anxieties in a major way.

Operation HOSPICE stands for the following:

- Heartwarming

- Obtainable

- Sociable

- Peaceful

- Impactful

- Compassionate

- Enjoyable

Now, y'all, try not to be underwhelmed by those simple words! They represent very big, *comforting* ideas that are crucial to providing

excellent hospice care. As I champion the cause of hospice in my community, I keep them at the forefront of my mind always. Let's go over them.

Heartwarming:

Contrary to what most people think, hospice is one of the most heartwarming experiences a person can ever come into contact with in their entire lifetime, whether you're the patient or the caregiver or a family member. There's a lot of love involved. Love is what happens when we make sure our loved ones pass from this world with lots of TLC. That's a comforting thought!

Obtainable: So many people don't realize hospice is obtainable for all members of our society. You don't need to be rich to get access to it. The word *obtainable* reminds me that we need to educate everyone about their *options* too—another good *O* word—to make sure they receive the hospice care they deserve. You always have options. That's a comfort!

Sociable: Hospice care is one of the best ways to show the patient that they are still part of the fabric of life. They're not going to be left behind because of their diagnosis. We still want to talk with them, to make them feel as if they belong here with the rest of the world. Hospice is a very sociable experience, and most people nearing the end of their lives crave companionship and social opportunities. We want friends, and you make lots of those in hospice. Friends equal comfort!

Peaceful: I had so many good *P* words like *powerful* and *playful* that would have worked well here to describe hospice, but *peaceful* is such a good one. You may wonder: How can there be peace in the middle of such a stressful time? Sleep is lost, heartstrings are pulled, tears often flow, and worries may weigh you down. Peace seems an impossible goal. However, hospice is the calm in the eye of the storm, providing patients and their loved ones the true peace that comes from knowing they're in good, caring hands as they navigate this challenging journey.

You really can't put a price on peace; it's a gift of the hospice experience, a by-product of checking off all the boxes of caregiving attended to by knowledgeable, mission-driven people. Talk about a profound comfort!

Impactful: Hospice makes a huge impact—it's life-changing. Patients who go through hospice tend to live longer and with better quality of life. Scientists say so. Can you beat that? No! Isn't that a wonderful comfort? Hospice makes such a positive difference in people's lives that I can't say it enough. Everyone needs to know about hospice. Help me spread the word!

Compassionate: Yes, yes, and yes! Hospice shows the patients that they matter. We care about them. We *see* them. They are not forgotten, nor will they be forgotten. Few acts are more loving than hospice care. Compassion for the vulnerable among us gives meaning not only to their lives but also to ours. Comforting the patient brings comfort to all involved in the hospice journey.

In fact if you've lost your way and can't find meaning in your life, consider volunteering with hospice care. Fill yourself up with compassion, and you'll be right back on track.

Enjoyable: People just don't know until they experience hospice care that there are plenty of happy, even joyful, moments. Patients truly enjoy music therapy, pet therapy, massage therapy, paint therapy, getting to know their hospice team, and telling stories about their lives. We do our best to fulfill patient wishes, whatever they are. It can be a magical time in so many ways for our patients. Moments of enjoyment add sparkle to what otherwise might be a hard day. How comforting is that?

Nurse Debbie, that awesome acronym HOSPICE helps me feel a lot better about hospice! But there's a family member who still doesn't get it. Can you explain what hospice is one more time in a different but equally creative way, please?

It would be my pleasure. Back in the 1960s, there used to be a daily cartoon called *Love Is …* drawn by New Zealand cartoonist Kim Casali. It was two little smiling people who looked like gingerbread cookies. Every day Kim would show a different aspect of what "Love Is …" in a short but sweet way that resonated with folks all around the world. Fifty years later that cartoon is still being drawn fresh each day.

That's a lot of definitions of love!

Let's do that with hospice, without drawing the gingerbread cookie people (smile). We'll do a top ten list with an important reminder at the end, which I mentioned earlier in the book:

---

1. Hospice is … the five-star TLC we would all want if we were given a life-limiting diagnosis.
2. Hospice is … making sure the patient's physical, emotional, and spiritual needs are met.
3. Hospice is … letting the patient always rule.
4. Hospice is … providing what the patient needs and wants in a compassionate manner.

5. Hospice is ... a combination of professional medical care and pain management.
6. Hospice is ... a team coordinating all the decision-making and goal-setting for the patient's care with the patient and family.
7. Hospice is ... creating that team from different health-care disciplines.
8. Hospice is ... striving to help patients live their *best* lives for as long as possible.
9. Hospice is ... not forgetting that the patient's family needs support too.
10. Hospice is ... providing respite for family caregivers and thirteen months of bereavement counseling.

There! That about covers the very basics. But if you need a really quick explanation of hospice to give someone who doesn't understand it, remember that Kim Casali's very best cartoons were always super short. So I believe the following explanation of hospice packs the most punch: *hospice is ... about caring, not curing.*

Hospice is ... about caring, not curing.

Nurse Debbie, what kind of patient, really, is best suited for hospice care? I've been told my dad is probably going to die in the next six months. He's a military veteran and a *very* independent guy who doesn't like to admit he's ever in pain, so I'm not sure he's a candidate for hospice care. But should we consider it?

First of all, thanks to your dad for his service. As you know, we keep our personalities until the very end. In your dad's case, a soldier is always a soldier, a sailor is always a sailor, and an airman is always an airman, long after they retire. Military folks are often very stalwart people who hesitate to call on help, even if they might need it.

So this is a great question. Whatever our life's calling, our experiences and our personalities help define each and every one of us. Some patients push back hard when they're confronting serious medical issues that could compromise their independence. Other patients crave big support.

Hospice works well for patients who are very sick and possibly uncomfortable, either because the illness makes them feel bad or the treatments they might have undergone for it are still making them feel under the weather. They might feel weak or nauseated. They could be in serious or mild pain that puts a real damper on their daily life.

Other good candidates are patients who feel a lot of anxiety or fear and could use some counseling or medication for it. We also see that patients who need spiritual support really benefit from the comforting guidance they receive in hospice care from spiritual leaders who will totally respect their personal spiritual journey.

Hospice can provide tremendous relief to all these patients.

It would be so awesome if your dad won't require pain relief or need any support as he declines. If that's the case, hospice is still there to support his family. Please take advantage of it. And if your dad does start getting uncomfortable or uncertain about whether he needs extra help, remind him that hospice caregivers are there only to help him feel better. They will still respect his scrappy personality and the decisions he makes about his own care.

Nurse Debbie, this may sound silly to ask, but is hospice only for people who are dying? Or can my mother who's really sick and might be told she's going to die in the next couple of years get hospice care?

First off, no question is too silly to ask. You're talking about your loved ones here! And maybe even yourself. All questions are on the table.

So here's your answer: hospice is for patients who doctors think could possibly die *in the next six months*. It doesn't mean the patient will, only that it's a possibility.

If your loved one hasn't been specifically told that by the doctor, then hospice care isn't in the plan at the moment. Make sure you ask, though. Ask the doctor to be straight up about your loved one's diagnosis. If there is any chance your doctor thinks your mother might die in the next six months, jump on the hospice train and get support for her and your family as soon as possible!

Nurse Debbie, I know someone can receive hospice for as long as six months. But how long would you say most people actually use it?

Oh dear. The sad fact is that over a third of patients use hospice for seven days or less! That is such a bummer of a statistic. Hospice isn't called in until that patient is very near death. Of course when death is unexpected and sudden, hospice can be there only for a short time for the patient. (Although in those situations, hospice can still benefit the family afterward.) But we can't deny that in many situations, patients and families have the option to call hospice much sooner and don't—usually because they're not aware of the tremendous benefits hospice brings to their situation.

In slightly better news, a little under a third of patients use hospice for a week to a month.

I wish the numbers were higher for the next figure: around 20 percent of patients use it between a month and three months. And it would be awesome if we could get the next two statistics much, much higher: under 10 percent of patients receive hospice care between three months and six months. And another 10 percent use hospice for the entire six months.

Only 10 percent use it for six months! My goal is to get more patients to take advantage of hospice sooner. One thing that holds back people with a terminal diagnosis is that they and their families believe hospice patients have to be bedridden. Not so. Many patients enrolled in hospice feel well enough to go on a little vacation, or see their family and friends at special events, or take walks around their neighborhood, or work on projects they feel passionate about.

The goal is to help hospice patients live their lives as normally as possible, and the longer patients use hospice, the more likely that is to happen.

But what happens if the hospice patient uses all six months and that person outlives their prognosis?

This does happen. A lot! I'm happy to tell you that hospice patients can get an extension. All they have to do is get their doctor to recertify them as "terminally ill." The physician can recertify the patient for up to two more six-month cycles.

So all together that's eighteen months of hospice care. That's a comfort to know!

My adult siblings and I are terrified that hospice means our very spirited momma will be put on drugs that make her sleep all the time, and we know she'd hate that. We don't want her addicted to anything either. That would mortify her! She's a dignified lady. Please help us feel better about what's going to happen.

God bless y'all—I totally understand your concern. We all want what is best for our beloved person in hospice care. We want them to remain *themselves*, not turn into a receptacle for a bunch of medications that turn off their personalities.

Here's what I hope brings peace to your heart: hospice caregivers want your mother to enjoy the remainder of her life. They don't want her to miss out on anything!

Also, understand that addiction doesn't happen when suffering patients truly need medication for pain. Addiction happens when that pain medication is no longer needed, and the person keeps taking it. When someone is at the end of life and under the care of a hospice team, a situation in which pain medication is abused is not going to come up.

And think of it this way: if your mother is given medication to alleviate pain, we are respecting her dignity. We're saying she doesn't deserve to suffer. She is worthy of tender loving care until she draws her last breath.

So you're saying bringing in hospice isn't the same as throwing in the towel?

That's exactly what I'm saying! A lot of people in desperate need of hospice feel ashamed to ask for it, and so do their families. One of the biggest misconceptions about hospice is that it means the patient, or the patient's family, has given up on the sick person's life. And they worry that facing the reality of the life-limiting prognosis by calling in hospice will hasten death somehow. But that's not true. Hospice is the opposite of giving up. It's believing that quality of life matters until the very end.

So ideal candidates for hospice are patients who want to focus on what makes their lives meaningful in their last days, like family and the comforts of home. These patients want to avoid pain and worry. They enjoy having the multiple levels of support hospice care brings. They're not surrendering; they're actively choosing life.

Nurse Debbie, about timing ... when should hospice care actually begin? And how do we get the ball rolling?

Hospice care should begin when that terminal diagnosis of having less than six months to live is received. Don't wait. Get started. You will be so glad that you're staying informed and preparing for the difficult days to come.

The first thing most people do is talk to their physician about hospice when that diagnosis comes in. Most often the doctor will

bring it up first. But if not, go right ahead and do so yourself. Don't be shy. It doesn't mean you're a Negative Nancy or an Eeyore. And it doesn't mean you're giving up. It means you're responsible and compassionate and want to be prepared. If the doctor believes hospice is appropriate, his office can start the process by connecting you to a local hospice care agency.

However, you don't have to wait to speak with the doctor and wait for his office to begin the connection to hospice care. You can also call hospice care agencies yourself and say you're ready for your loved one to receive their support. Their office will then make it official by getting in touch with your doctor and ensuring that hospice care is indeed needed—the patient has to have that terminal diagnosis.

Of course sometimes there is no time for a diagnosis. People can die unexpectedly and fast. In situations like that, hospice can start right away, and families in shock lean heavily upon the services they receive from hospice, funeral planning and counseling among them.

But when there's time enough for a diagnosis, there's a waiting period of a few days because a hospice nurse will need to visit the patient first to make sure they meet all the requirements for hospice care. All the paperwork is gone over, and procedures are explained. But it's not long before hospice care will begin, usually within a couple of days of reaching out.

Nurse Debbie, I'm one of those people who can't sleep at night when I think about what I will eventually face in dealing with my loved ones' passing. I want to get ready now. Is that normal? My parents are only in their early seventies. And I'm even thinking of my spouse and, dare I say it, myself. When is the right time to learn everything I can about hospice?

You are not only normal, but you're also smart! Dealing with issues around death is an anxiety-provoking experience. It's healthy to not want that buzzing around your subconscious mind for years. And nobody wants end of life to include awkwardness or discomfort. So I highly encourage everyone reading this book to learn about hospice, plan now, and then let it go, knowing you have done what you need to do.

That's what I did, and I'm a healthy woman who intends to live to be one hundred, at least! Even though that's decades away, I've already got a huge party planned out and budgeted for, my funeral arranged to the smallest detail, and most importantly my directives about my own end-of-life care put into the hands of people I trust. Speaking of which, it's always best to get input from loved ones before time constraints and stress start tightening the screws on your decision-making process.

Educating yourself about hospice care now is a great idea. You'll feel so much better, and you won't have those niggling thoughts waking you up after midnight!

I can't believe I haven't asked who pays for hospice, Nurse Debbie. And what kind of costs will the patient incur?

The only reason you haven't asked yet is because it's a really big topic with a lot of stress associated with it. I'm glad you're getting to the practical aspects of hospice care—it means you're becoming more comfortable with the idea.

Eight out of ten hospice patients get hospice paid for by Medicare, which covers all hospice costs with no deductible and no copayment. The patient doesn't have to worry about paying the hospice care team. Prescriptions and medical supplies related to pain and comfort management are also covered by Medicare.

But Medicaid and managed care/private insurance can also play roles. Medicaid eligibility varies by state. And people who use private insurance need to talk to their provider about deductions and copayments and what that private insurance plan's eligibility requirements are.

For people who aren't eligible for Medicare and can't pay any other way, charities often step in to assist.

Nurse Debbie, can I or my loved one receive around-the-clock hospice care seven days a week, and if not, how often will the hospice team visit the home?

All righty … there are a couple of different approaches to these questions, and it would benefit you to know your options. *Most hospices come to you,* and their offices typically don't stay open 24/7. They close daily like most other businesses. They are known as intermittent hospice care facilities; the caregivers might visit the home several times a week or even daily. And when I say home, the patient could be in their own house, or perhaps they're living in a nursing home.

When you're researching hospice care agencies that come to you, it's a good idea to ask what services they offer after regular business hours. They're required to have a nurse on call, and they might also have a chaplain and social worker available.

As for the number of times the team visits per week, each patient has different needs, so the patient, family, and team members work out a plan that best serves the patient.

But Medicare also recognizes when continuous home care may be needed. If a patient has an acute need for nursing care around the clock—not to prolong life through medical treatments but to provide palliative support at home, like monitoring oxygen or stemming seizures—then sometimes Medicare benefits cover this option. However, not many hospices provide continuous care because the practice invites a lot of federal scrutiny. The government doesn't want patients to receive unnecessary care, so they tend to inspect hospices that frequently offer this option to their clients.

Another way to receive twenty-four-hour daily care and avoid all the government red tape is to supplement Medicare benefits with private pay home care. Some hospices actually help the patient and families with this enrollment and have a list of reputable providers with whom they coordinate on behalf of the family. This twenty-four-hour private pay supplemental care again can take place at the patient's home or in a residential care facility.

Let's say the family doesn't have access to private pay home care. Their patient is receiving intermittent care at home, but the family is barely able to keep up with the stress, even with the hospice team support. In cases like this, Medicare *does* provide temporary inpatient hospice care to give respite to the family. It's five days of twenty-four-hour patient care in a home staffed by hospice workers, and while it doesn't seem much, it can provide the family a much-needed break. The hospice team usually has connections to a home they can refer the family to.

Can you tell me more about the hospice team, Nurse Debbie?

You mean the heart and soul of hospice, the people who make up our teams? I'd love to! The interdisciplinary team is composed of a doctor, social worker, registered nurse, chaplain, and hospice aide. They draw up the care plan with patients and families, and it's adjusted based on how patients fare medically through their time in hospice.

Volunteers also play a role on the team. We sure do love our volunteers!

The team is so important that we'll speak more about their particular roles later on in the book. As an added bonus, I also interview some team members who have worked with me and Serenity First!

I'm worried that hospice care is limited to people with a terminal cancer diagnosis. Is that true?

Absolutely not! Anyone with a life-limiting diagnosis of six months or under can get hospice. The category of illness doesn't matter. We have people with heart disease, respiratory illnesses, kidney disease, Lou

Gehrig's disease, AIDS, cirrhosis of the liver, and Alzheimer's disease as well as many other diagnoses.

Nurse Debbie, what if my father no longer lives at home? He's in a long-term care facility. Can he receive hospice there when the time is right?

Yes, he sure can. Hospice caregivers often work with clients with life-limiting diagnoses in nursing homes, memory care facilities, or other types of long-term care facilities. The home and hospice team will have a written agreement in place that details the services provided by the hospice care team. These specialized services are covered under Medicare hospice benefits and *supplement* the home's regular services that are billed separately to the patient (such as daily room and board). And if your loved one is eligible for Medicaid, it can even cover room and board.

It's a good feeling knowing that the hospice team—the doctor, chaplain, social worker, registered nurse, home health aide (HHA), and volunteers—is happy to work with your father, or any hospice patient, wherever they live.

And don't forget that the team also works with patients at hospitals, whether they are admitted mere days before they pass away or are there for an extended period of time.

You mentioned that the government inspects hospice agencies to ensure there are no legal problems, such as inappropriately overlapping Medicare benefits with private pay home care. Is there both state and federal government oversight? And does the government provide evaluations of hospice programs and make those assessments available to the public?

Yes. Clients can rest assured that hospice care facilities cannot operate without adhering to state and federal law. We have to comply with federal regulations to be approved for Medicare reimbursement. Hospices are also habitually inspected by the state to ensure regulatory standards are being adhered to. If the hospice fails the inspection, it loses its license to operate as well as the certification allowing Medicare reimbursement.

When you do your research, I highly recommend that you ask to see the hospice facility's inspection reports and proof of license to operate.

Are there other ways to find reviews on a hospice care agency? I want to be able to compare the three I'm looking at now, but I'm not sure how.

You're doing the right thing—research before you choose one! And yes, there are measurements on paper you should be able to review that will help you make your final decision.

A good hospice care facility monitors itself to ensure it is consistently meeting standards of practice for hospice care programs as outlined by the National Hospice and Palliative Care Organization (NHPCO). NHPCO even provides its members a self-evaluation tool. So when you do your research into programs, first ask if the hospice care agency belongs to NHPCO. They should. Then ask whether they employ NHPCO's self-evaluation tool. They should do that too. If their answer is yes, then ask to see their latest self-assessment and discuss with them any concerns you have.

Another way to evaluate a hospice care program is to ask to see the satisfaction surveys they offer their clients' families. Most hospice care programs provide these. If they don't, that's not a great sign. If the facility *does* use a family satisfaction survey, what kind of feedback are they getting? And are they using that feedback to continuously strengthen and improve the services they have in place? Have a discussion with the leaders of the program.

You can also ask to see their latest state or Medicare inspection report. These should uncover any care provision issues. So would a list of complaints they've had in the past year. A quality hospice provider doesn't hesitate to offer any of this information to a prospective client, and they're happy to listen to any of your concerns regarding feedback they've received.

Y'all, speaking as a nurse, as a businesswoman, *and* as the loving daughter of a wonderful father in hospice, I'd like to remind you that a good hospice care program is on the ball and craves being the best in the business, as we do here at Serenity First. The only way to be the best is to have high, measurable standards, meet them, and exceed them. Then that hospice care program should want to share their success with the public. Transparency matters. Facilities with wonderful records don't want to hide anything. If you ever get that vibe—that they are reluctant to speak with you about their track record—walk away.

And don't forget, you want to evaluate unmeasurable standards too. Those come from your gut. It's the feeling you get when you talk to the folks who run that hospice care facility. We all know the difference between a business that's all about crunching the numbers and one that wants to make a positive difference and is fueled by compassion. We recognize when a smile is genuine, when passion for the mission is evident. So keep those standards in mind too.

Nurse Debbie, I keep hearing the phrase *palliative care*. What does it mean? Is it the same as the end-of-life care provided by hospice?

I'm thrilled that y'all are so smart and curious! You're asking such important questions. Most people have no idea what the phrase *palliative care* means, and that's because they're not in the medical profession or, thankfully, not immersed in a serious medical situation involving themselves or a family member.

And, y'all, I have a favor to ask. I want you to hang around for this explanation, complex as it may appear on first reading. Why? Because knowing what palliative care is can truly affect your treatment, or your loved one's, in hospice. The more educated you are about it, the more power and control you will have in times of serious discussions with your doctor.

Let's start by saying all hospice patients receive palliative care. They have been told they could possibly die within six months, and the curing phase of their treatment is over. But the caring side of their plan, which has been ongoing, is still in place and will not be removed. *That's what palliative care is … the caring side of the patient's treatment.*

Palliative care is the caring side of the patient's treatment.

But not all palliative care patients are in hospice! They're struggling with an illness that the doctors are still trying to cure, and they're offered palliative care in addition to an active curing plan.

I hope this is making sense to you. I'll say it again: palliative care is *not* about curing the patient. It's meant to bring comfort, relieve pain, and improve, or at least maintain, a patient's quality of life. The medical team also wants to set up conditions where further disease like infection won't happen.

Palliative care is about understanding a patient's particular situation and giving them appropriate comfort and support. It complements the curing plan, or it remains when the curing plan is removed.

Let's start with a situation in which the patient is nowhere near being declared a hospice candidate. Say you're a person with no family, and you hightail it to the emergency room and are immediately admitted to the hospital with an inflamed appendix. The doctors want to cure you, of course. This means they will get that diseased appendix out through surgery ASAP!

But curing the illness isn't all there is to medicine. What about the patient's pain? Sure, the docs could operate without anesthesia—gulp!—but how medically practical and humane is that? It's not! So enter anesthesia. It doesn't cure the disease, but it's still considered part of the curing side of medicine. Why? It's an essential part of the operation! Imagine not putting the patient to sleep. That patient, cut open while wide awake, could easily go into shock and die during an operation. Picture an awake patient writhing on the operating table and knocking the doctor's hand while he's trying to stitch up an incision. Gosh, that's the stuff of nightmares!

However, by bringing up anesthesiology, we are now crossing over into the palliative side of medicine: alleviating pain. This is one of the greatest missions of palliative care.

Palliative care for this patient admitted through the ER starts when the operation is over. The yucky appendix has been removed, and back in the patient's hospital bed, there might be a warm blanket to help them feel secure and cozy, and a chaplain is standing there when they awake to bring them comfort. If the patient is highly anxious, maybe a sedative will be offered to help them stay calm and sleep. As the patient heals, bandages are constantly replaced with clean ones, and the patient is bathed and fed. If the patient has no family to take care of them, maybe a social worker will come in and help the appendix-free person figure out a ride home and a way to get emotional and physical support during recovery.

Put another way, palliative care is assessing the patient's whole picture—psychological, social, and physical—and seeing what needs to be treated, apart from actually curing an illness.

Notice that nothing in palliative care *cured* that particular patient's infected appendix. But those palliative care services contributed to the patient's overall well-being. They enhanced the cure by preventing infection and adding to quality of life for the patient through pain management and providing social support with that talk from the chaplain. Or maybe the nurse brought in the patient's favorite flavor pudding as a snack. A comfortable, stress-free patient tends to heal faster and better.

Palliative care also extends to family members. In cases where the patient has an illness that goes on a long time and could sap the energy of the family, the respite care offered to the family is also considered palliative care.

In a medical situation unlike the burst appendix where the disease can't be reversed—that is, if it can't be cured through medicinal means such as surgery, or chemo and radiation, or a variety of other medicinal options—palliative care is still essential. We all deserve to feel cared for, right? No one deserves to suffer needlessly.

But the questions about palliative care are complex. Oftentimes medical and palliative care overlap. What if a disease that can't be cured goes on for years? That happens all the time! COPD patients use oxygen tanks to alleviate their breathlessness. That's medical care—providing oxygen to starved lungs—but it's also palliative care because shortness of breath is so uncomfortable. COPD patients might require those tanks for years before they die.

A patient with cerebral palsy often uses crutches. An amputee might have a leg prosthetic to help with walking. Those are palliative care solutions to ongoing medical problems without a cure.

How does palliative care relate to hospice care? Remember that not all palliative care patients are in hospice. They might receive palliative care for many years before their actual death. Palliative care overlaps hospice care when an incurable disease is predicted to take the patient's life *within six months*. Hospice care *is* palliative care for those patients.

Sometimes, on the outside looking in, it appears a patient in hospice is getting curative care, such as chemo. But in that case, the chemo is a palliative measure. It's not about curing the cancer. The chemo is used to improve that hospice patient's quality of life by helping shrink the cancer, reduce the patient's symptoms, and possibly even extend their life.

Oh my goodness, you can go out now and give a whole talk on palliative care! The medical teams you encounter in your life will be so impressed you know your stuff. You'll be relieved that you really understand what's going on with your own medical treatment or a loved one's when it comes time for end-of-life care.

It's all about caring, not curing. That's palliative care. And I want you educated about it so you can fight for it if you have to. If your doctor is reluctant to give any sort of traditionally curative treatment in hospice because they're no longer going to try to cure the disease, if you think that treatment should be designated *palliative* in your case or your loved one's because it might lessen symptoms and improve quality of life, you ask for it! And you state your case!

Nurse Debbie will be so proud of you.

Should we wait for our family doctor to suggest hospice?

No. It's so important that before hospice even becomes a necessity, patients and their families discuss it among themselves and bring it up as an option to their doctor as soon as they feel it's necessary. It's a sad truth, but a lot of doctors don't refer patients to hospice soon enough. They wait until the patient is very near death, which means that the patient and the family have missed out on possibly six months of incredible support from a hospice team.

Some doctors worry that calling in hospice too early will make the family think the doctor has given up, when they are really simply recognizing that the illness is beyond curing. The doctor also sees how hope is sustaining the family. It's awfully hard to be the bearer of grim news, so the doctor might avoid mentioning hospice until the end.

But doctors need to be reeducated about hospice. Yes, patients and families want hope. But the biggest hope we all have for our loved ones at the end of their lives is that they are happy and comfortable. Doctors need to let patients and families know the tremendous benefits of hospice. Facing the reality of the patient's dwindling days and calling hospice makes it easier for them to receive the gamut of support they want and need.

Nurse Debbie, my sister with a cancer diagnosis loves her family doctor. Once she enters hospice, can she keep that family doctor involved in her care?

Yes! It's a comfort for most patients to know that entering hospice doesn't mean having to say goodbye to their family doctor. A favorite personal physician can be on the hospice team, no problem! In fact we love when our clients' doctors become part of the team because they often already know that patient well. With the knowledge they already have, family doctors can help the team get situated faster and better.

This is a crazy question. Can you leave a hospice care program, Nurse Debbie?

I told you no question is crazy! You're brave to take on educating yourself about hospice. You should be proud!

And the truth is, people do sign out of hospice sometimes. My own father, Pappy, did. His health started improving, and his doctor said leaving hospice care was fine because he didn't think it was likely Pappy would die within six months anymore. (And that doctor was right!) Pappy really didn't need hospice-level attention from his medical team at that point. So out he went. You could say he graduated.

Later on, however, Pappy's illness progressed. He had several diagnoses going on that the doctor said could possibly end Pappy's life within six months, so with another medical referral to hospice in hand, he reentered it.

You can also leave hospice if you decide you and your doctor want to try a new plan to cure the disease. Sometimes this means trying an experimental new drug. Other times it means using a more aggressive approach with treatments you've already tried. People in the curing phase of treatment aren't eligible for hospice.

But don't forget what I said earlier when we talked about palliative care. Medicare allows only patients on palliative care into hospice. But sometimes traditionally curative treatments such as chemo and radiation can be used as palliative measures. For some patients, they can slow the rate of decline and assist with quality of life.

It is because of this overlap between curative and palliative treatments that occasionally a terminally ill person wanting to enter hospice as a chemo or radiation patient might receive pushback. It's a very complex situation, and so it's important to have a doctor on that patient's side explaining to Medicare that some cures can be used simply to ease a hospice patient's suffering, making that treatment serve in the patient's case only as a palliative measure. This distinction between palliative and curative treatments, which is so important, can be used to persuade Medicare to allow that patient to enter and remain in hospice.

Nurse Debbie, you're telling me about all the valuable services hospice provides, so I want to get my loved one with a serious, life-limiting diagnosis enrolled. But I can't decide what to do about timing!

Indecision is natural, but I promise you that the right time to start hospice is when the patient first qualifies for it. I can't tell you how many patients and families wish they'd started sooner than they did. Hospice relieves so many burdens on the patient and the family. A team comes in to provide a friendly ear, offer nursing advice, give spiritual support, meet daily needs like bathing, provide medical equipment, and stay on top of pain relief. Often the increase in quality of life because of hospice care actually lengthens the patient's life expectancy. Plus, families who enroll earlier adjust better to the bereavement period than do families who get hospice at the last minute.

At least three months of hospice care *or more* is considered optimal. So go ahead and get started. You won't regret it.

What do I need to know about medical power of attorney, Nurse Debbie?

Excellent question! And I'm going to take my time answering because this is important—I mean, *incredibly* important. Please put a bookmark on this page because I want you to get working on it right away.

COVID-19 has proven that we don't feel nearly as secure about our prospects for good health as we would if a worldwide pandemic weren't raging. And even if it's over when you read this (as I surely hope it will be), the memory of the uncertainty COVID-19 brought into our lives should spur us to act in our best interests and plan for our medical futures.

One of the most comforting things you can do for yourself and your loved ones is to get yourself a medical power of attorney. I know, I know … this isn't something anyone wants to dwell on. After all, your children, parents, other family, and friends have your best interests at heart! So if you're suddenly incapacitated—say, you're in a bad car crash and unconscious or a virus has stricken you so hard you're in the ICU—of course your loved ones will know what to do.

Right?

Think about it. How would

One of the most comforting things you can do for yourself and your loved ones is to get yourself a medical power of attorney.

you feel if *you* got a surprise phone call that your dear friend or relative was in an awful automobile accident and was clinging to life? I pray this has never happened to you. Anyone who has ever been in that position knows you're not going to be thinking exactly straight—you'll be scared and anxious. On the way to the hospital, your thoughts will race with lots of what-if questions. You might catch a glimpse of your loved one on the gurney, completely unable to make decisions for themselves, or maybe you never get to see your loved one at all! They might be in emergency surgery.

It's not unheard of for doctors you've never met before to come up to you and say something along the lines of "Your loved one didn't designate a medical power of attorney and is in critical condition. Should we resuscitate them or not if their heart stops? Or if their brain ceases to function?"

Ugh. No one wants to be put in an extremely frightening situation like that with no notice. But it happens all the time. Every day people across the world accidentally get seriously injured or get acutely ill, and they leave the finer aspects of their medical care—beyond what doctors are required to do in the emergency room—completely up to chance. And believe it or not, a lot of people who know they are declining and have plenty of advance notice *still* don't establish medical powers of attorney!

But do you really want to put your loved ones on the spot like that at the hospital, especially when you, as the patient, are unable to contribute any opinion yourself? Shouldn't these decisions be made when everyone is calm, cool, and collected? Do we really want to wing it when it comes to undergoing medical crises?

Absolutely not. A medical power of attorney is what we all need, and it's not nearly as hard as you think to set one up. At Serenity First we provide our clients the paperwork to get one going. You will *never* regret it, I promise you.

However, if you're still hemming and hawing, think about how grateful your loved ones will be. Do you want them wondering if they made the right decision by you or not? Imagine them being plagued by worries, sometimes for the rest of their lives, that they might have chosen the wrong options for your medical care. What a burden that would be to their spirits!

They're going to want your input. Of course they will. So please put their minds at ease and tell them exactly what you want *now* before any crisis happens. You may be reluctant to get the conversation going, but think about how much it will benefit everyone involved for you to speak up when you have the chance to. It's a *blessing* that you have this option now to steer your medical future in a way that you think is best for you—and for those loved ones responsible for you when you can't be responsible for yourself. So take advantage of this time to plan, and please prepare for your future.

Once you get your medical power of attorney set up, you'll have such peace of mind! Honestly a lot of us fear serious illness and death because we feel we have no control over what happens at such a momentous, often frightening time. This way you'll at least have some input into vital decisions because you will have put them in the hands of someone who has your best interests as their number one priority.

Make sure this is a person you trust implicitly and talk to fairly regularly. They should be willing to have multiple discussions with you about how you want to be cared for in a medical crisis, long before these tough personal decisions come up.

The situation will be extremely stressful as it is, even with a medical power of attorney in place. But having one will make everyone feel much more secure: the doctors, your loved ones, and you.

What keeps us up at night? Often we regret not doing right by the people we love. *A medical power of attorney means you'll have no regrets.* This is a chance to make sure your loved ones can have peace during a turbulent, emotionally draining, physically taxing time. And it's an opportunity for you to be empowered in the midst of a crisis that has taken your ability to contribute your opinion.

I want you to remember this*: if you're a loved one with medical power of attorney, remember it's not about you!*

I've had a lot of experience navigating my role as the person entrusted with my dear Pappy's medical power of attorney. Not everyone in the family likes the decisions I've made on his behalf. But he and I have had lengthy discussions about what he wants. It's not about what I want or anyone else in Pappy's circle. *It's about what Pappy wants.*

So really think this through—and I mean thoroughly—when you're choosing the person you'll grant a medical power of attorney to when you're incapacitated. The best candidate is someone who is going to stand up for what *you* want. They will not cave to pressure from other people, no matter how much they claim they know what's best for you.

Look for a strong person you trust to handle all the opinions that are sure to come out of the woodwork. And don't forget, whoever holds your medical power of attorney will be collaborating with the hospital team or hospice team. They need to be available to make decisions for you, and I promise that they will be called upon to do just that. It's a position of high honor to be chosen, so only work with someone who deserves that honor. And if you're the medical power of attorney yourself for someone else, never lose sight of the fact that that person's life is essentially in your hands during a medical crisis in which they cannot contribute their opinion.

I told you this was a long answer! But it's vital you read the whole thing. Here are some short facts about medical power of attorney:

1. A medical power of attorney is always a durable power of attorney. That means it's valid even when you're incapacitated, and it won't come into effect until you are unable to make decisions for yourself.

2. The person you choose to hold your medical power of attorney is called an attorney-in-fact (even though they're not required to be a lawyer). Most people appoint a family member or close family friend as their attorney-in-fact.

3. A living will is not the same thing as a medical power of attorney. A living will is put in use only when you are permanently incapacitated. It states your long-term medical wishes, and doctors and family members can read it and take your requests into consideration. But a living will doesn't give a particular person the legal right to make medical decisions on your behalf in a temporary emergency.

4. Whoever holds your medical power of attorney should have access to your living will or, at the very least, know your

wishes about the kind of healthcare you want to receive if you are unable to speak for yourself.

5. Some states allow certain loved ones priority when it comes to making medical decisions on your behalf if you're unable to. If you're not happy with who the state would choose, a medical power of attorney allows you to bypass this problem. You can choose for yourself who will call the shots. You want to choose someone who respects your wishes, your religious convictions, and the moral choices you would make if you could decide for yourself.

6. You can limit your attorney-in-fact to certain types of decisions, or you can allow them to make all medical decisions on your behalf. Some decisions your attorney-in-fact may make for you include giving or withholding consent to medical or surgical treatment. But the person with your medical power of attorney also often makes day-to-day decisions, the way I do for Pappy when I talk to his hospice nurses and doctor about his diet and his activities.

7. Rest assured a doctor can't say you don't have the capacity to make healthcare decisions just because you're old or have a mental illness. The doctor must complete a thorough evaluation before they determine that you can't make medical decisions on your own behalf.

8. That being said, if you are truly incapacitated, make sure you truly trust the person holding your medical power of attorney. I can't say this enough. I've witnessed sad situations in which the person holding the medical power of attorney clearly did not respect the patient's wishes. Don't let this tragic situation happen to you. Choose the person holding

your medical power of attorney wisely. I selected two friends who know me extremely well and whom I trust with my life and my death ... because y'all, that's what you're doing, choosing someone who will defend your wishes, even if death is the inevitable outcome.

9. You can choose a backup representative if your first choice for medical power of attorney is unable to meet your needs. But put this backup's name in writing in your document. You can also change your mind and revoke a person's medical power of attorney and choose a new representative. Don't forget too that if you get a divorce and your former spouse was your attorney-in-fact, they will automatically lose this status. However, if by any chance you still want them to represent you, you'll have to start all over again with a new document.

10. You can't choose your doctor or nurse or anyone treating you to serve as your attorney-in-fact. None of their employees can serve as your attorney-in-fact either unless they are related to you.

Whew! I feel better knowing you are now well aware how important medical power of attorney is. Thank you for getting through those facts with me! And remember, choose your people with care. Also, if you accept the responsibility of becoming someone's attorney-in-fact, you have a duty to follow their wishes, no one else's. Period.

I am so glad I learned about medical power of attorney and everything else you've taught me, Nurse Debbie! What are some interesting facts about hospice you haven't shared yet?

How about this? Most hospice patients are over sixty-five, but patients of any age with the proper diagnosis can enter hospice.

Not many people know that if your loved one dies *outside* of hospice care, the family can still receive bereavement support services.

Furthermore, when a public tragedy occurs and communities are having trouble coping in the aftermath, hospice can provide grief support.

Nurse Debbie, what are some basic questions to ask when we're choosing a hospice care agency?

There are definitely some common questions you could ask a hospice care agency directly. If you don't know how to find one or where to start, feel free to call the NHPCO's HelpLine at 800-658-8898. But you can also check in with any healthcare professionals you trust, your favorite clergy or counselor, a social worker, and your friends and neighbors who've experienced what hospice care is like.

In the Appendix section, you'll find a wonderful checklist of questions that NHPCO put together to help consumers choose the right hospice agency for them.

I'd also love to tell you about a terrific resource set up by the Centers for Medicare & Medicaid Services (CMS). It's a web-based Hospice Compare tool that allows people to compare ratings of Medicare-certified hospices. This can be a useful tool to help people select one hospice program over another. Visit the CMS Compare website at www.medicare.gov/care-compare and select "hospice" as the provider type.

Hopefully you'll feel so much more confident now about how to find the hospice care agency that's right for you and your family. And if there's only one hospice care option available where you live, at least now you know the questions to ask that agency to ensure that you or your loved one is getting the best hospice care possible.

CHAPTER 3

The Hospice Team

I've been looking forward to writing this chapter. I tear up thinking of how wonderful Pappy's hospice care team is! They've added so much joy and love to his life. I can never repay them, but I can pass it on. It's why I started my own hospice care agency, Serenity First, so other families and their loved ones can feel the same sort of warm, happy love and care Pappy and his entire family have basked in during his time in hospice.

So we're talking about Pappy here, the ultimate good guy. And I simply cannot think of him without being reminded of those movie trailers when the good guy and his sidekicks walk straight toward the camera and show by their determined expressions (and their heavy weaponry!) that they're going to save the world and be our heroes. Pappy, who served in the US Air Force, loves action hero movies. He starts eating his popcorn faster and takes a big sip of his drink because just like you and me, he loves the part where the good guys show off! The music gets loud and dramatic, and sometimes a giant ball of fire appears behind the team, an inferno they recently set off to defeat the bad guys. The whole scene, hokey as it is, shows us that the good guys are powerful. They're in control. They're bringing the happy ending.

And we love it!

Then we get a reality check. After the actual movie, we stand up from our theater seats, go outside, blink in the light of day again, and realize it's time to go home and pay the bills or do some chores. Or we were watching on Netflix, so we get up from our couches and eat ice cream to compensate for the disappointment that, gosh, those heroes were only a Hollywood fantasy.

Ah well.

If we're smart, though, we remind ourselves that real heroes are usually pretty ordinary, like my darling Pappy, who should win all sorts of medals for being wonderful. But he's content being a great dad and patriarch of his big family. You have personal heroes too. We also have collective ones to admire. Look at what happened during COVID-19! We saw heroes in action all around us, among them our medical community, which saved lives daily while COVID-19 terrified the world, and they did it in the face of tremendous risk. Many of those medical heroes lost their lives trying to save others. We truly can't put a price on the sacrifices they made on our behalf.

My point is, next time you think of heroes, or next time you watch a movie trailer with those brave, big-hearted people striding toward the camera, I would love it if you imagine them as your loved one's hospice team members. You will meet heroes on the team, I promise. And you will feel the goodness, the compassion radiating from these people, even as they show by their tremendous expertise how skilled they are at what they do professionally.

Heroes Comprise Your Hospice Team

Don't forget you're part of that team, so you're a hero too. When life throws lemons right at you, you're catching 'em single-handed and squeezing those suckers into lemonade. You're staying positive. You're keeping your heart and your head aligned, and you're doing whatever you have to do to help yourself or your loved one have a peaceful, meaningful hospice experience.

And as a member of the team, you get a say in what's going on. And just like you would in any team, you'll cling to the other team members in stressful times. You will laugh and perhaps weep with them, and you'll be grateful forever that you called them in your time of need—and that they came.

Your hospice team members are reliable and compassionate and oh so smart because they are trained. They're extremely familiar with end-of-life scenarios, and they will hold your hand and walk that road with you. You'll never forget that they showed up and gave you and your loved ones the support and understanding you needed as you embarked on a journey that isn't easy.

So let's talk about who those hospice team members are. You'll work with a doctor provided by hospice. You can also use your own doctor, if you prefer, or both. In any case, the hospice care medical director will be aware of the setup and will be involved. You'll also work with registered nurses, social workers, HHAs, a chaplain, counselors, and perhaps a speech, occupational, and/or physical therapist. Last but definitely not least, you'll work with trained volunteers. They go where they are needed.

The team's goal is to help keep the patient as pain-free as possible, to control symptoms, and to support the patient in any way they can, including socially, psychologically, and spiritually. They'll also be there to provide medication, medical supplies, and equipment. And they do this while interacting with and coaching the patient's family about caregiving skills. Those moments are some of the most valuable—the simple conversations the team holds with the family. The family members are oftentimes the primary caregivers and will need multiple levels of support.

Various team members will not only share with the family techniques of caregiving. They might also even coordinate phone calls or Zoom sessions between the patient and faraway loved ones.

The team's goal is to help keep the patient as pain-free as possible, to control symptoms, and to support the patient in any way they can.

And it's not uncommon for team members, such as the chaplain, to pray with the patient or family. Everyone involved will monitor the family's overall stress levels and, if necessary, provide respite care for them by checking the patient into a short-term care facility.

And let's say symptoms or pain become too difficult to manage at home, the team may temporarily remove the patient or even recommend a permanent move to a hospice care facility.

Finally, besides providing day-to-day comfort and support for the patient and family, a big part of what the team does is offer grief support and bereavement counseling to the family after the patient dies. Bereavement support lasts one year, and it includes giving individual counseling through the hospice or making referrals to a community resource.

Y'all, the hospice care team is invaluable. Please take advantage of their professional wisdom, experience, multiple skills, talents, and the unique, loving personalities they bring to a stressful, momentous time in your family's life.

Doctors

I say this time and time again: I'd rather be a nurse, but I am so thankful for the MDs. We all have our roles to play, and doctors bear an awful lot of responsibility on their shoulders. Plus, they have to be smart as a whip and never forget why they went into medicine in the first place. It's all there in that Hippocratic oath they take. It's a doozy of an oath to live up to, not to mention all those years of medical school, so I am thankful we have people willing to take on this tremendous calling.

Let's start out by distinguishing between the doctor who makes the hospice referral and the doctor who is involved in the hospice care plan. *They are not always the same doctor.* Sometimes the referring doctor steps back, and a new doctor steps up to create the actual hospice care plan and direct it. We will get to that possible transition between doctors momentarily.

The first doctor involved in the hospice care process is the patient's own personal physician. This doctor does the following three essential things:

1. The personal physician identifies when the patient qualifies for hospice. How? By evaluating the patient's condition and coming to the conclusion that there is *a possibility* the patient could die within six months. It's not a stone-cold fact, only a possibility. Doctors aren't God, but they have a responsibility to alert their patients at this juncture that the patient should prepare for possible death within half a year.

    Let's pray every doctor we know does this with grace and compassion. It can't be easy to hold that conversation. Doctors actually receive training in how to do this properly. And from what I understand, they learn to ask the patient questions along the way, such as "How do you feel about this?" so that the patient feels ownership of their own story.

2. The patient's doctor then makes the actual referral to a hospice agency. Nothing can happen without the physician's signing off on paperwork that says a patient is eligible for hospice. Y'all, just take a deep breath and remain as relaxed as possible at this point. Paperwork makes the world of government go 'round, as we all know! The doctor sends this referral to the hospice people and may also make a call to say it's on its way. At this point the hospice care ball truly starts to roll.

3. This next step is so important. The personal physician has a responsibility to explain to the patient exactly what hospice is. It may be an overwhelming conversation, and the doctor's conversational skills matter a lot, especially in light of the fact that they want to check in with the patient's feelings as the discussion unfolds. Some patients barely remember what happened because they may be in shock at the news or in denial. That's normal.

But it helps when you come home to have a book like this to keep the information straight for you.

Now let's stop for a minute and talk a little bit more about how personal physicians approach talking to the patient about hospice. You'll hear stories about some doctors not telling the patient or family soon enough about the possibility that the patient has six months or less to live. Sadly this happens sometimes because no doctor wants patients to believe their personal medical team is giving up on them! Some patients see a referral to hospice as just that—a surrender of sorts by their physician.

But a great doctor will assure the patient that hospice is not about giving up. It's shifting hope from curing to caring. It's focusing on giving that patient the best possible life for as long as possible. That includes helping them live their life as they wish, get their affairs in order, and connect with the people important to them.

Because we know that patients who call in hospice as soon as they find out they have a terminal diagnosis tend to do better (they usually live longer and with better quality of life), it's especially imperative that a personal physician talk to the patient as soon as it's determined that hospice may be needed.

But what if the doctor still hasn't spoken up about potential hospice care for the patient and that patient or family member has questions about how long the patient can live?

Bring it up. Don't be shy. If you're either the patient or a loved one, and you're starting to think you or your loved one could die within a year, then you should ask the personal physician if they believe that scenario is possible or even likely.

In other words start the conversation if this concern is niggling at you. If you need a boost of confidence, remember that your personal physician will do a better job knowing where you stand on all matters concerning your healthcare.

I mentioned at the top of this section that sometimes there's a transition from the referring doctor to a hospice doctor. After the patient's personal physician is done explaining what hospice is to the patient, that doctor may step back and allow the hospice care agency's medical director, or one of their staff doctors, to take over a patient's care plan.

That's not a bad thing. Hospice care doctors are very familiar with palliative care (which you'll remember from last chapter is all about caring, not curing). They stay abreast of the latest scientific advancements, and they understand that ethical issues sometimes inform a hospice patient's situation. They make sure the treatment plan is in compliance with Medicare rules and regulations specific to hospice. They're also used to managing conflicts that may arise on the hospice care journey. Sometimes not everyone in the family is on the same page about the care plan and needs convincing, or they simply want to understand better what's happening. Other team members may need to consult with the hospice doctor about the care plan—that includes the nurse and the personal physician. The hospice doctor has to manage all sorts of communication, so getting across important messages so everyone hears them is a big part of the hospice doctor's job.

It's also reassuring to note that doctors who focus on hospice care often come from medical backgrounds that enhance the hospice mission. The majority of patients in hospice are elderly, so the fact that many hospice doctors are board-certified and/or have specialized in geriatric care and internal medicine is comforting to patients and families. The hospice care doctor also may come with a lot of family practice experience, which is handy. Family practice doctors are used to looking at the big picture, and that can be reassuring to families.

With years of practice behind them managing pain and symptoms, these doctors with hands-on experience create specific hospice care plans unique to each terminally ill person that maximize their quality of life.

In summary hospice care doctors manage the hospice care team's mission: to make the patient comfortable and give them the support and tools they need to fulfill their life goals in the time they have left.

But back to the personal physician … in many cases, the patient's doctor may not want to be involved in hospice care for the patient. Why would they be reluctant? It could be that the personal physician is not very familiar with end-of-life care and what it entails, including what medicine and equipment to provide in hospice. Or the personal physician may believe the patient needs around-the-clock care or at least access to medical help day and night. Depending on their own career situation, not all doctors have that kind of time to devote to their patients.

But sometimes the family doctor does stay involved. It's helpful to hospice teams when they do because they already know the patient well and can offer a lot of clinical insight. The personal physician can even lead the interdisciplinary hospice team, and the hospice care doctor can be there to offer support. Or vice versa: the referring doctor can stand by to assist the hospice physician. Creative solutions can be found. The family doctor may be available on certain days or times to attend the patient, and the hospice doctor can cover the other times a doctor's presence is needed. The personal physician and hospice doctor should be able to work together and support each other. The patient and family are an important part of this dynamic. So make your preferences known so they can be considered as the plan rolls out.

The bottom line is that if you would feel more confident and comfortable having your personal physician stay a part of the hospice care team, hold that conversation. Make clear how much it would mean to you if they could help set up the hospice care plan and stay closely connected to either your or your loved one's care.

Registered Nurses

All right, when I get to this part, I have to admit some bias. As I've told you, I'm a registered nurse. And I think it's a pretty cool job. In fact just like any medical profession, nursing is more than a job—it's a calling. The life of a registered nurse is an extremely challenging, exhausting, *and* fulfilling one. I'm so proud that I can call myself Nurse Debbie!

Let's face it. Who do you want to come over first when you don't feel good, either physically or emotionally? Someone who's going to bring you chicken soup, a smile, and the assurance that you'll make it

through just fine or the expert on whatever ails you? To be clear, that second person may be just as nice as the first. They'll outline exactly what is wrong with you, what tests you need, and what sort of medicines you require. All things you really need to know to get better.

Both are caring roles, but let's not beat around the bush. We want TLC when we're feeling under the

weather, so we call our mother first, or our best friend, or anyone in our lives who is super nurturing. We crave being around people who are warm, caring, and *see* us. And by that I mean we don't have to explain what's wrong. This person intuits it. They get our fear, confusion, or irritation. Their presence alone brings comfort, and comfort opens the door to healing.

So in the case of end-of-life care, we want to hang out with the registered nurse. Hands down, they're the support we need if we're feeling emotionally fragile or physically sick. Of course we want to have a great relationship with a doctor too and the other hospice team members, but there's something about nurses that is so special. A lot of people see us as angels walking the earth, which is a very sweet sentiment, and I happen to believe it's true of all my registered nurse sisters and brothers, although I'd never call myself an angel—I leave that up to my patients and their families (wink).

But without a doubt, registered nurses are loving and giving and seriously know how to do just about everything! I think of us as the MacGyvers of the medical world. Give a nurse a problem to solve with very few resources and she'll find a way. We have to think on our feet and be extremely flexible, and all the while we stay calm and loving and guide our patients as they navigate some very tough roads and lead them toward wholeness and well-being.

Indeed there's a kind of registered nurse—the hospice nurse— who wears more hats than any other. They have so many skills and talents that one can argue that their impact on the hospice operation itself and on the patients and families is unsurpassed by anyone else on the team. Hospice nurses, like all nurses, are committed to providing the highest quality of care possible. They need compassion, great communication skills, tremendous empathy, a level head, and an ability to pay attention to the smallest details. But the hospice nurse also has a very big responsibility—that of bridging communication between the team and the patient, family, and caregivers. When there's an impasse, as sometimes happens, it's often the hospice nurse who finds a solution or brings everyone onto the same page again.

Among their many duties, hospice care nurses administer medications; regularly check patients' vital signs and document them; manage symptoms and pain; give social and spiritual support to the patient, family, and caregivers; step in during emergency situations; and know when to intervene and when not to. They also educate caregivers on all aspects of hospice. Above all, they want the patient to feel as much control of their situation as possible.

There are several types of hospice nurses the patient and family will encounter.

First we have the **admissions nurse**. They play a pivotal role because they're the ones who visit the patient to assess their eligibility for hospice. While this process goes on, the admissions nurse learns more about the patient's medical needs while teaching the patient and the family about what hospice does. This nurse also helps prepare the hospice care plan in conjunction with the doctor and the rest of the team.

The next nurse the patient and family work with may be the **case manager**. The case manager has the most direct nursing role to play in hospice care. The case manager is often a registered nurse. (Note: Sometimes the case manager is a social worker. We will get to that scenario eventually. Either way, a registered nurse is always involved in the patient's care.)

The case manager oversees the day-to-day management of a patient's hospice care plan, adjusting it as time goes on if needs be based on their continuing assessment of the big picture, which is to figure out the patient's medical needs and requirements of social services. To achieve this perspective, the case manager stays in communication with the doctor and other team members, including social workers, spiritual advisors, and mental health specialists, to ensure the patient is receiving the treatment they need.

But case managers also talk with patients, families, and caregivers constantly, holding their hand (sometimes literally) through any ups or downs of care and fighting for the patient's voice to be heard. If the case manager is a registered nurse, they may also provide hands-on nursing care to the patient. Real bonds of trust are formed among the patient, the family, the caregivers, and the case manager.

The patient, family, and caregivers will also get to know the **visit nurse** really well. This nurse carries out the hospice care plan on a daily basis, administering medicine, cleaning wounds, chatting with the patient, and helping them achieve whatever it is they want to do, like taking a walk around the block or dressing. This nurse does a lot of paperwork too to document the visit and what happened during that time.

Triage nurses are the on-call nurses whom patients and caregivers contact when there's an emergency at home and they need an expert medical opinion to determine what care should be provided. The triage nurse will also work with the case manager or the visiting nurse to determine whether a medical professional needs to visit right away.

Two other nurses who work in hospice care are **dietitians** and **hospital liaisons**. The main goal of the dietitian is to help the patient eat nutritious food that will help them feel good. Dietitians consider a patient's current condition, their diagnosis, and their medications before coming up with a nutrition plan. Hospital liaisons are nurses who coordinate between a hospital and a hospice care facility when the hospital refers a patient to hospice care. This nurse makes sure communication links and relationship ties are strong between the hospital and the hospice care facility so patients' needs don't get lost between the transfer from the hospital to hospice care.

Social Worker

The patient, family, and caregivers will get to know a social worker really well in hospice care, particularly if that social worker serves as case manager. As I noted earlier, sometimes they act in that capacity, managing the hospice care plan, which they help construct as the team member charged with looking at the overall picture of that particular patient's situation. If the case manager is a social worker—and not a registered nurse—that social worker will have special certification to be the hospice care case manager.

Often a social worker is *not* the case manager. Instead they will work with the registered nurse who is serving as case manager. That nurse consults with the social worker to determine what social services the patient may require based on the social worker's assessment of the patient.

Either way, a social worker is involved in the patient's care. But let's pull the camera back a bit and see what hospice care social workers do in general terms. Their mission is to advocate for their clients, to improve the lives of the patient and the family. If they're struggling with social and/or personal issues, the social worker tries to help solve those problems. They gently observe the family's unique dynamics to assess how they impact the patient's and loved ones' well-being. And they find out the wishes of the patient and the family to further customize the hospice care plan.

The social worker's greatest goal is to see that their clients' overall well-being is maximized. They have a keen interest in protecting the patient's and the family's human rights and their safety. The social worker often serves as counselor to the hospice care patient and family (a job that the registered nurse doesn't take on) and can refer them to a spiritual advisor. If needed, the social worker also connects patients with community services like Meals on Wheels and support groups.

Social workers can assist with legal issues too, such as helping document the patient's end-of-life wishes, including setting up advance directives like "do not resuscitate" orders. Patients often deal with serious financial stress, so the social worker will attempt to relieve some of that by helping track down disability income and assist with researching insurance coverage and medical or veterans benefits. With their knowledge of financial resources, social workers will also help the patient and family handle other bills. They're happy to assist with Medicare/Medicaid paperwork.

A social worker helps familiarize the family with the dying process, including helping them plan the patient's funeral. And after a hospice care patient passes away, the social worker ensures that the family has access to bereavement counseling.

Social workers generally do *not* deal with the patient's medical treatments. They leave that to the nurses and doctors. However, they often educate patients and families on coping strategies for managing pain and other symptoms of their disease. They can help translate medical jargon and explain procedures to make them more understandable to the patient and family. And as an up-close-and-personal advocate for the patient and family, they are able to provide valuable insights to the other hospice care team members.

This description of social work may sound clinical, but the reality is that when you need their help if you or a loved one is in hospice care, the stranger with the job title *social worker* quickly becomes a friend and is very important to both the patient and family.

Home Health Aide or Certified Nursing Assistant

Another hospice care team member sure to bond with the patient, caregivers, and family is either the home health aide (HHA) or the certified nursing assistant (CNA). Many times HHAs are also CNAs, but the separate job titles are there for a reason, which I will explain.

The CNA, or the HHA, visits with the patient between one and three times a week, usually for about forty-five minutes, to provide essential services that ensure the dignity and comfort of the ill person. They also provide much-needed companionship to the patient and are naturally friendly, warm people with big hearts. Talk to any HHA or CNA and you'll find out they're drawn to hospice care because they want to help alleviate suffering and help their patients have a good day.

The two positions overlap, but they're not quite the same. A hospice patient will work with at least one of them. CNAs and HHAs both provide basic personal care and do light household chores, but the CNA can perform a few job duties not usually performed by an HHA, such as giving medications, monitoring vital signs, reporting to doctors and nurses, documenting changes in the patient's health condition, and transferring the patient in and out of a bed, chair, or wheelchair.

CNAs are often the primary caregiver in nursing homes and other long-term care facilities and have more contact with the patient than any other staff member.

There are some states that allow HHAs to administer meds and watch vital signs under a nurse's or doctor's supervision, but generally HHAs stick to nonmedical, personal care.

The HHA's or CNA's intermittent presence gives the family caregivers a much-needed break and a sense of security too. To know that their loved one is receiving compassionate care from a professional who is familiar with the dying process helps scared, stressed family members and caregivers relax. The HHA's visits also prevent the family from experiencing a sense of isolation, which can be so debilitating to caregivers. It's not uncommon that the family caregivers need guidance too when it comes to day-to-day caregiving. The health aide is well able to provide tips on daily caregiving and encouragement.

The duties of the CNA or HHA depend on the particular patient's needs and typically include bathing, shaving, dressing, washing hair, combing hair, oral or denture care, help with toileting or incontinence, care and cleaning of Foley catheters, nail care (not always cutting but at least filing), back rub/massage care, turning and repositioning bed-bound patients to avoid bedsores, wound care, transferring the patient from bed to chair or chair to bed, assistance with walking, range of motion exercises, changing bedsheets, and light housekeeping. Some HHAs prepare light meals, such as sandwiches. They also may accompany patients to activities outside the home.

HHAs and CNAs are certified to do their work. But they aren't nurses, so they can't give the patient or caregivers any medical advice or professional nursing care. They follow the hospice care plan and report to a registered nurse supervisor, who occasionally accompanies the HHA or CNA on a patient visit to see how things are going. The nurse will observe the care provided and lend additional support or guidance if needed. HHAs and CNAs provide invaluable input to the hospice team because of the close relationship they usually form with the patient, caregivers, and family.

Note that if your patient is receiving hospice care in a freestanding care facility such as a hospital, nursing home, or a hospice home, the care provided by the HHA or CNA goes beyond the routine care the facility is already providing. In these circumstances HHAs and CNAs offer supplemental care.

Spiritual Advisor/Chaplain

When you think of a chaplain or spiritual advisor, your first thought isn't usually *medical professional*. But that's exactly what chaplains and spiritual advisors are in the hospice care setting. Their job is to plan, assess, and care for the patient's and family's spiritual needs in the patient's twilight days.

They've usually completed studies in clinical pastoral education and received accreditation in the field. They've also usually been ordained or received an endorsement from a denomination or faith group. But some chaplains are not actually ministers or rabbis; they can be laypeople with a strong spiritual interest who have received the appropriate training to be a hospice spiritual advisor.

As representatives of religious traditions, hospice chaplains rely on their background in theology, spirituality, and religion to support patients of all religious faiths. *Hospice care chaplains do not try to convert a patient or the family to their personal beliefs.* They're trained to know how to support people of many faiths and cultures. Their ultimate goal is to help the patient and their loved ones find peace during an extremely challenging time. Whether that is helping Hindu parents make funeral arrangements for their sick child to be buried, or coleading a Native American funeral, or even officiating at a wedding as a hospice chaplain, they are ready to take a unique journey with the patient and their family.

Hospice care chaplains also offer guidance and solace to patients with no religious faith or interest in spirituality at all. Again, their goal is not to change the patient's or the family's beliefs. Their goal is only to reassure the patient and their loved ones that they are *seen*, that they matter, and that peace is possible for them. As you may think, hospice chaplains need excellent interpersonal and communication skills. They're gentle, wonderful listeners, and they're respectful, sensitive conversationalists.

A hospice chaplain's main focus is the spiritual needs of the patient, but they're adept at supporting caregivers and families too. The process of witnessing the patient die has implications for them as well. It's a stressful, emotional time. Sometimes difficult family dynamics require the chaplain to help lead the family through rough patches.

Hospice chaplains must prepare the patient and family for the eventual death of the patient by using everything the chaplain has learned about that particular patient's situation. In other words spiritual care in hospice is not a one-stop-shop sort of affair. A lot of thought and care go into the chaplain's approach to each patient and family.

Chaplains are often on call twenty-four hours a day and provide pastoral care wherever the patient is living—at home, a hospital, a nursing facility, or any long-term care facility. And pastoral care is always optional. A hospice patient can decline it. Whatever the patient decides, the hospice chaplain is always willing to assist the family members cope with the diagnosis by offering emotional and spiritual support to them. Sometimes people start to question their spiritual beliefs, and the chaplain helps them explore spiritual grievances while also helping them reclaim their spirituality identity and see it as a source of strength.

Hospice chaplains look at spiritual care for the whole person. They want to restore a patient's sense of purpose and meaning, reinvigorate anyone involved in the situation who is feeling detached from their own spirituality, and provide spiritual counsel that aligns with the hospice patient's wishes. The chaplain prepares the terminally ill person for the end of life by reminding them of their life's value and the positive impact the patient made in this world. If there are complex feelings that come up—anger, guilt, and regret are a few—the chaplain knows how to redirect the hospice patient to a spiritually healthy state of being. Sometimes this means the chaplain helps the patient find rituals, prayers, and other spiritual coping methods that offer comfort.

Hospice chaplains also strive to make sure their patients don't die alone and that they feel love and compassion at their passing. And if any caregivers or family members have difficulty coping after their loved one's death, the chaplain is prepared to recognize their distress, including depression, and provide spiritual care.

Finally the hospice chaplain acts as a bastion of spiritual support for any hospice team members who need pastoral care to sustain them in their fulfilling but highly stressful careers. The chaplain also plays a vital role in helping the team understand the spiritual and cultural perspective of the hospice patient and their family, which, of course, facilitates better communication between the team and the patient.

Counselor

Counseling is indispensable to terminally ill patients and their families. In such a difficult time, people want to be heard, and that requires a dedicated listener. Often a hospice counselor's primary job is listening to the concerns of patients and their loved ones. They may have a fear of dying or have questions about death. Or they may be depressed or angry about the patient's illness. Sometimes there are problems within the family that need resolution. After the patient dies, the counselor is still there for the family, offering support and directing them toward appropriate community services.

The counselor also works with the entire hospice team as they share insights with each other about how best to maximize that particular client's well-being.

The most challenging aspect of counseling in hospice is the fact that the clients die at the end of counseling. So unlike counselors working with healthy clients, who can look at their lives from the short and long term and often set goals they can build upon over time, hospice counselors help their patients focus on short-term goals that will bring them peace before they die. Like healthy people, hospice clients often want to work on improving relationships or altering difficult situations with their counselor. But the lack of time means that the hospice counselor has to excel at unraveling personal stories quickly and help the patient establish achievable goals within the time the patient has left.

A good end-of-life counselor will get to know the beliefs and customs of the clients and their families as well as their particular adversities—financial, social, cultural, or otherwise. All of these can impact upon how the counselor approaches therapy with that patient. Hardships are woven into our personal narratives and are often revisited at the end of life. Hospice patients may want to recall both the happy experiences they have had and the difficulties they have confronted. So knowing and appreciating the lived experience of the patient, including in context of their race, ethnicity, socioeconomic status, gender, or sexual orientation, will make the counselor even more able to bring grace and dignity to that patient's time in hospice.

Hospice counselors can come from varied educational backgrounds. Many have nursing degrees and decide they like counseling hospice patients so much that they go into the field. Others are social workers or chaplains who specialize in bereavement. They may pursue certification through the Association for Death Education and Counseling, which administers the nationally recognized certification in thanatology, the study of death, dying, and bereavement.

Speech, Occupational, or Physical Therapist

Therapy often plays a role in hospice care, although not long ago, Medicare didn't cover **physical therapy** for hospice patients. A physical therapist (PT) is a movement expert. Their job is to help the patient move more freely and safely without increasing pain or creating further disability. Normally PTs also want to rehabilitate, or restore, function in their patients, but hospice physical therapy isn't as concerned with restoring function as simply delaying decline. PTs accomplish this mission of maintaining as much stability as possible by prescribing exercise for the hospice patient as well as by hands-on care and patient education.

It's such a valuable therapy that why would Medicare not have recognized its worth as little as ten years ago? The rationale was that if the patient had "plateaued," more therapy was unnecessary. Improving or maintaining function apparently didn't rate as highly as improving a hospice patient's symptoms, social conditions, and spiritual needs.

Yes, hospice patients will eventually decline functionally and die. But we know that offering them physical therapy to either maintain or improve function is a worthwhile endeavor. It's also helpful with managing and relieving pain. It isn't the same as trying to cure a hospice patient. Helping a patient not get worse meets the hospice mission of being part of a caring plan, not a curing one.

So if physical therapy will help a patient retain mobility, keep their functional independence longer, relieve pain, prevent bedsores, aid in managing edema, conserve their energy, and offer therapeutic measures like massage, then physical therapy is helping that patient live their best life until the end.

If it means patients will have a greater likelihood of avoiding falls, which can lead to surgery or a need for extra assistance, then physical therapy—part of which is home modification, if necessary, and equipment training—is again a valued aspect of hospice care for some patients. Of course no patient is the same as another. Not all terminally ill people want to participate in physical therapy, and some simply can't.

It's a relief to know that Medicare will now pay for ongoing physical therapy for hospice patients if the treatment will improve, maintain, or prevent decline in the patient's condition.

So how will your loved one qualify for "maintenance" therapy?

1. If a doctor has written orders for therapy. Find out why the doctor feels physical therapy is necessary, and ask how many sessions are needed and how often.

2. If the patient needs services Medicare finds "medically reasonable and necessary." That is, doctor's orders for physical

therapy are fairly expected for a patient with this particular illness.

3. If the patient requires a skilled therapist. That is, an untrained person, like a concerned loved one, can't assist properly. Some movements take much more skilled help than others to achieve. An example would be going upstairs. That's a more complicated action than walking across a room. Although even in the crossing of a room, a patient can encounter hazards like a slippery rug. The PT's job is to remove dangers and provide equipment if needed, like a cane or a walker.

Functionality is so important and can remove some stress not only on the hospice patient but also from the caregivers and family as well as the hospice medical team. So a great PT is an active, alert listener and observer of the patient's environment.

Speech-Language Pathologist

Another therapy helpful to many hospice patients is provided by the **speech-language pathologist** (SLP). The SLP diagnoses and treats a wide range of speech, language, cognitive, and swallowing disorders. When they work with a hospice patient, their job is not to rehabilitate but to facilitate, and usually their biggest task is to work on helping the patient with swallowing and speaking. They want to make it as easy as possible for the hospice patient to not only enjoy their favorite foods but also get the most of out their social time with loved ones.

If an end-of-life patient has difficulty swallowing, for example, the SLP works with the patient and caregivers on strategies to keep the patient eating by mouth for as long as possible and to keep nourishment activities with loved ones positive. When feeding tubes or breathing difficulties prevent the patient from being able to speak, the SLP helps develop alternative methods of communication. The SLP wants to preserve the patient's role in decision-making and to help patients maintain as much social contact as they desire.

Probably one of the hardest issues the family confronts in a hospice situation is the choice to put their loved one on a feeding tube, if the patient hasn't been put on one already during palliative care. The SLP's recommendation to the hospice care team is crucial. They may conduct a swallowing evaluation to decide if the risk of aspirating or choking when eating and drinking by mouth outweighs the benefit of remaining on some form of oral intake.

The SLP hopes to keep a patient fed by mouth comfortably and with the minimum of distress for as long as possible to optimize their quality of life. Sometimes to avoid a feeding tube placement, the SLP can make adjustments in the care of the patient to increase safety, such as modifying the diet, making sure the patient is positioned correctly, and giving small, frequent meals with a high number of calories.

There is also research that a feeding tube may do more harm than good in some cases, especially in patients with dementia, so an SLP's advice to the family is crucial. Food is considered love in many cultures, so it can be hard on a family emotionally to consider the option of no feeding tube at the end of their loved one's life. A hospice care team with an SLP involved can educate the family on all their options as they go through this decision-making process. One question to ask is "Would my loved one have wanted aggressive care or comfort care at the end of life?" The SLP's job is also always to remind the family that what they are seeing is part of the natural course of end-stage illness.

Occupational Therapy Practitioner

The **occupational therapy** practitioner (OT) plays an important role on the hospice care team. OTs identify life roles and activities that provide some meaning to their patients, all while addressing obstacles that may keep the patient from performing those activities. OTs not only look at the patient's physical needs, but they also assess their emotional, social, and behavioral health needs. OTs prioritize what is most important to the terminally ill person to accomplish before they die and consider whether the resources available, the patient's environment, and the patient's abilities make it possible to achieve these goals.

Maintaining independence to maximize quality of life can dramatically change a person's experience. A simple adaptive utensil can allow a person to feed themselves for an additional month or two. Maybe the patient wants to shower by themselves or get in and out of bed independently. They may want to keep seeing their family and friends for as long as possible, so the OT will assist with making that happen. This can mean that the OT monitors and changes meeting times and locations as the patient declines and fatigue sets in. Or the patient

Maintaining independence to maximize quality of life can dramatically change a person's experience.

may choose to work on reducing anxiety and addressing pain management with the OT, which can be done in a number of ways, including lowering fall risks with adaptive measures and using manual therapy techniques to increase range of motion.

Whatever the patient's wishes, the OT's big goal is to foster a sense of independence and well-being in the hospice patient to help enhance their quality of life.

OTs can work in a hospital setting, a specialized hospice facility, or an individual's home. Typically their duties would include designing a plan that assists the terminally ill patient with dressing, which could mean helping the patient and caregivers adapt new ways of dressing the patient that avoid pain and overexertion; often bringing in benches and grab bars to help with bathing and showering the patient; and

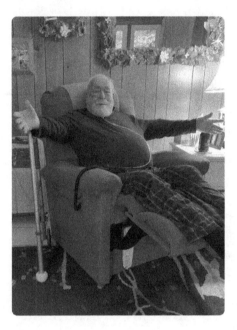

looking at keeping the patient safely mobile, which could mean improving lighting or removing slippery rugs in the patient's home.

As for meal preparation, OTs may reorganize an entire home kitchen to provide better access for the patient, and they will encourage the patient to adopt a healthy diet, providing the patient or caregiver resources to guide them. OTs also will observe a hospice patient's ability to manage their home. Can they do laundry or any cleaning? The OT will then work with the hospice care team to establish a support system or improve an existing one based on their assessment.

As the disease progresses, interventions may shift to focus on making practical preparations as death comes closer. This can involve an OT helping to pack up the patient's home and assisting them with giving away items and belongings to their loved ones. An OT may also be involved in helping the patient get closure through looking back at their life, saying sorry to anyone they might have hurt, or reuniting with a loved one. OTs may also help set up opportunities for the patient to say a final goodbye to their loved ones.

Hospice Volunteers

How many of us have volunteered for committees at school, church, work, our neighborhood, a service organization, or maybe even on a political campaign, hoping we're going to make a positive difference in this world? Hopefully all of us are raising our hands. The reality is, occasionally we're disappointed at how little impact we seem to actually have when we volunteer. It doesn't feel so rewarding when we get folding and stamping duty with those all-important flyers that have to be mailed out, or we're sweepers of floors in the workroom. Both those jobs matter, of course, as do all tasks related to carrying out the big mission at stake. But it sometimes takes us a long time to see *why* our actions matter.

When we volunteer, we want to be content doing our part, and we try not to second-guess the impact we're having. But every once in a while, as volunteers, it feels so good to be the stone thrown in the pond that creates a big splash and leaves a ripple effect.

In other words we want to see meaning happen before our very eyes, meaning that we are fully immersed in and helped make happen.

I promise you that as a hospice volunteer, you'll find that meaning every day.

Some of the things hospice volunteers do are

- chatting with and listening to the patient,

- playing games with the patient,

- reading to the patient,

- grocery shopping,

- making light meals,

- driving the patient to doctor appointments,

- doing light housework, and

- letting the other hospice team members know of any patient needs.

Sometimes hospice volunteers are needed away from the patient's bedside. They may do administrative work, such as answering the phone in the hospice office, helping fundraise, preparing mailings and leaflets, and performing data entry and clerical tasks.

Then there are the volunteers who provide music therapy, pet therapy, massage therapy, narrative therapy, and art therapy. Sometimes volunteers may help with legacy projects. Whatever a person is skilled at, the hospice team can use those skills and adapt them so that they benefit a patient's particular situation. And if a person who wants to volunteer feels they lack applicable skills, I promise, the hospice organization will train you. Never fear! All we need are willing hearts to work with, and before you know it, you'll be a trained hospice volunteer.

CHAPTER 4:

Expressive Therapy and Hospice

How many days have you woken up and weren't sure what life was about—and what your own life means in the great scheme of things? It's happened to all of us. It's a part of what it means to be human. None of us wants to depart this world without making some sort of impact. And we don't want our loved ones ever to feel their lives don't matter either.

One of my favorite parts of hospice care addresses this age-old, sometimes anxiety-provoking questioning about our life's meaning. It's called expressive therapy. It's an alternative medicine that complements regular medical care and has been shown to benefit patients in a variety of ways—and I have seen it work firsthand with my dearest Pappy. He may be rolling along having a ho-hum day, and then he gets his music therapy, and it's like his whole body gets a megadose of joy.

The experts agree that expressive therapy can help boost a hospice patient's quality of life by alleviating depression and reducing agitation. In a more intangible sense, it can often help a patient connect to themselves and the world—to create and claim a sense of meaning—through a review of their life. I've seen all these benefits in Pappy.

Expressive therapy is an integral part of most hospice programs and includes music therapy, massage therapy, art therapy, narrative therapy, and even pet therapy. All these interactive treatments engage the physical body and the mind and promote well-being. The concepts behind them evolved on a separate but parallel track to the development of modern Western medicine. What I really mean is that it took us a long time in the West to truly accept that the mind, spirit, and body are all connected! They've known this in the East for a much longer time. So if you work on improving one aspect of your health—the mind, the body, or the spirit—you are actually helping your overall well-being.

> **Expressive therapy is an integral part of most hospice programs and includes music therapy, massage therapy, art therapy, narrative therapy, and even pet therapy.**

These days expressive therapy is seen by most doctors as an integral part of healthcare. Even better, as these life-affirming services grow in popularity, so does the trained and certified pool of paid and volunteer staff that offer them to hospice patients.

Here are what expressive therapies can help patients do:

1. Manage their pain

2. Decrease their isolation

3. Find a creative outlet

4. Move and engage with others

5. Think about their lives

6. Create their legacy

Wow. Talk about impact! You may find one or two forms of expressive therapy resonate with you or your loved one more than others. Whatever kind you choose, just remember that the *expressive therapist is part of the patient's hospice team.* The expressive therapist will report back to the hospice team how things are going and be open to feedback from the other team members, the goal being to make the patient's quality of life the best it can be until they draw their last breath.

Which brings me to my final big point about expressive therapies: it's important for you to know that all these therapies can be used at any point in the patient's end-of-life journey. They may participate more actively near the beginning of their hospice experience and, as they approach their final days, only be passive recipients of the therapy. But at any stage of hospice, these are valuable therapies that can enrich every patient's life.

Music Therapy

Music therapy is an established allied health profession. That means it requires certification. In other words you can't just call yourself a music therapist and start playing guitar in hospital rooms, although that's a very nice gesture. Music therapy involves more than entertainment (as awesome as a live performance is). It's about meeting goals for the patient's overall health and well-being, so training is essential.

In an end-of-life hospice situation, music is such medicine for the patient! The therapist uses both active and passive techniques to meet their patients' social, emotional, cognitive, physical, and spiritual needs. The goal is to relieve loneliness, boredom, anxiety, depression, fear, disorientation, confusion, and pain. Sometimes the music therapist will help the patient maintain spiritually based rituals and connections, whether it's through hymn singing or playing songs that reflect a patient's own personal walk with their higher power.

It's also not uncommon for a music therapist to write songs with a patient. Or they may sing together. Pappy's music therapist recorded him singing his favorite songs. I treasure that CD more than anything I own!

You will often see a music therapist play an instrument, chat about lyrics of the patient's favorite songs, ask about the patient's favorite singer or band, or use guided imagery and music together to promote relaxation. Music therapy is lively and thoughtful, fun and enriching.

A couple of things to think about: Patients who receive repeat music therapy sessions do better than patients who only get it once. The more music therapy a patient receives, the higher quality of life they report, even when they are steadily declining. Live music is also more effective than recorded music for decreasing pain symptoms and discomfort. And interestingly music therapists spend more time with hospice patients in nursing homes than nurses and social workers do.

I interview a wonderful music therapist named Anna in part two of the book, so look for that to find out more about what they do!

Massage Therapy

I can see why surveys show that patients in end-of-life care rank music therapy and massage therapy as their two favorite alternative therapies. Music brings us such joy and peace. And who doesn't love to be touched? We all do. Touch is the first sensation that welcomes us into this world, and it seems fitting that it would be important as our lives draw to a close.

Remember those studies about the babies in orphanages who were never picked up and held in a caregiver's arms? They weren't nurtured, so they either wasted away, fell ill, or wound up never being able to connect with other people. Humans *need* touch. Our nervous systems crave touch, and so do our spirits.

Of course massage therapy in end-of-life situations isn't the same kind of vigorous, deep tissue massage therapy you may receive at a spa! Hospice patients can be frail. At the very least, they are more vulnerable than most people. So the massage therapist uses compassionate, gentle touch to ease discomfort, soothe the patient's anxieties, and help them achieve the best quality of life possible.

Most people don't know that massage therapy is not just a feel-good therapy. It can also help medically stabilize the patient. It can reduce high blood pressure, steady the heart rate, improve circulation, decrease pain and joint stiffness, and promote the release of endorphins.

Just wow!

Now as the patient declines, they may not be able to tolerate a lot of physical contact. In those cases the massage therapist will use *focused touch*, which can mean simply holding that patient's hand. From the outside this doesn't look like massage at all, does it? But massage therapists adjust their expectations in hospice. They keep their eye on the big picture—massage in hospice is about *caring*. Focused touch reminds the patient they're not alone. In the active stages of dying, focused touch is particularly reassuring.

In hospice patients who can tolerate more physical contact, massage therapists promote deep relaxation by massaging arms, hands, legs, and feet. A slow-stroke back massage helps relax patients too. Trouble sleeping is not uncommon in hospice patients, so a relaxing side massage can bring on those blessed moments of slumber an agitated patient needs.

The healing presence of a massage therapist is worth its weight in gold. Staying with the patient in the present moment through physical touch brings them peace and comfort in a highly stressful time. Through compassionate massage, a patient feels that they matter and they are not alone. What a valuable source of comfort this ancient art is!

Visual Art Therapy

Exploring painting, collage, photography, video making, and even sculpting or pottery making is a meaningful way for a hospice patient to reconnect with themselves and the world. Personalized art therapy sessions can be healing and transformative, helping the hospice patient focus on an identity beyond their illness. The visual arts also help create space for deep listening during a very difficult time. They're a way to validate a patient's life story and do so in a safe space that allows for that person's individuality to shine.

A patient with their guard down, painting happily away or enjoying creating a photo album, is less stressed, which is always a good outcome in a hospice situation. But besides the physical, psychological, and spiritual benefits dabbling in the visual arts brings about—relaxation, fulfillment, and joy—this form of therapy can also help dementia patients maintain their cognitive functioning or at least slow the decline.

Of course art therapists are sensitive to the fact that many people don't think they're able to create art. The last thing a hospice patient needs is more anxiety, so one goal of the therapist is to build rapport with the patient. They will want to understand something of how that patient views the world before guiding them toward what art medium they may like to explore. One person may love collage. Another may decide creating a video or a photo album is their preference. Still another patient may want to choose an art project tied to their culture.

Often the family is involved in the creation of the art. They may want a portrait painted of their loved one, or they may take part in filming the video or taking photos for an album. Painting on canvases together or making a mobile or scrapbook is another way to create happy memories. Many a treasured family keepsake has been created through visual art therapy.

And in the final stages of life, surrounding your loved one with beautiful artwork handmade by a grandchild, or even a famous painting the patient has always enjoyed, or a vase of gorgeous flowers is another way to use the visual arts to bring that patient peace and comfort.

Narrative Therapy

Everyone has stories to tell, and no one is more expert at talking about your life than you. Narrative therapy in hospice is about using words and language to see the patient's life experiences through their unique viewpoint. At the end of life, there are so many feelings, ranging from anger to fear to hope to confusion. Sometimes patients give up on having a sense of peace in the midst of the turmoil that terminal illness brings. But with the guidance of a narrative therapist listening to their stories, hospice patients can better sift through those complex emotions, reevaluate their life, improve their sense of self, and separate problematic experiences, such as their illness, from their identity as a whole person.

A special aspect of narrative therapy is how it can help the patient and loved ones create a shared story that can be passed down. It can anchor them as a family unit and bring a level of comfort and understanding of each other. No life is perfect. But we can make peace with that. From negative experiences, positive lessons can be learned. When we tell our stories, we can reclaim our lives by creating meaning and forging connection with our listeners.

Interestingly narrative therapy can also help hospice patients with their experience of pain. By identifying and naming aspects of their life that are larger and stronger than their pain, the patient can feel psychologically empowered. In turn the grip of pain on their identity can ease, improving their quality of life.

Narrative therapy is also helpful to the patient and family seeking comfort through spirituality. The therapist can help reframe the patient's end-of-life story in the context of their personal spiritual journey.

Storytelling is nothing new. Humans have been telling stories since the dawn of time, passing them down through the generations. So we should take more advantage of this incredible opportunity to name who we are, to claim our lives, to stand in our unique space and say, "We were here. Don't forget us." It's in our DNA to share our stories and to learn from each other's life experiences. Offering this therapy to a hospice patient is a gift not only to them but also to their families and, ultimately, to all of us, including future generations.

Legacy Projects

So now we come to one of my favorite parts of expressive therapy: creating legacy projects. A legacy project is something physical created to honor someone's life and is passed down to loved ones after that person is gone. The idea is that everyone has a story to tell and share. How they choose to do so is up to them. Visual art therapy, music therapy, and narrative therapy are excellent venues for creating legacy projects.

Legacy projects help boost a hospice patient's spirits and provide an opportunity for the family and patient to celebrate that person's life together. And after that hospice patient has gone, the project provides comfort to the grieving family. A legacy project is a reminder of who that person was as well as who and what they loved while they were with us.

Examples of legacy projects are a cookbook with the patient's favorite recipes, a Christmas ornament, a portrait, a memory box, plaster handprints, a scrapbook, a music CD, a sculpture or some sort of pottery made by the patient, a memory garden, a painting, a journal, a bracelet, poetry or stories (printed and bound in a book or recorded on audiotape or videotape), a shadow box with memorabilia, cards and letters written for future birthdays or special events, and an embroidered or cross-stitched pillow. Digital legacy projects are becoming more common now too as people preserve their photos and narratives online.

Whatever the legacy project, the specialness of it lies not in the objective quality of the final product but the intention behind it and the memories creating while making it. For an example of a legacy project I did with Pappy that you may enjoy doing with your loved one, see page 107.

Pet Therapy

I saved this expressive therapy for last because it is borders on the miraculous to me. Pet therapy is all about promoting the natural bond between humans and animals to bring comfort and peace to terminally ill patients. My dear father in hospice recently lost his dog, Blaze. They'd been together for fifteen years. Those two were joined at the heart. You and I both know that pets enrich our lives during normal times when we're healthy and not thinking too hard about how close we actually are to leaving this planet. But when a person is nearing the end of their life and scary thoughts of death intrude, and pain becomes almost unbearable, pets become our superheroes. They *know* their person is stressed to the max. Ever loyal, they rise to the occasion by showering extra love upon their beloved human. They stay close to their chair. They guard their precious family member. They are the most dedicated hospice volunteers ever. Blaze certainly was, so losing him was not easy.

Did you know Florence Nightingale was the first person to bring small animals into a hospital setting? But a famous psychotherapist named Boris Levenson is credited with really inventing pet therapy. He noticed that taking dogs to work to mingle with his young patients helped them communicate better.

Pets bring out the best in us. They remind us that we can claim joy until the very end. It's amazing to see how hospice patients react to pet therapy. Some people who haven't responded to other therapy absolutely brighten up at the appearance of an animal. They might even speak when they haven't for days. Hospice patients especially could use a dose of joy, don't you think? So the pet therapist should be a part of every hospice team, in my opinion, unless the patient truly doesn't like animals. If a patient is simply allergic to a type of pet, usually the therapist can find a different animal to come visit.

Dogs, bless their furry heads and brimming hearts, are the most common pet therapy animal. There are two types that visit hospice patients. Both provide distraction from pain, calm agitation, and help lighten a patient's mood.

The first kind, the comfort dog, is simply there for companionship, which is very important, of course. A happy patient is enjoying life more than a lonely one. Give most of us an adorable canine with soft eyes and a thumping tail and all our cares seem to disappear, at least for the moments the dog is with us.

Another type of dog visits hospice patients too. This one is specially trained to work as a therapy animal, which means the therapist uses the dog to meet goals beyond providing companionship. One mission of pet therapy is to promote active movement in hospice patients as they play and cuddle with the animal. Often active movement is neglected at this stage of life, but pet therapy can have a real impact on a patient's range of motion and bodily strength. Studies have also found that pet therapy engages people's brains so much that it can slow the rate of dementia and the decline of verbal skills associated with the disease!

Both the comfort dog and the therapy dog have to be able to stay calm and obey commands from their handlers. Most hospices mandate that the handlers are certified in pet therapy and that the pets pass a rigorous screening and a certification process too. Of course any pet and caring owner can provide comfort to a sick person, but screened and trained animals working with certified handlers are trusted to be especially calm and obedient, which is important because they are usually visiting people unfamiliar to them. They have to be able to navigate rooms containing clunky hospital equipment and not be bothered by noisy machines, get tangled up with wires and tubing, knock over canes, or get in the way of wheelchairs. And we definitely don't want the pet therapy animal jumping on patients or eating their meals!

Cats, rabbits, pigs, horses, and birds can be used in pet therapy too. Animals bring peace, love, and their own quiet wisdom to the hospice sickbed. They seem to intuit that terminally ill patients need extra TLC, and they provide it. The love story between Blaze and Pappy is living proof of pet therapy's value to me.

Humor as Therapy

I hope you enjoyed learning about expressive therapies. There's another kind of therapy I wanted to talk about too. It seems obvious because we've all heard that laughter is the best medicine. But it really is—I mean, science says so. Laughter produces all those feel-good chemicals that give us another knot to tie onto the end of our ropes, not just for the patient and the family but for the hospice team too. Humor—appropriate humor, the kind that doesn't make light of suffering but somehow makes

suffering easier to bear—can be a big part of keeping a hospice team working well together and with their patient and the family. Everyone involved in end-of-life scenarios need some release from tension.

Humor is an excellent coping mechanism! When you hear a hospice patient laughing, that usually means they've entered the realm of processing what's happening to them. They are beginning to accept their situation. When a caregiver laughs with a patient, it means bonding is going on, which is always a good thing. Laughter staves off loneliness, even pain! And it's great to use humor to get through those moments of embarrassment for the patient, like having to accept help to use the bathroom.

Using humor in a medical situation is always a balancing act. But it's possible to respect the patient's dignity while still allowing ease and warmth to enter the hospice space through gentle humor.

In its own way, laughter can also help create a bit of needed distance when emotions are surging. Have you ever laughed while you cried? That's how we deal with tough emotion sometimes. It's normal and nothing to be ashamed of. Or someone may tell a joke just when everyone is really down, and the sheer absurdity of it may remind folks that we are in this crazy thing called life together.

Pappy has dementia and is in hospice, but he still makes me laugh all the time. I do the same for him. His eating is slowing down, and I said, "Daddy, I'd really like you to take two more bites of the chicken pot pie for me, please. Would you do that?" He said, "Okay, I don't want to, but it's for you. Right?" I said, "Yeah, for me. I want you to do it for me." So he took two spoonfuls and put it on *my* plate! Boy, did we get a chuckle out of that.

When we're in the middle of a difficult situation we have little control over, it's the small things, the light moments, that keep us brave *and* flexible. We are all humans riding on the same spaceship called Earth. Humor reminds us we have so much in common, and that's a true comfort.

Nurse Debbie's Legacy Project for Pappy

I came up with my legacy project for Pappy on my own, but if you're not sure what to do, ask your hospice team. They'll have lots of ideas, I'm sure, especially if you're working with a music therapist, visual art therapist, or narrative therapist. But I'd love it if you decide you want to use the idea I'm presenting here. It's very simple, but it will mean a lot to you and your loved one. And when they're gone, you'll remember sharing it with them.

I promise you'll never regret reading this project out loud to your special person, no matter how much it makes either of you cry. When we say our loving words out loud, we feel how powerful love is. Admit it. It's scary to love. It breaks our hearts. Yet we wouldn't choose anything else, would we? And by making that choice to love, no matter how much it hurts, love, in turn, empowers *us*. I promise you, our big hearts will carry us through the grieving, each of us at our own pace.

After you read this out loud to your person, you can frame it or put it into a scrapbook by their bedside for them to see and read every day.

So what is this project, really? Well, with my favorite guy Pappy in hospice, it became very clear to me how important it is to stay positive for him. But all too often, people are extremely willing to tell us what we're doing wrong. I see negativity on social media and hear it on the radio and TV. And there are people in every person's life ready to jump on what we do wrong. We waste so much time on the negative. But when we're staring death in the face—the passing of one of our loved ones, or maybe we're facing our own transition—we realize more than ever how amazing life is, how lucky we are, and how special each and every one of us is.

We are. Believe that. And spread the message with me.

But back to our loved ones in hospice. They don't have a lot of time. We need to tell them, while we have them with us, how important they are to us. It means so much to get words of affirmation, doesn't it? This project is all about telling your beloved hospice patient what makes them so special to you. All you have to do is take time to think of at least ten things you love about your person. You can think of big or small things. You can talk about their dimples, or their laugh, or some great accomplishment they had, or their wonderful hugs, or one small thing they do out of love that you always took for granted. Those little things you remember sometimes mean the most.

You can choose things you love that no one else will even understand, except you and your loved one and maybe a few family members. It's up to you. Thinking of these things might make you cry. Or chuckle. Either way you'll be honoring your loved one. You're taking the time to show simple gratitude. While I was coming up with my list, I really enjoyed thinking about Pappy. It made me realize how precious our bond truly is. He's totally unique. He's my Pappy. There will never be another one of him, and I thank God he was put into my life.

When you're done with your list, you can present it just as it is. Or you can go to town and make it into a big poster and decorate it with your favorite pictures. Or like I said earlier, you can type it up or write it in a pretty color ink and frame it. Or glue it into a special notebook and keep adding wonderful things about your loved one. Maybe you can even ask visitors to your hospice patient's room to add their favorite things about your person! Keep it going!

I'll add too that if the hospice patient is doing well enough, give them the opportunity to draw up their own list and say out loud things they love about *you*. Even hearing one reason why your person loves you can bolster you for life! It can carry you through the bereavement process like nothing else.

So I'm suggesting this could be a two-way street, a fun activity for everyone in the inner circle of this hospice patient's life.

Ten Things I Love About You, Pappy!

1. First and foremost the thing that sets you apart from all the men I've ever known is how much I love that you adopted me when I was three years old, and you were twenty-one. You were just a boy! Yet you made me your daughter, and you never looked back. You are the best father a girl could ever ask for.

2. Pappy, for you, family always came first. Always, always! There was never a doubt about that. Never a question mark. I just love how you loved my mother. You have set the bar so high. You were a wonderful husband to Momma and an amazing father to all your children.

3. You are brutally and 100 percent honest. What you say, I can count on. You wouldn't know how to pull the wool over anyone's eyes. You say what you believe. This has meant so much to me. I can trust you to tell me the truth.

4. Pappy, you are loyal. It's such a hard virtue to find these days. So many people don't think loyalty is important, but when

the chips are down, we need to know we can rely on our people. I have always been able to rely on you, through thick and thin.

5. You are such a hard worker. Because of you I am a hard worker. I see how it gives a person dignity and pride and how fulfilling it is to do your very best and not give up. Thank you for being such a great example to me that way.

6. You have a huge sense of adventure. You love life, and you took risks. And you still managed to have fun. You've taught me to embrace my dreams too and not be afraid, even if success is not guaranteed. Because it's all about the journey, Pappy. You taught me that. Thank you for the lesson.

7. Pappy, you are fearless. Any time I'm tempted to be afraid, I remember you. I buck up. I tell myself fear cannot control me. Fear will not lead my decision-making. Whenever I'm brave, that's thanks to you.

8. You sing the craziest song, and no one likes you to sing it! I confess, I'm laughing just thinking about it. You're so good at getting a rise out of people! You're such a jokester! You passed that playful attitude down to me, and I love you for it. Sometimes we just have to be silly. A sense of humor keeps us flexible! You taught me that.

9. I do love your smile. You're already so handsome, but that smile of yours simply blows everyone away. People write to me about your smile all the time. You always look so cute and happy. I'm never going to forget your smiling face, Pappy. When I'm down, I'm going to think of you and that special inner light you have had your whole life.

10. Pappy, you have always been the caretaker, the protector, the person who makes sure no one else is left behind. I can't tell you what this means to me. Thank you, Pappy, for cherishing me. That's what keeps me strong. You are why I have such a loving heart, no matter what life throws at me. I also want to thank you for taking care of all the people you and I both love, like Momma and my siblings. Hey, you even take care of people who don't always appreciate what you've done! That's a noble heart you have, to love with no expectation of return. I'm so glad God decided to give you to us, Pappy. I love you with all my heart.

So that's it. That's my legacy project for and about Pappy. I plan on doing other things too. I love the idea of honoring him with a garden. He was a country boy. He loved the earth and making things grow! I could also donate to my local veterans hospital. He was in the air force and loved his country very much. He'd like for me to help

veterans. Or maybe I could set up a nursing scholarship in his name because he's the one who encouraged me to be a nurse. I like that idea too of a young nursing student being helped by Pappy in his own way.

Just thinking of potential legacy projects to honor Pappy bolsters my spirits. It's very easy to focus on the sad parts of a loved one's passing, isn't it? But I know Pappy will be so proud of me if I create something positive from this experience. After he leaves me, I will still be reading my ten things I love about him, and I will remember how much it meant to him too.

Like me, you have an amazing chance to enhance your life and your loved one's with a legacy project. Don't be shy to express your love. You'll never regret it.

PART 2:

Hospice Team Interviews

Talking one-on-one to members of a hospice team is a great idea when you're learning about hospice. The more you know about what the team does, the better informed you'll be when you or your loved one needs the special kind of care hospice offers. So in this part, I want to provide you a glimpse into the hearts and minds of skilled hospice team members I've worked with personally. They are all great people and have tremendous insights and advice to offer. Enjoy!

Sharon, Hospice Volunteer

NURSE DEBBIE:

I'm really thrilled I get to talk to you, Sharon. I want to know if you could take me through what a day in the life of a hospice volunteer is like. What does a hospice volunteer do? What do you do, in particular, and how did you decide to get into it?

SHARON:

Well, I first decided to get into it because my sister has been involved in hospice for many years, and she shared a lot about her experiences and how positive it was. And also I had been through hospice on the receiving end when I had family members and friends who were dying and going into hospice. So I had several experiences that were very positive, and I saw how much value it was for my family and friends and also to me. It was a great comfort. I recently retired and was looking for a volunteer opportunity. I thought about hospice, and then my son suggested it too. He's training to be a physician's assistant. He went through the hospice training and had a really positive experience.

NURSE DEBBIE:

How did your training go?

SHARON:

I was very impressed with my local hospital's training program. It's quite intensive. It's several days that you have to commit to, and you're going through with a number of other potential volunteers. The volunteer coordinator was fabulous.

NURSE DEBBIE:

Did you actually report there in person and take classes?

SHARON:

Yes. The classes were at the hospital. It was very structured—three days where you have various people who are part of the hospice team, including physicians, nurses, social workers, and pastoral/counseling people, come in and share their roles. They do that so you can understand where your role will fit in. And then you learn all about the death and dying process and what kind of issues come up for people, both those who are going through the dying process as well as family members.

And then we did role playing. We saw a number of videos that they had done about hospice, a lot of different situations. It was really enlightening. We had to share a lot of our own feelings about death and dying and our experiences about that too. They're very careful about making sure potential volunteers are a good match for the program. Our volunteer coordinator told us that. She screens you on the phone first. Then you have an interview with her in person, and if you get through that, you're admitted into the training program.

NURSE DEBBIE:

They sound very responsible with their screening.

SHARON:

Yes. You're not guaranteed a role because they do want to make sure people are going into it for the right reasons.

NURSE DEBBIE:

Do they do a security check on the volunteers?

SHARON:

Oh yes. A background check. We have to give all that information. And health information. Because you're going into people's homes. You're dealing with people during very vulnerable situations in their lives. Same with their family members. Everyone is in very vulnerable situations. But I was impressed about how thorough the training was. Obviously you had to be committed that this is something you want to do.

NURSE DEBBIE:

Does the hospital system that trained you have their own hospice care facility?

SHARON:

Yes. So if somebody at the hospital needs to be admitted to a hospice situation and they don't have access at home to the level of support they need while going through this process, these patients can go into this hospice care facility called the Cottage. It's really nice—set off in a little wooded industrial park. It's also used to provide respite for caregivers who need to go away on a trip or just need a break.

Family members can come and visit their loved one. And as a volunteer at the Cottage, you go around to the rooms, bringing water or talking to people, supporting family members coming in. You can answer the door, sit at the front desk, all kinds of different things. I've helped out there a couple of times, but my preference from day one was to go into homes because I wanted more of a one-on-one, close relationship with the patient and family. So I've supported them when they've needed me at the Cottage, but my preference has been volunteering in patients' homes.

My first home visit was with a gentleman who was close to passing. He had moved into a little apartment above the garage of his stepdaughter. She had offered to take him in. She herself really didn't have any other family. It was interesting because she was a young mom going through her own transitioning about his upcoming death. She was having a very hard time with it. She has young children, and she was worried about them too, which we see a lot.

NURSE DEBBIE:

I'm sure there are lots of emotions to deal with in the family.

SHARON:

Yes.

NURSE DEBBIE:

How did you get connected with this man? Did your volunteer coordinator call you and say, "I have a gentleman above a garage I need you to go visit?"

SHARON (CHUCKLING):

Yes. Something like that. She'll call when she thinks she's got a good match for you. She'll describe the situation and give you a rough outline. And then you can say yay or nay. Also, I haven't mentioned that they like you to go visit not more than once or twice a week.

NURSE DEBBIE:

And do you have to set that first visit up beforehand with the family?

SHARON:

Yes. You set it up yourself. You work with that individual and the family. So when the volunteer coordinator gives me a name, I call and say, "Hey, I'm a hospice volunteer. I was given your name by so-and-so, and I'd like to come in and meet with you and talk with you and your family member about my coming to visit you regularly." They know the process ahead of time because the coordinators talk to them about it. By the time I call, they're actively enrolled in hospice. By the way, to get into hospice, a doctor has to recommend them first.

NURSE DEBBIE:

Oh yes, you need that physician referral.

SHARON:

So you set up a mutual time that will work for the two of you, and then you go visit. The focus of hospice as a volunteer is to be there as a listening post and let people talk. You're told not to share about your own life. It's not about telling stories about yourself. It's about having them open up and communicate whatever it is that they need to talk about.

NURSE DEBBIE:

Do they teach you skills about how to get people to open up?

SHARON:

Oh yes, they do. You go through lots of training on active listening. They also train us on how to navigate conversations that might be difficult. For instance, if you're not a religious person and you've got somebody who's really religious—and obviously they want to talk about that and the next point in their life—you want to just let them talk. You don't want to, obviously, share your points of view on that. You're there to bring them out and let them communicate what they need and then help facilitate if they really want to reach out to a family member. Or if they want to talk to a social worker or chaplain. You would let the social worker or chaplain know through online team conversations. These patients in hospice are being visited by various members of the team regularly. I'm only one part of this team.

NURSE DEBBIE:

How long do your visits last with each patient?

SHARON:

Usually for a couple hours because it takes a while for people to unwind and say everything they want to say, not just the patient but the family too. I've had experiences of all kinds. The gentleman above the garage, I actually probably spent as much time with the stepdaughter as I did him. She obviously needed to talk. The patient also had so much to say. He wanted to talk and reminisce about his life. I only saw him a couple of times. Sadly he passed away shortly after I started as a volunteer.

NURSE DEBBIE:

Do the hospice trainers encourage you to hold the patient's hand or stay apart?

SHARON:

Yes. You can touch and help them, like a caregiver. That includes giving them their medicine. They have to take it themselves, though.

NURSE DEBBIE:

Can you tell us about another patient?

SHARON:

Sure. The second person I visited for around six months. She had dementia, late-stage Alzheimer's. She was not too communicative at all, but I found a way to connect. She loved music, and so I'd find a lot of music from her generation. I would play it, and then because she couldn't talk, I would talk. I was mainly there to give respite for the daughter she was living with. The patient had full-time caregivers. I'd be there between them coming and going so I'd have time with her. And I'd take her for walks in her wheelchair.

NURSE DEBBIE:

Wow.

SHARON:

It was more of a one-sided thing. Different from the first patient I worked with. Then my next one blew me away. It was just very powerful. She was an amazing woman. A young woman in her forties dying of cancer. I got very close with her and her husband. She was just a brave, positive person. She took this on with such grace and strength.

NURSE DEBBIE:

Aww. Did she have children?

SHARON:

Stepchildren she was close with. She actually went back to die with her family out of state, where she had sisters. The step-kids lived there too. I think she was only there with her sisters a couple of weeks, and she died. But she was so happy. That's really what she wanted to do. It was hard because we had to convince her husband here that that was something he needed to do for her. Take her there, back home. He didn't want to. He wanted to keep her with him here, just the two of them. He had a business. They owned their own business. There was a lot of stress on them.

NURSE DEBBIE:

Did her husband wind up going with her?

SHARON:

Yes, he did. But there was a lot of drama in the family, which is not uncommon in hospice situations. I met the sisters. They came to visit here. You get very close with these people during this very intimate time. Her husband was totally into the idea that there was going to be a miracle from God. They were religious, and God was going to save her. It got to the point that his minister tried to help him come to closure and to realize that she was going to die. The patient herself knew. I mean, she had hope up to nearly the end, but then she realized. I mean, she was really accepting. And so it was all about trying to help him let her go.

NURSE DEBBIE:

I applaud you for being supportive to all the patients and their families. Do you talk to the other hospice team members sometimes?

SHARON:

Oh yes. What we do is, every time you visit, you write up a report online. You send that in, and then they share it with the rest of the hospice team. You see their reports also. So you're kept apprised of the patient's health, the different dynamics, what they're learning so you can work together. Obviously you don't want to be in the dark about the patient's situation. And quite often I will find myself crossing paths with the social worker or with the nurse, and we chat in person.

NURSE DEBBIE:

In your volunteer training, what did they tell you about handling your emotions?

SHARON:

They said you've got to remember you're there for them, for the family and for the patient. And they do tell you've got to know how to handle your feelings. But if you're overcome—I mean, I had tears in my eyes many times with this last woman—they say it's okay. I was extra close with my last patient. We would tell each other we loved each other and hug. We really did get close.

NURSE DEBBIE:

Here you are, a stranger coming into her life at the end, and she feels so much love for you. That's wonderful. And you loved her?

121

SHARON:

Yes, I did. At this point, when people are willing and able to do it, you can get very deep quickly because everybody is so open. They're willing. If you're willing, you can go to some interesting depths in your relationship. I was sad when she died, but I also knew her suffering was over. She was dealing with a lot of pain in and out, and it takes an emotional toll. I knew she felt complete and was able to do what she wanted to do at the end of her life. So I felt good about that.

NURSE DEBBIE:

So when you're working with a patient, how many hours a week do you think you spend with that patient?

SHARON:

If you count travel and everything, about three hours a week.

NURSE DEBBIE:

Do you ever have more than one patient at a time?

SHARON:

You can. They suggest that you don't. Also, sometimes you can't make your appointment for personal reasons. When I had the one patient with dementia, I had to be gone a couple of weeks. And so they had other backup volunteers that filled in at that stage. They came and took my shift basically.

NURSE DEBBIE:

That's good.

SHARON:

It always seems to work pretty well. And then, of course, our volunteer coordinator has been deeply involved in hospice for many, many years. So if you have questions, or if you're going through something emotionally with a patient, or you're finding some hard times, the coordinator is always there, ready to talk.

My sister is a hospice volunteer. She's a more open heart-and-soul person. I'm probably a little more pragmatic than she is. And sometimes she would try to help the family out more than she should. The hospice team doesn't want you to get too intimately involved in the sense that you're supporting the family beyond the parameters of the position. It's tough. We need to know our role.

NURSE DEBBIE:

You mean, some people want to give the family money or something else that might be considered too much involvement?

SHARON:

Oh yes. Or you might say, "What a shame your car's broken down. No problem. I'll pick you up and drive you here and there." But we're not supposed to get that involved. My sister had to be coached a little bit about holding back the tendency to over-involve herself. And we are taught how to decline if the patient or family asks us for assistance beyond what we are supposed to offer. Of course we can go and help make dinner. If you want. If you don't want to, no, you don't have to. You just say, "No, I really don't think I can help you with that." But, yeah, I've tidied up the room a little bit. Or I help them with some craft project that they might want to do. You're there to do that, but they don't want you going beyond your regular visiting time. They don't want you taking additional roles as a helpmate outside that.

NURSE DEBBIE:

So if you had to give one bit of advice to me or anybody else who is thinking about becoming a hospice volunteer, what would you say?

SHARON:

I'd say do some reading first about death and dying. I've researched a lot to understand what it's about. And if you're not familiar with hospice—if you haven't had anybody around you die or you haven't experienced hospice before—I think it's helpful for you to read a little bit about hospice too. But definitely read about the death and dying process. That's essential.

NURSE DEBBIE:

Good advice.

SHARON:

So then you know you'll be comfortable and that this is something that you want to do. I've always felt it was such a privilege just to be part of it. I mean, birth and death are the two most intimate times of our lives. Midwives and doctors are there for birth. For someone to invite you into the last phase of the cycle of life, to share that with them, I think of it as an honor. It is. You see the strength of people and the strength of families. You see families going through all kinds of stuff. But everybody processes differently, and you have to really learn to respect that and to understand it. There's no one right way.

NURSE DEBBIE:

Excellent points.

SHARON:

And I think that's probably the biggest piece of advice. Learn as much as you can. Talk to people who have done hospice so you know if that's something that's right for you.

NURSE DEBBIE:

That's really good advice. Do you feel you've changed at all, either in a big way or small way, as a result of being a hospice volunteer?

SHARON:

Yes. I think I've learned how to move into intimacy more quickly with people. I think before … well, I'm more of a natural introvert. I'm not necessarily an extroverted person. And so I just don't open my arms and want to get deep with somebody right away. I'm a little more cautious. But I've learned in these situations that these patients and their families are so ready for it, in most cases. We need to be there for them and respond to them, to that desire for intimacy. The strengths of people and the purity that comes out of people at the end of their lives is very interesting.

NURSE DEBBIE:

Really?

SHARON:

I've only seen this shining light from people. When you come to terms with your passing, if you have time, if you're lucky enough to have the gift of time to process, it's amazing to see how people move through it.

NURSE DEBBIE:

Wow. That's awesome.

SHARON:

It is great. And it doesn't require a lot of the volunteer's time. It's just a couple of hours a week. But they are very powerful, those few hours. They can be life-changing.

Anna, Music Therapist

NURSE DEBBIE:

Hey, Anna. I so appreciate your talking to me. You're an amazing person with a lot of gifts you're sharing with the world through music therapy.

ANNA:

Aww. Thank you.

NURSE DEBBIE:

You started a music therapy business in Richmond called Healing Sounds, LLC.

ANNA:

Yes. We stay quite busy. I love my work.

NURSE DEBBIE:

I can see why. I think my favorite part of the whole Serenity First care experience, speaking from the viewpoint of someone whose own dad has dementia, is the music therapy. I cannot talk about it enough.

ANNA:

I'm so glad.

NURSE DEBBIE:

It's a wonderful thing that you do. Many people reading this book have probably seen high school students come in and sing old songs to nursing home residents. The residents sing along and look so happy. Is that music therapy?

ANNA:

Not exactly. There's a little bit of a difference between music therapy and high schoolers coming in to play music. We all know that music is beneficial to everyone. Most people listen to music to pump them up, to make them feel better. And most people know that live music carries a different amount of energy. We appreciate going to see live musicians in any shape or form.

NURSE DEBBIE:

Yes, I love a live band.

ANNA:

I do too. But there's a big difference between music therapy and entertainers, such as a band, a choir group, a handbell choir, or a solo guitarist who might come in to a nursing home. Even though we're all using music to benefit our listeners, a huge difference is that *music therapists are using music to work on nonmusical goals.*

NURSE DEBBIE:

I see—nonmusical goals. How fascinating!

ANNA:

Yes. So a music therapist's reason for meeting with a patient could be to help with physical symptoms, like reducing pain or agitation. Or we might be helping alleviate depression or isolation.

NURSE DEBBIE:

Such important objectives.

ANNA:

Yes. Sometimes the music therapist comes in to help patients who feel confused or frustrated with their loss of independence. We can also help with spiritual needs. As people come to the end of life , we can certainly improve the quality of their last days. And so it's different from musical performance because an entertainer is there to only bring music and joy. We're there to do a bit more than that.

We're celebrating the person's life, we're providing support and comfort in the dying process, we're helping them leave a legacy or inspiring connection with family members. And we're doing all that through music. It could be live music or recorded music. It could be the discussion of the patient's favorite music and the memories that might be connected to those music selections. It could also be music making. We have a lot of clients who play the maracas and the drums along with us. So then there's that, the actual physical stimulation that comes along with it.

NURSE DEBBIE:

My most cherished possession is a recording of Pappy singing. I will treasure that the rest of my life. So that's part of the legacy goal of music therapy.

ANNA:

Yes, it is. So when we do a legacy project, it has to be with somebody who is cognitively able to do something like that. It can be a recording of them singing or playing their favorite songs. Or it could be that we've written a song together.

NURSE DEBBIE:

I love that!

ANNA:

We can record one song, or it could be a full album, which is pretty awesome. But it has to be when the patient is at the right state of mind cognitively.

NURSE DEBBIE:

So there is a point where that kind of project is no longer possible.

ANNA:

Yes. So it's a good idea to get music therapists involved early. We are here and available, and we're doing good work. But many people don't know about us. And certainly the lawmakers and some insurance companies don't always respect that it's a valid aspect of hospice care.

NURSE DEBBIE:

We need to let everyone know about music therapy! Can you tell me what happens during a session with a hospice patient?

ANNA:

Sure. Music therapy is an incredibly broad field to learn about, but here's a typical scenario that might take place between any music therapist and a hospice patient. Let's say a patient is referred to music therapy by a hospice nurse due to his emotional outbursts, anxiety, and irritability with staff and other residents at his care facility. The patient's past history with music included playing piano as a young child and singing in the church choir as an adult. He prefers '50s and '60s rock and roll, although his daughter tells the therapist he likes hymns.

When the music therapist does the initial assessment, she finds the patient asleep. When she eventually is able to interview him, the patient says he doesn't need therapy, and he doesn't like music. Nevertheless the music therapist persists. It's not unusual for patients to be skeptical at first about music therapy's benefits. But music therapists are patient. They know how to work with the person's personality and physical limitations to get to a point of true connection.

So let's say this particular music therapist shares a list of rock songs from the decades the patient prefers, and he immediately starts talking about concerts he attended, records he coveted, and music he would dance to. The therapist asks if he wants to hear some of the music, and he says yes. When the therapist tries to sing along with the recorded music, the patient becomes agitated. Even so, he agrees to meet with the therapist weekly. It's clear that music therapy can support his emotional regulation and decrease his anxiety and agitation.

Over subsequent sessions, the relationship grows, and the patient is willing to sing along with the music therapist to his favorite music without the recording. He even begins to prepare a list of songs for the therapist to learn. She asks the patient if he would like to record some of the songs, and he agrees. They begin to record the patient singing while the music therapist provides guitar accompaniment and harmony. Soon they have several songs recorded.

Then the music therapist suggests they write their own song. The patient is starting to decline and does not have as much energy to sing. However, he is able to give the therapist ideas for their song and determines the tempo and framework for the accompaniment. They record their short song and call it "Song for My Daughter." The music is shared with the family and cherished.

Soon the patient is declining so much that he's asleep during most of the music therapist's visits. The therapist provides guitar renditions of the songs they sang in previous sessions. Occasionally the patient will awake and smile at the music therapist. On rare occasions he will make a request. The music therapist is able to provide support in the dying process. That's our ultimate goal, to be of service to each and every patient, using the language of music to ease their suffering and enhance their quality of life until they pass away.

NURSE DEBBIE:

And such a worthy goal it is. Thanks, Anna, for sharing what you do in music therapy at Healing Sounds!

For anyone who wants more information about Anna's wonderful company in Richmond, Virginia, go to www.healingsoundsrva.com.

Jo, Registered Nurse

NURSE DEBBIE:

Jo, you're an RN like me, and I love your passion for patients and your whole take on hospice. You've been involved in the field a long time.

JO:

Yes, about thirteen years. I've had a variety of hospice roles, from being a case manager in the field taking care of patients to quality improvement, making sure that we're giving the best care, the highest quality, and meeting all our goals and standards. I've also been an administrator running and coordinating the care of hospices. Currently I'm working on the other side, helping with educating on the documentation side of it with the electronic medical records. So throughout my career, I've done a little bit of everything in hospice—from patient care to making sure the agency is running the way it should and that we're taking the best care of the patients.

NURSE DEBBIE:

So many people don't know a patient can get hospice for six months—it can start as soon as the doctor gives the diagnosis.

JO:

That's the biggest misnomer. The actual criteria, according to Medicare, is that you have to have a prognosis of six months or less if your disease follows its normal course. Now, of course, nobody really knows exactly when a person will die. It's really aimed at people for whom treatment is no longer available, or they don't want to seek any more active treatment to cure their disease. They're at a point where they just want supportive care. They want to focus on being comfortable. They're not wanting to go back to the hospital anymore and have that aggressive treatment. There are patients that are on hospice for a year sometimes, and we even have patients that graduate from hospice because they get better. So, I mean, I would say one of the biggest things that I tell people is it's not about giving up.

NURSE DEBBIE:

That's worth repeating: hospice is not about giving up!

JO:

Exactly. And we find that a lot of patients, once they come on hospice—because you've got a nurse and a medical director, and sometimes a nurse practitioner, who are focused on looking at and adjusting your medications—sometimes these patients have been seeing six or seven doctors, all prescribing different things. Sometimes when you get control of those medications, the patient actually starts to feel better for a while.

NURSE DEBBIE:

That's what happened to Pappy.

JO:

Yes, it's amazing. I've had patients who have graduated hospice and come back five years later. So it's definitely not about giving up.

NURSE DEBBIE:

I'll bet psychologically that's why people steer clear of hospice. Like if someone's mother decides she wants hospice, the grown kids might say, "No, Mom! You're giving up," and then the mother would feel guilty, and the kids would feel mad or upset or hurt. It's so psychologically fraught when you say, "I'm going to hospice." Same with saying, "Mom, you should go to hospice," because people are assuming that the person saying it—in this case, the grown children—are giving up on their mother's life. And none of that is true. Hospice *helps*.

JO:

Yes, absolutely. Hospice helps. Even so, you do find a lot of patients or families who have that guilt. They feel they need to keep fighting for their family, or the family feels guilty for putting them in hospice because they feel like they're giving up on their mother, or their brother, or whoever the patient is. Nothing could be further from the truth.

NURSE DEBBIE:

Right. I wonder if there's a new way to frame that. Like instead of saying, "I'm giving up on life," we can say, *"I want the best for my loved one in the final part of their life."* Something more positive that people could see.

JO:

Yes. I think the key is, hospice is not about dying. It's about improving the quality of life.

NURSE DEBBIE:

That's a good way to put it.

JO:

Whenever I tell people I've worked in hospice, they immediately go, "That's so depressing." And it's really not because we're not focused on the death. We are focused on making sure every single day the patient has left is the best day possible. So we're making them all comfortable. It's as much about the family unit as it is about the patient.

Recently I coordinated a FaceTime session for a patient with her daughter who lived in New York so the patient could actually see the birth of her grandchild. That was what was important to her before she died.

Hospice is a lot like the concept of Make-A-Wish. It's finding out what is important to that patient and the family and doing everything to help support what their goals and wishes are, whether it's the last few days, weeks, or months. There's actually research to prove that the earlier terminally ill patients get hospice, the longer actually their life expectancy.

NURSE DEBBIE:

That makes so much sense.

JO:

Yes, and the hardest thing is, when people come into hospice at the last minute because they have anxiety and guilt, it's much more difficult to get their symptoms under control and really have that impact and help the family because there's a lot the hospice team does. You have a team of a director or doctor, a nurse, a social worker, a chaplain, and it's the only area of medicine and healthcare where you're required to have volunteers.

NURSE DEBBIE:

That's so cool. *Required* to have volunteers.

JO:

They have a whole team of volunteers! We're not just focused on the physical aspect of the patient's situation. It's the whole person. It's being holistic—their social well-being, psychological and spiritual well-being too. And then once the patient does pass, the hospice team offers bereavement counseling to anyone in the family for thirteen months. So for over a year after the patient dies.

NURSE DEBBIE:

That's how it should be, the family being looked after.

JO:

Right. The care continues far beyond the patient's passing. I mean, there's so much with hospice. It's funny. I just got off the phone with a good friend of mine who is going through this with her aunt, and she knew nothing about hospice. She was asking, "Why can't the hospice people stay twenty-four hours a day?" That's probably one of the biggest myths about hospice. People don't realize the team members come and go. And the other myth is that most people believe hospice is a place patients move into.

NURSE DEBBIE:

That's what a friend of mine used to think. She thought it was a building!

JO:

Right. Almost everyone thinks that, and it's not. The idea of hospice is that we take care of the patient wherever they are, or wherever they want to be. We have patients in group homes, in nursing homes, and some who live in independent living. So it's not a place. And as I said, we're there to support the family, not to *replace* the family.

NURSE DEBBIE:

That makes sense. Hospice is helping the family. Not taking over.

JO:

Exactly. I'd love to talk a little bit more about volunteer programs. They can be very creative. So you could have a volunteer who does massage therapy, a volunteer who does pet therapy. We've even had Reiki. I've worked in hospices where they had a volunteer vigil program. For example, you might have a patient in assisted living, and there's no family that live nearby, or maybe they can't be there and they don't want their loved one to die alone. Some hospices develop a vigil program where they have volunteers on call, and they'll say, "We need you to go sit with this patient." And so they will go and sit so that they can ensure that no patient dies alone.

NURSE DEBBIE:

That is so important!

JO:

It is. Some of these volunteers are retired nurses. Others may have a history in spiritual care. And of course we have music therapists who provide music therapy to patients. I've seen patients, nonverbal patients with dementia who just came out of themselves with music therapy. It's amazing. It's very moving to see it. It's incredible.

NURSE DEBBIE:

Can you just locate a hospice company and say, "I want to volunteer?"

JO:

Yes. Look up hospice companies, or call your local hospital. They will put you through training. They do quite significant training with all the volunteers. They will have a volunteer coordinator who meets with every patient so they can make sure there's a good fit between the volunteer and the patient. Because not all of them are good fits. They might want to have someone who has a similar background.

NURSE DEBBIE:

That's what I heard already from my friend Sharon, a hospice volunteer. But it bears repeating that volunteers aren't placed willy-nilly. I'm glad you brought that up because I wanted to ask you about cultural issues with hospice. Different cultures have different ways of approaching death. How does hospice accommodate for that and maybe for different religions and countries?

JO:

Good question. There is a lot of diversity between cultures and countries of origin. In some cultures it's disrespectful to shake hands, or what we consider a greeting here in the United States could actually be considered offensive in some cultures and religions. So on the hospice team, we need to be respectful and sensitive to these differences. For instance, the hospice team has a chaplain on it. And probably one of the biggest myths we have to overcome is that people think the chaplain is there to convert them to their particular religion. But they're not. The chaplains are there as a nondenominational spiritual support.

NURSE DEBBIE:

That's good to know about the chaplain.

JO:

It should be very reassuring to the patient and the family. The chaplain will have an understanding of people from every spiritual or religious background. And part of their role is to connect with an advisor from the patient's religion. Say, for example, if we had a patient who is Jewish. The chaplain will reach out to a rabbi. Maybe this patient hasn't lived here very long and doesn't have a religious connection, but they want it, so the chaplain will connect with someone from the patient's religion to help facilitate whatever their spiritual needs are related to their religion.

So chaplains are not there to pray and preach Christianity to someone who's not Christian. We get patients who are agnostic or atheist, and the chaplain is there as an added spiritual, psychological support for the patient and family. It could be that a family member needs spiritual counseling too.

NURSE DEBBIE:

Addressing spirituality is a big part of hospice, as much taking care of the patient's physical and psychological needs.

JO:

Yes. And as far as languages go, the hospice team has access to a language line, so they do have translators available. It's not uncommon for us to have families in which nobody speaks English. So the team will either try and match the patient and family with a nurse who speaks that language, or the team has that language line where they can get a translator on the phone to be able to translate.

NURSE DEBBIE:

So cultural needs matter and are met in hospice care.

JO:

Yes, definitely.

NURSE DEBBIE:

What else will a newbie to hospice appreciate hearing about?

JO:

One of the benefits of hospice is that once you're signed up, hospice will pay for any medications that the patient needs to manage symptoms related to their diagnosis, as well as any medical equipment they need, and supplies. There's also a level of care where the family can get respite for five days. So if the caregiver needs a break, hospice care pays for that.

NURSE DEBBIE:

Medicare pays for that?

JO:

Yes. You'll have caregivers who are exhausted or maybe called away. The patient can go for five days to a contracted care facility, and it's covered a hundred percent.

NURSE DEBBIE:

Wow. This is so good to know. Now I'm wondering about patients who might have a little bit of dementia, who might live alone, who really don't have a whole lot of connections in their community. They're sitting in their house, and they've gotten a terminal diagnosis. How do we connect them with hospice? How do we connect homeless people with hospice? There's so many people who won't read this book and who don't have a loved one to support them. I'm just curious about that. I hate for anyone to get left behind.

JO:

Me too. I've seen such a change in the way hospices get referrals now. There are a number of ways people get referred to hospice. One is their primary care physician or any physician in the community. A lot of patients get referred from hospitals because you have patients who have never been to the doctor and wind up in emergency rooms. They might be homeless. The hospitals are very aware of the benefit of hospice, so they will refer from there.

Any organization can connect someone with hospice. For instance, community churches may have hospice contacts. People who work with Meals on Wheels—any kind of community resource. It's very important to educate the whole community at large, even homeless shelters. They might have people coming into the shelters really needing hospice.

But for the majority of patients today that don't go to see doctors, or who don't have that community contact, it's usually, unfortunately, when they end up in the emergency room. The hospital physicians or hospital team will identify that the patient would benefit from hospice.

NURSE DEBBIE:

So you're saying we all need to educate ourselves, our families, and people we work with about hospice. It could be that we are able to connect someone to hospice care who really needs it.

JO:

Yes. Let's spread the good news about hospice. No one should die alone. Everyone deserves comfort and support and the best quality of life possible.

NURSE DEBBIE:

I agree completely!

Crystal, Hospice Aide

NURSE DEBBIE:

Hi, Crystal. You work with my father, Pappy, as his health aide, and he adores you. How long have you been a certified nursing assistant or CNA for short?

CRYSTAL:

I've been a CNA for going on twenty-nine years in November. And I love your dad. I call him Mr. J.

NURSE DEBBIE:

Thank you for all you've done for him. I firmly believe aides are the unsung heroes of hospice care. Y'all are the eyes, ears, hands, and heart of the whole operation because you're there with the patients the most, of all the team members. And so the other team members rely on you and your observation to make the hospice care plan work.

CRYSTAL:

We're the first point of contact with the patient. So we see them more than the nurses, the doctors, the social workers, and therapists. Sometimes we're with them daily, although it's usually three or four times a week. So we learn their routines and become friends with a lot of them.

NURSE DEBBIE:

Is it hard to stay professional?

CRYSTAL:

It is at times. When you get attached to them, it's hard.

NURSE DEBBIE:

What is something you never expected when you entered this field?

CRYSTAL:

I had no idea how much I would learn about life from my patients in hospice. Sometimes we talk about what they went through as a child. Or we talk about their jobs and their accomplishments. You learn about their families and how they operate. It's not always good, and sometimes it's very heartbreaking. You'll see the way some children treat their parents, how they fight over family issues. It really crazy to see how death can change your whole family.

NURSE DEBBIE:

So you see family dynamics get stressed out from the new situations.

CRYSTAL:

Yes. I've seen them get stressed. I've seen very loving families, of course, too. Absolutely delightful people. But I've also worked with families where the siblings have fought so much to the point where one sibling or a few siblings wouldn't come to visit the parent. This one wonderful woman I took care of, she and her husband had a daughter who never came to visit. She had some underlying issues with her dad, and because she was mad at her parents, she stayed away. So her mother passed away without ever getting to clear things up with her daughter.

NURSE DEBBIE:

That's so sad.

CRYSTAL:

It's really sad. But I have to say the hardest position I've ever had as a hospice aide was taking care of my own grandfather. That reminded me how emotionally stressful this time can be for family members. My grandfather lived only nine days after he left the hospital. I had to stay and take care of my grandma afterward. I'm still taking care of her.

NURSE DEBBIE:

God bless you! I want to know if you and most hospice aides get the emotional support you need. It must be so draining!

CRYSTAL:

It is. You get what's called caregiver burnout. Because you're constantly caring for everyone else. You forget to care about yourself.

NURSE DEBBIE:

That makes sense. Good for you for recognizing it. So what do you do for self-care?

CRYSTAL:

I like to go get my nails and my toenails done. Just to relax and get my legs massaged. Sometimes I go sit in the park for peace and simply sit there and listen. I recently came back to work because I had my knee replaced because being an aide for so long, I've blown out both my knees.

NURSE DEBBIE:

I'm so sorry.

CRYSTAL:

Before they came up with mechanical lifts, aides did all the lifting. I had to lift patients from their wheelchairs to the bed, from the bed to shower chairs. It took its toll on my knees.

NURSE DEBBIE:

I sure hope those knees of yours are better. Can you tell me about your training?

CRYSTAL:

Sure. When I went to school for my CNA license, I went ten weeks to get my certification. And then I had to go and take a state board. But now they're doing it in like sixteen weeks.

NURSE DEBBIE:

That's interesting. Do you have to have your certification renewed?

CRYSTAL:

Yes. I have to renew my license yearly.

NURSE DEBBIE:

And what does that involve?

CRYSTAL:

You have to show you've done at least eight hours of care to keep your CNA active. You also need to have twelve hours of in-services a year. If you work for a facility or hospital, they do in-services once a month to help the aides keep up with their training. You have to be present at those. With private care, you don't have to. You can be an independent contractor.

NURSE DEBBIE:

Are you in demand all over the place? I mean, you've been doing this for twenty-nine years.

CRYSTAL:

Yes. I can leave my current position right now—not that I ever would leave my precious Mr. J.!—and have a job before tonight. That's how much the demand is for CNAs.

NURSE DEBBIE:

Whew! We don't want to lose you, Crystal. Thank you for being such a big part of Pappy's life. Now what can you tell me about the difference between hospice and palliative care? My clients ask me all the time, and I'm curious how you'd explain it, in the simplest terms possible.

CRYSTAL:

No problem. Hospice is going to stop all your preventative medications. For example, you're not going to take blood pressure or anything for sugar issues. With palliative care, you take all those medicines. Although patients can be on a line, teeter-tottering between hospice and palliative care.

NURSE DEBBIE:

Pappy teetered for a long time. Hospice is all about caring and not curing, right?

CRYSTAL:

Right. It's all about comfort. That's it. My job is to bring comfort and be as loving as I possibly can. If you're my patient, when I see you, I come in with a smile. There have been days I've had to leave everything at home, and it was tough, but I do my job. For instance, when my mother passed away, I had to come into work and put a smile on. You can't let your personal life interfere with your professional one, especially when you're working in a hospice situation. You don't want to go in a patient's house being unhappy. The sick feed off of your mood. If you're not happy, you're going to make them unhappy. So you go in and put a smile on your face and get moving.

NURSE DEBBIE:

I admire that selfless attitude of yours. So when you see some family dynamics in shambles, do you do any sort of counseling with the family members? Or mediation?

CRYSTAL:

No, no, I would not. When I notice something like that, I report up to the higher members of the team, like the nurse, because they can bring in a social worker. Social workers can help counsel families so they can communicate better.

I mentioned earlier what a tough time I had working with my grandfather in hospice. It got to a point that required intervention. I knew I had to give him his medicine every two hours, but my heart was saying he didn't need it. So I was caught between myself and my nursing degree. Finally the nurse on the hospice team said, "I know you're having an issue, but he *has* to have this medicine." And then it just clicked over to where I realized that even though he's my grand-father, I'm here to do a job.

NURSE DEBBIE:

I feel for you. Is it difficult for you to share some of the more emotional aspects of your job?

CRYSTAL:

It is. I get very emotional because I connect to my patients.

NURSE DEBBIE:

You're a human being, and you've got a huge heart to do this kind of work because most people are too afraid to even contemplate it. It's hard taking care of another human being approaching death. Why did you get into this line of work?

CRYSTAL:

I became a CNA because this is what my mother did. I watched my mom take care of patients, and I enjoyed the relationship she had with them. It was something I realized I wanted to do. I wanted to take care of people too.

NURSE DEBBIE:

I love that your mother inspired you. Is there anything that you particularly love in your daily work?

CRYSTAL:

Yes, I love the one-on-one relationship I build with my patients. They ended up trusting me because they often see me more than they see their family. So I become their family, their first line of contact. When they see me, I brighten up their days. And I like that. I like to see them smile and laugh. I do crazy things to make my patients laugh, be silly.

NURSE DEBBIE:

I already know the answer because I've seen firsthand how you act with Pappy, but for people reading this, what do you do to cheer them up? Do you dance? Do you joke?

CRYSTAL:

Yes, I've danced, and I joke all the time. I've walked in and dressed up like a clown for a birthday for one of my patients. I do stupid things to get a grin. I go the extra mile for my patients. If they want a hot coffee, I get them hot coffee. I just try to make sure all their needs are met because I look at them as if they could be my mother, my grandmother, or my grandfather. I treat each and every patient as if they are my own relative.

NURSE DEBBIE:

That is so wonderful. Have you ever worked with anyone younger, or is it generally older people? Though don't tell Pappy he's old. He still thinks he's about thirty-nine!

CRYSTAL:

Mr. J. is definitely young at heart. That's another thing—my patients remind me of my own blessings. If Mr. J. can smile when he's got so much going on with his health, I have no excuse not to bring the sunshine myself. As for children, when I first became a CNA, I tried working in pediatrics. But when we had a baby pass away, I decided that wasn't the field for me. I went into geriatrics instead. It feels more natural. The patients have already done a lot of living, and I'm just there to make the rest of their life happy.

NURSE DEBBIE:

I understand why you made that choice.

CRYSTAL:

It's where I'm best suited. Helping older people is what I was meant to do. It's not about me. It's about my patients.

NURSE DEBBIE:

How did Pappy act when he saw you again, after your knee surgery?

CRYSTAL:

Oh, he was so happy. He's ecstatic that I'm here. He's wanting to know where I've been because of his memory. He didn't remember.

NURSE DEBBIE:

That's right.

CRYSTAL:

I told him I had the surgery and showed him my scar. He's the sweetest patient. He'll say, "Is there anything I can do for you?" And that just melts my heart because even in his state, Mr. J. is trying to help me. You can't take the caring nature out of the elderly. Not all of them are caring, of course, but when they are naturally that way, like Mr. J., they stay that way.

NURSE DEBBIE:

How do you help your hospice patients feel they're in control when they have dementia, like Pappy?

CRYSTAL:

Even with a sweet memory patient like Mr. J., you still have to let them feel like they're in control because if not, they'll just quit trying. And we don't want that. So instead of coming out and saying, "We have spaghetti or tacos for dinner," I'll say, "Mr. J., would you like to have spaghetti or something else?" And he'll say, "No, spaghetti is fine." Or if I say, "You have to take a bath today" or "Today's your shower day," if he says he doesn't want to, it's not a big deal. As long as he showers the next day. As long as he feels like he's in control of himself. Of course sometimes you have to put your foot down and say, "You have to do X or Y." But usually, if you use the right words and the right tone of voice, you can get any dementia patient to cooperate.

NURSE DEBBIE:

Pappy adores you. I have one last question, and it's a repeat, sort of. I just want to make sure I got this right. Anytime you have a concern about your patients, you bring it to the registered nurse who's on your team, and then they bring it to whoever else they need to?

CRYSTAL:

Right. You always report to the next in command. Not always an RN in my case. Sometimes it's an LPN, a licensed nurse practitioner.

NURSE DEBBIE:

Okay. Gotcha.

CRYSTAL:

It just depends on who's next, whoever is the in-charge nurse on the floor if you're at a facility. But in a home environment, when I see something different with a patient, I also tell a family member because they are the RP.

NURSE DEBBIE:

What does RP mean?

CRYSTAL:

Responsible party. The family is a big part of the hospice team, and ultimately the patient and family call the shots.

NURSE DEBBIE:

That's good to know. Thanks, Crystal. And thanks for being Pappy's dear friend.

Dr. Miranda, Hospice Physician

NURSE DEBBIE:

Hi, Dr. Miranda! I feel so fortunate that we work together at Serenity First. I'd love to talk to you about what you do as a physician for our clients.

DR. MIRANDA:

I'm happy to. My life's work is to bring hospice care to every person in need of it.

NURSE DEBBIE:

Well, let's start at the beginning—when a patient receives a terminal diagnosis stating they might die within six months. Their family doctor, or the specialist, or the ER doctor at the hospital who makes that diagnosis will refer that patient to hospice. But this referring doctor isn't always the same as the doctor who gets involved with the actual hospice care.

DR. MIRANDA:

Correct. This is where I come in. I will take over the care of that patient in hospice.

NURSE DEBBIE:

Sometimes the family doctor stays involved, though, right?

DR. MIRANDA:

Oh yes. Patients often don't want to leave their family doctors. They want them to stay part of the picture. The hospice team always welcomes the family doctor's involvement. And I should point out that even though I am a hospice medical director, I still see patients in primary care. When I refer them to hospice, I remain their caregiver. I often play both roles on the referring and hospice side.

NURSE DEBBIE:

That's reassuring to know that the referring doctor and the hospice doctor can either be one and the same—or if they are not, they can work together.

DR. MIRANDA:

Exactly. They can work out a plan that best suits that patient's needs.

NURSE DEBBIE:

So are there any insights you can offer into your daily life, Dr. Miranda, so people can understand a little bit more of what you do?

DR. MIRANDA:

Yes, absolutely. I finished internal medicine twenty years ago and have been with hospice for about a decade now. Before I became involved with hospice, I was and still am a medical director of multiple care facilities in and around Richmond. My goal has always been to care about the patients holistically. I want to integrate all their care under one roof to make it a better place for patients to live.

So as a medical director, I would find myself saying, "What will I do with these terminally ill patients who are very sick? Nobody wants to decide anything. Not the primary care, not anybody. What am I going to do with this patient? Just watch them die?" Of course I didn't want to do that. So I contacted one hospice that worked in the building.

That was my first medical directorship with hospice. I saw the benefits of it. Care became a lot better with those terminally ill patients and not only to the patient but also their family members.

When you have an arsenal of people in the building—great people like nurse practitioners, nurses, clinical nurse assistants, volunteers, a chaplain, the music therapist, a massage therapist—the quality of life improves for residents, including the ones in hospice.

NURSE DEBBIE:
Of course.

DR. MIRANDA:
I became such an advocate of hospice. I didn't know that there is software where you can actually check all the providers nationwide and how many of them use hospice. Because I had been working with multiple hospices, my name was at the top of the list. Why? Because I was using them all the time. Now I am extremely familiar with hospice, including knowing how to help hospice patients apply for Medicare, Medicaid, or whatever private insurance they have. Nothing comes from the patients. Everything they need will be supplied by hospice. We take the stress off them. Instead of them dreading the end of life, some of them will tell you they're living the happiest days of their lives.

NURSE DEBBIE:
I love how you remove the burden of worry from them.

DR. MIRANDA:
It is a game changer for me to the point that I can't work without hospice anymore. As a primary care doctor, I still see patients on their regular diseases, diabetes, hypertension, whatever. But at the same time, I'm a medical director of hospice. I can integrate it holistically to those patients who we know are likely to be dying in the next six months or less. So it's really a gift for me as a doctor.

NURSE DEBBIE:

Wouldn't that be great if people knew about hospice's tremendous benefits?

DR. MIRANDA:

Absolutely. I believe being admitted to hospice is not a death sentence. As a matter of fact, studies say that you live around three months longer when you are admitted earlier.

NURSE DEBBIE:

Yes. As soon as someone received the diagnosis, they should enroll in hospice.

DR. MIRANDA:

If the family will embrace it, the patients will accept it. And vice versa. Meanwhile, as a physician, I know what the course of the disease is. And I can alleviate all those questions that you have. As the hospice doctor, I hold your hand and walk you through it.

I have patients' family members who appreciate me a year or two after the patient dies. We don't forget them or their family. In fact the family receives thirteen months of bereavement counseling. We ask them, "How are you doing? What are your coping mechanisms?" And then I make sure that after one year, we have a prayer service for all of the hospice patients who passed away in the past year. We invited the family members. I ask them how they're doing. We have refreshments. We say our prayers for the souls of whoever died to let the families know their loved ones haven't been forgotten.

NURSE DEBBIE:

It's a wonderful thing to remind the families that we haven't forgotten them or their loved one.

DR. MIRANDA:

Yes. After death, our patients are still going to be remembered. And 99.9 percent of the families appreciate what hospice is. They tell other people. They spread the news. They say, "This is what hospice did for my mom. This is what they did for my wife." They become advocates of hospice, like me. If I'm about to die, I'll be in hospice on the day that I know my diagnosis, you know?

NURSE DEBBIE:

Yes, and that's what we want people to do. I have a friend whose husband is just now going into hospice. He's supposed to die within two weeks. It's sad that they didn't consider hospice sooner. He's had his diagnosis for a long time. So for months, you know, they went without hospice care.

DR. MIRANDA:

I try to educate every patient about what we do with hospice. I say, "It's okay, I'll be there. I'm not going to leave you, but now I have all these hospice people working with you. You're not going to sign anything unless you and I agree on what's best for you. If you don't like it, just say no. If you like it and you're going to benefit from it, then I'm still going to be there until the end. I won't leave you." You know?

NURSE DEBBIE:

That must be so reassuring.

DR. MIRANDA:

Nobody wants to die alone.

NURSE DEBBIE:

No.

DR. MIRANDA:

End of life is about more than the morphine, the lorazepam, whatever you give for the pain. Those are very important. But nobody wants to be alone during their death.

NURSE DEBBIE:

No, no.

DR. MIRANDA:

I want connection for my patients to the people they love or with hospice team members, who know how to provide comfort and support.

NURSE DEBBIE:

Let's say I had to consider whether to put my mother or father in hospice care—what's the one piece of advice you might give me?

DR. MIRANDA:

Easy. Hospice is not a death sentence. It's a better way of exiting the world. My ongoing mission is to add more arsenal to the care of a dying patient.

NURSE DEBBIE:

Yes.

DR. MIRANDA:

I'd also say don't be scared of dying. Your loved one will be *our* loved one in their dying moments.

NURSE DEBBIE:

That's what I love most about you, Dr. Miranda. You understand what hospice is really about.

Joanne, Social Worker

NURSE DEBBIE:

Hi, Joanne! A social worker is such an important part of the hospice team, and you often wear many hats, including that of bereavement counselor.

JOANNE:

That's right. I'm a social worker who worked in acute care in a hospital setting for many years. I worked with oncology patients during their chemotherapy treatments. I'd get to know these individuals. So when their treatment was not working, and the doctors started talking about transitioning from acute care plans to comfort measure plans, I was part of that discussion, which included talking about hospice.

I had a patient for many years who was transferred to a higher level of care, waiting for a stem cell transplant, and one day the phone rang, and he was on the other end at the hospital, saying, "Joanne, they're saying it's not working. And now they're throwing around the word *hospice*. What does that mean?" Even though his new team had their own social workers, we had developed a real relationship over five years of treatment. So I was the one he called to say "Tell me what to do."

He wound up going home with hospice and, with the supportive care of the hospice team, died at home. That's mainly the plan with hospice—to make you comfortable in the surroundings of your own home, if at all possible. But they also do hospice in alternative living situations like nursing homes and assisted-living facilities, which may be the patient's home. The hospice team tries to make the experience enriching for the patient as well as the ones who are left behind. Which brings me to bereavement counseling and how important it is.

NURSE DEBBIE:

What exactly did you do for the families left behind?

JOANNE:

I led several bereavement groups for surviving partners or family members. Under hospice guidelines, you follow the family for a year. Medicare pays for their counseling.

NURSE DEBBIE:

I like that.

JOANNE:

It's important. It's amazing how the loved ones left behind evolve during an eight-week bereavement program, from crying the first night to planning what they're going to do together after the last week. You see, for two months they're together every Tuesday night. So you see them grow. They develop a bond through this experience that continues even after our group ends. It's neat to hear them talk about whether they'll meet at someone's house or at a restaurant. They're there for each other.

NURSE DEBBIE:

Wow. That is wonderful.

JOANNE:

We sometimes have people in the group who lost a loved one suddenly. And others, it took years for their person to pass. There is always the discussion about is it better to lose your loved one suddenly or have someone with you and be able to be with that person as long as you can be with them?

The peers essentially run the group. They have a topic for every week, and they just run with it. The first meeting everyone tells their stories and cries the whole hour and a half. They might bring in a picture of the loved one they lost and talk to us about what they were like. I love that the camaraderie and the shared suffering turns into friendship and support for each other.

There are always a lot of feelings, a lot of turmoil. Sometimes there are unresolved issues. How do you learn to deal with that? Sometimes the group leader will suggest that the person get more intense therapy separately from the group.

NURSE DEBBIE:

It doesn't sound easy, a bereavement group, but it certainly sounds effective.

JOANNE:

It is.

NURSE DEBBIE:

Is there anything else you'd like to tell families when their loved one is in a hospice care situation?

JOANNE:

It's a good idea to plan the funeral together, if the patient and family are willing. It can be very therapeutic. The patient might ask for certain pictures or a collage or a song to be sung. That planning makes it a healing process for the people left before the patient even dies.

NURSE DEBBIE:

That makes so much sense. What about getting the family ready for some things that might happen during the patient's last moments? I just read an article about the dying process and how some very common things like "the death rattle," which is agitated breathing, can be agonizing for the family. The article was written by a doctor who said it's actually not bad for the person experiencing it, but to witness it is a trauma. Most people have never heard of the death rattle. I'd rather know about what could happen before the actual passing occurs, wouldn't you?

JOANNE:

Yes. It's so important to get everyone as comfortable as possible. That's the hospice team's number one priority. Let's say the patient has trouble breathing. They'll likely receive medication for that. Not only does it help them. It helps the family. They're sitting there watching their loved one have difficulty breathing. That can be very hard to witness. It becomes a memory, their mother or father or spouse or child gasping for breath. So hospice does their best to bring ease to the patient's situation.

NURSE DEBBIE:

Thank goodness for hospice. Do you have any other advice for the families?

JOANNE:

Yes. I say you need to take a break. You can't be there all the time. For your own sake, if you need to go to the bank, if you need to go to a movie, use hospice volunteers to sit with your loved one so you can take a break from it because you have to take care of yourself in order to take care of your patient. That is very important.

Another bit of advice: I find that when people enter hospice too late, it's often because the doctors kept offering different types of treatments because the patient and/or the family weren't ready for death. As a result the patient did not get the full benefit of what hospice can bring to both the patient and the family. I would say that happens more so than not.

I used to say to the spouses all the time, your loved one is tired. They're doing this because you are not giving up. That's difficult to say to these loving families, but sometimes they have to hear that from a caregiver they trust.

NURSE DEBBIE:

I was in that position with my mother. I just didn't want her to quit her treatments. And finally she let me know she was ready to stop.

JOANNE:

Sometimes patients continue to be pushed for treatment because of the family's reactions. They're not ready to let their loved one die, and the patient knows this and doesn't want to make them sadder. So the patient goes along with it.

NURSE DEBBIE:

I so relate, Joanne. I'm so glad Momma finally spoke up to me about what she wanted.

JOANNE:

I love that story you told me about how she said she was heading to a wedding.

NURSE DEBBIE:

That's right. She's there at a wedding in the sky.

JOANNE:

That's such a lovely thought to hold in your heart. Meanwhile we can all work together to make sure people still here know exactly what hospice is. So many people think about hospice and think about cancer. It's not always about cancer. You can have a patient with end-stage dementia, ALS patients, and MS patients, for example.

NURSE DEBBIE:

Right. That's another good point.

JOANNE:

I do advanced care planning now. I help people actually write up a medical advanced directive to indicate their wishes if certain things happen.

NURSE DEBBIE:

These are people who might themselves need hospice in the future?

JOANNE:

Yes. So when you're alert and oriented, you should name people that you trust to make decisions if you ever become incapacitated to make medical decisions. That's when an advanced directive comes into play. You might change it over the years too. It's all about balancing quality and quantity of life.

So I did my first one when I was forty-eight. At that age I want to live, right? But when you're seventy-five, you might feel differently about medical procedures available to resuscitate you or cure you. People in hospice—remember, hospice isn't about curing—can get very specific about how they want to their team to approach their eventual passing. So think about what future healthcare you want.

Because you never know. You could be in a car accident. When I work with couples, I'll say, "Both of you could be in the same car accident and not be able to make decisions for each other. So if you have this legal document, if you name each other as your primary decision maker, it allows you to name another person. So if you can't help each other, we'll bring that secondary agent in to make decisions on your behalf.

NURSE DEBBIE:

That's so smart. Thank you, Joanne, for caring so much about hospice and what it can do for patients and their families.

JOANNE:

I'm happy to share. I can't talk enough about bereavement support under the hospice umbrella. It truly helps the ones left behind.

Greg, Hospice Pastor

NURSE DEBBIE:

Hi, Pastor Greg. We're so fortunate to have you with us at Serenity First. You're a ray of sunshine for so many. Can you tell me what the chaplain's role is on the hospice team?

PASTOR GREG:

Thank you, Debbie. And of course I'd love to explain my mission on the team. One of the goals of hospice is to make the patient's transition as smooth, as peaceful, and as relaxing as possible. And so hospice, with its team members, gives each patient that opportunity to do so. The role of the chaplain and the bereavement coordinator is to talk with those who may be very spiritual or to those who have no spirituality whatsoever. We're there as a sounding board. Just to listen.

NURSE DEBBIE:

Ah. You're there to connect.

PASTOR GREG:

Yes, to listen and let them share their life stories and to talk with the family. And in a lot of cases, the patients may go through a period of dementia. In that case they may not be able to converse as much. But we're also there for the families as well, helping them deal with the process because in a lot of instances, it's more difficult for the families than it is for the patient themselves.

NURSE DEBBIE:

I understand that. I needed support when I lost my mother.

PASTOR GREG:

Yes. And so we're there for support for the families, to help them go through the process.

NURSE DEBBIE:

What is your day like?

PASTOR GREG:

Today was pretty typical. I had a funeral. Chaplains go through the whole process of dying with the patients and their families, so we're there with them at the funerals. We hold their hands, and we cry with them and laugh at their stories with them. We help them do obituaries and all those sorts of things. We're just there as a comfort and support. I have to go visit another family today where the daughter has not grasped the idea of losing her father. And so I'm helping her understand what's actually going on. It can be difficult sometimes for the family.

NURSE DEBBIE:

Yes.

PASTOR GREG:

Even though the patients themselves are quite aware of what's going on.

NURSE DEBBIE:

Gosh, your job can get so complicated and stressful.

PASTOR GREG:

Well, it has to be something you want to do.

NURSE DEBBIE:

Being a chaplain is a calling.

PASTOR GREG:

Yes. I've spent many years as a pastor, so it's already in my DNA to do this sort of thing. And so it's a whole lot easier for me to help the patient and their loved ones. And by the way, we're not trying to win them to any denomination. We're not trying to browbeat them about religion and God. We're just there to give them the support that we think they need. Some patients say, "You know what, thanks, but no thanks. We'll do this on our own." They're very rare.

Usually when people get to this period of life, it's a very intimate, vulnerable time. Most people know they need help to get through it. I mean, the medications and all those things are good. But after that, somebody needs to talk with them, let them cry on a shoulder and let them maybe ask the question "Why?" Not that we have the answers, just a listening ear. And so we give them that.

NURSE DEBBIE:

That's a blessing.

PASTOR GREG:

For me, hospice is a gift. And what I've learned, it's a gift in that you see patients in their weakest time, but when you look on the walls of their homes and in their rooms, you see how beautiful they were, how young they were, and how vibrant they were. Everybody says to me, "I wish I could get more time."

NURSE DEBBIE:

That breaks my heart.

PASTOR GREG:

Yes. When you hear that, you realize how valuable time is. With our patients, it's kind of like watching the movie *It's a Wonderful Life*. I get to see their lives played out. And so when I come back to my reality, I cherish the time I have with my children, my wife, and my family. And I make sure I have my life in order. Because we're all going to die. That's the reality of life. The question is, how are we going to do that? Hospice helps people do that with dignity.

NURSE DEBBIE:

Amen. Thank you for what you do. Say I were meeting with you for the first time, and I just found out my parent, spouse, or sibling is about to enter hospice. Let's say I do attend a particular church. Does my church leader work with you? If so, how does that work?

PASTOR GREG:

Involving the patient's church is an integral part of being a hospice chaplain. We coordinate with local pastors, rabbis, and other spiritual leaders. We stay in touch with the community the patient cares about. We also consult with funeral homes.

In many instances, someone who is a devout churchgoer might get support from their own pastor and church members. I know a hospice patient in his nineties whose church gave him over a hundred greeting cards, all from different members of the church. And so we help coordinate and even build upon that type of relationship. We don't get in the way of that at all. We are there to support our patients' spiritual needs, and for those who don't have a spiritual community or a family, the hospice team becomes their families, their support.

NURSE DEBBIE:

Thank goodness.

PASTOR GREG:

The key is no one should have to suffer and grieve alone. And so that's what we do. We make that process more peaceful and comforting as much as we can.

NURSE DEBBIE:

Yes. During COVID it must've been so emotionally difficult for everyone—the patient, the family, and the hospice team.

PASTOR GREG:

Yes, COVID was difficult. Because I think as human beings we're meant to be social. We're meant to be together. COVID separated us from touching and hugging and that sort of thing. So it was difficult, especially for those who lost loved ones and could not be with them.

NURSE DEBBIE:

Yes. I'm so glad we're putting those days behind us. But we can never let it happen again. That's on my mind a lot. This most likely won't be our last pandemic. We need to prepare for the next one by figuring out how to keep dying patients with their families.

PASTOR GREG:

I agree.

NURSE DEBBIE:

Can you tell me what bereavement coordination means for a chaplain? You help with the funeral and direct the family to counseling?

PASTOR GREG:

We do a little bit of everything. Again, the patient drives the direction in which we go. Everyone grieves at a different pace. And so we have many resources. It's twelve months of contact with the loved ones. So every month we see them. The first month, it's a weekly thing. And then from there on out, we stay in contact with them, either by way of calls, a visit, or a card, for twelve months.

So we're in their life. Again, that's if they want that. Some people may get to the six-month mark and say, "We're okay. Thank you for all you've done." And some will go the whole year. You really develop into a family. I just met with an aunt of one of the patients. She said, "When this is all over, we want to bring you and your wife to dinner."

NURSE DEBBIE:

That's so nice.

PASTOR GREG:

That's what hospice should do. That's the goal so that we become family. No one has to suffer and grieve alone.

NURSE DEBBIE:

Let's say someone is really suffering terribly after a patient's passed on. Do they ever need more counseling than what you can offer?

PASTOR GREG:

Yes. It's usually rare, but sometimes that happens. We always know our limitations. There's a healthy grief, and then there can be an unhealthy grief. If it looks like the family member needs a little bit more than we're able to give, we have resources that we direct the loved one to— psychological counseling and that sort of thing. But our support groups are there all year long. Anytime the family member wants to come, they can sit and listen or share.

NURSE DEBBIE:

Is there any other tidbit of advice you might give a newbie to the hospice care system, who's either entering it themselves or has a family member or friend doing so?

PASTOR GREG:

I would say the hospice process is nothing to be afraid of. Hospice is to help people cope with the unknown, I guess you would say. It's not so much the death but the process of going through it that scares people. And so let us help you. Our desire is to help our patients transition and their families get through the grieving process. Nobody has to grieve and suffer alone.

NURSE DEBBIE:

I'm so thankful for chaplains like you, Pastor Greg.

Conclusion

Y'all, we've been on a quite a journey together! I hope you learned a lot about the nuts and bolts of hospice. Even more importantly I hope you sensed the true *spirit* of hospice, which is focused on compassion and comfort for every single person on this earth who has been given a terminal diagnosis of less than six months. Hospice puts a heartfelt, caring spotlight on this vulnerable population.

At some point in our lives, you and I will be there. Maybe you or a loved one already are. If so, I hope your current hospice care exceeds your expectations. We all deserve to be celebrated at life's end! Wouldn't it be great to draw our last breaths feeling that we matter? That's the goal, to let everyone know they truly matter.

Trends in Hospice

So what is happening now in the hospice industry? What should we all be aware of?

Telehealth: COVID-19 changed everything, of course, causing a massive and at the time necessary shift across the healthcare continuum toward telehealth. And it looks like the genie can't be put back in the bottle. More than ever, payers like Medicare are reimbursing for many telehealth services. In light of this new reality, hospices are working to find the right balance between virtual and hands-on care with their clients.

Of course the cornerstone of hospice is in-person care, but top-notch hospices like Serenity First stay abreast of the latest advances in telehealth practices and are prepared to adapt the best aspects of them to support their mission.

Predictive analytics: That's a fancy *Star Wars*-level term that means anticipating how something is going to play out using all sorts of data brought in from different sources. Technology that collects patient information has made it possible for healthcare staff to see patterns in their patients' health conditions and act faster if they see their health deteriorating. This ability to track changes means the patient is much more likely to receive appropriate care and comfort. Healthcare professionals can communicate with the patient and their family about the data they're observing and coordinate a plan of action with them, which means less confusion and a smoother hospice experience for everyone.

LGBTQ+ care: We are learning every day that just as individuals have unique wishes at the end of their lives, certain populations have particular concerns that until now haven't been adequately addressed in hospice situations. But we are now at a time where those voices are being heard. Many members of the LGBTQ+ community fear discrimination at the end of their lives. Not only do they have to deal with their deteriorating health, but they also may feel compelled to hide their support network from healthcare professionals or family who may not approve of their lifestyle. And sometimes they struggle with unclear legalities regarding their relationships, a problem that can jeopardize their basic rights and protections.

So sadly these patients often don't seek the hospice care they need, or if they do, they delay asking for help. This can result in social isolation, depression, anxiety, and even premature death if they don't reach out for support.

Sensitivity training is a must, and more hospices are training their teams to be aware of the particular concerns of the LGBTQ+ community. Death doesn't discriminate. It comes for all of us. So we want to ensure that LGBTQ+ patients and their partners receive compassionate care.

Community-based hospice care: This is a major trend that integrates hospice with assisted-living communities. When a resident needs to transition from palliative care to hospice care, there is no major move involved. They can seamlessly switch to a new care team. The beauty of this trend is that patients' comfort and dignity are prioritized. Often the patient can avoid unnecessary hospitalizations as well.

Those are current hospice trends. But what do we want to see in hospices of the future? Darrell Owens, a doctor of nursing practice who runs palliative and supportive care at the University of Washington Medical Center Northwest, said something very relevant to this topic in an interview with NPR: "As much as we are obligated to save people's lives, we are obligated to save their deaths."

Amen to that! We deserve dignity, compassion, and recognition of our individuality at every stage of life, including at our passing.

The Future of Hospice

Demedicalizing the dying experience: Echoing the powerful statement Darrell Owens made, the future of hospice is going to be about *demedicalizing* the dying experience. This does not mean denying a patient healthcare. It simply means that there is more to dying than the medicinal side of it! Somehow the mysterious, multi-faceted, powerful experience of dying has been reduced to something clinical. And if you're not in healthcare, the topic of dying is often ignored because no one wants to talk about it. Many of us are afraid to face it. In denial, we are missing out on so many opportunities to enrich the lives we have left to live.

Y'all, if I can get only one message across to you in this book, it would be this: we really need to live until our last breath. Every moment is precious! When we don't talk about death, when we distance ourselves from it, the end of our lives can become a perfunctory, almost impersonal topic. But we are doing ourselves a disservice with this avoidance strategy.

It's so important to remember that the same way our births are awe-inspiring, our deaths also reflect our dignity and value as human beings. We don't like to talk about it, but our deaths are going to be extremely personal to each one of us. This final experience of life is as much a part of who we are as our births. We deserve the chance—if we're lucky enough to have some notice before our passing—to help shape that experience so that our unique social, emotional, and spiritual needs are met.

And we especially need our healthcare professionals to give the experience back to the patients. Listen to the patients' wishes. Empower them with the truth, even if that truth is difficult to hear. In most cases terminally ill people will choose quality of life over pursuing medical options that ultimately won't help them.

Planning advanced care: COVID-19 proved to us how quickly our medical situations can change. Life is fragile. A pandemic brought that home to us in a brutally clear way. So more than ever, we need to move toward advanced care planning, letting others know our end-of-life wishes when we are unable to voice them ourselves.

We will never forget the terrible stories we all heard (or might have experienced ourselves) about families not knowing what to do when their loved one landed in the ICU at their local hospital with COVID-19. Trying to work these issues out on the phone with a nurse or doctor is the stuff of nightmares—and yet that nightmare came true for so many.

Before COVID-19, only about a third of Americans had completed any advance directive. Often we tend to wait for the doctor to bring up end-of-life strategies. But that era must pass. We need to make advanced care planning part of routine care. And that plan should evolve as you age. It's not a one-time conversation. Keep it on the front burner or at least simmering on the back one when you see your doctor. Become familiar with it, and you'll get more comfortable discussing it.

Improving bereavement care: Individual hospices like Serenity First do a great job helping grieving families. But overall, as a culture, we need to improve bereavement leave policies for devastated mourners. This is a national public health issue, and these systemic changes should begin at the legislative level.

Thankfully we have nonprofits like Evermore, founded by Joyal Mulheron, working on getting the word out. Currently we are failing many of these burdened families. The lack of support for them causes enduring and negative economic, social, and health consequences. And that's the last thing they need after their loved one passes—to be ignored or unsupported. Let's lift them up by putting laws into place that ensure their well-being is a priority for their entire community.

A name change?: I'm a big cheerleader for hospice, and it's still shocking to me how few people think of it as a positive thing. It's because they don't know what it is. They've never known anyone who's gone through it or been a member of a hospice care team. It's why education about what hospice does is so important. (I hope you feel good about it after reading this book!)

However, as integrated, community-based hospice care continues to evolve, don't be surprised if the word *hospice* goes out of style. Insurance companies, healthcare systems, and even grassroots pop culture movements can play a role in how we label our medical care options. And lately, as hospices grow their portfolio of services, some are rebranding to reflect that development. But the idea is the same— that the patient's needs and wishes come first.

* * *

Wow. We've come to the end of the book. Thank you for taking the time to read this. I hope you felt my compassion and understanding throughout. Every word was written with the hope that I can bring you comfort. I also hope I provided you knowledge that can assist you on this journey. Like you, I know what it's like to spend many a sleepless night worried about my loved one's last days. How can we make sure they feel loved? How can we help them through it?

Or you might be asking these questions about yourself if you've been given a diagnosis that makes you eligible for hospice.

Either way, the feeling I'm feeling as we wrap this up is love for each one of you. Life isn't easy, and as we approach sunset, the shadows that gather can frighten us. But please remember, you are not alone. You never have to go through this experience alone! I promise, that setting sun will light up the corners of the world that want to ease your suffering. People care. And until the last rays disappear below the horizon, you and your loved one deserve to be seen. All of us deserve to be celebrated for as long as we live—and through wonderful memories after we're long gone.

So here's to life. Here's to you. Here's to the wonderful service that we call hospice. May your experience with it lift you and your loved ones up and bring you true peace and comfort when you need it most.

Finally, coming from my platform as Nurse Debbie, the director of Serenity First, and as a loving child to someone in hospice right now, I hope I can count on you to help me spread the word about what hospice has to offer. I especially need your help advocating on behalf of people in our communities who may not have access to any support system at all.

Hospice is a validation of our dignity. Hospice is a celebration of what it means to be human. Hospice is love in action, folks. Thank you for caring and for sharing this great news!

Appendix

Here are the questions the National Hospice and Palliative Care Organization (NHPCO) has put together to help consumers choose the right hospice agency for them. If you need additional help, their helpline is at 800-658-8898. But you can also check in with any healthcare professionals you trust, your favorite clergy or counselor, your social worker, and your friends and neighbors who've experienced what hospice care is like.

Is the hospice Medicare certified?

Most hospices are certified by Medicare and are therefore required to follow Medicare rules and regulations. This is important if you wish to receive hospice care as part of your Medicare/Medicaid coverage.

Has the hospice been surveyed by a state or federal oversight agency in the last five years?

Ask when the last survey was and if any deficiencies were noted and, if so, have they been resolved.

Is the organization an NHPCO member, and does it comply with all aspects of NHPCO's Standards for Hospice Programs?

Ask if the hospice is a current NHPCO member, if it complies with NHPCO's Standards and has completed the Standards Self Assessment, and if so, how recently they completed it.

Is the hospice accredited by a national organization?

Several organizations accredit hospices, surveying them to ensure they meet quality standards. Hospices are not required to be accredited, but accreditation can be a reflection of its commitment to quality.

Does the hospice conduct a family evaluation survey?

Many hospices ask family members to complete a brief evaluation of their services after the death of a loved one. Ask for their most recent scores so you can see how previous patients and family members have rated their services.

Does the hospice own or operate a care facility to provide homelike care in a hospice residence, hospital, or nursing home?

This may be important to you if the care needed is complex and/or family caregivers cannot care for the person at home.

Are clinical staff (physicians, advanced practice nurses, nurses, nursing assistants, social workers, and chaplains) certified or credentialed in hospice and palliative care?

There are several credentials that hospice professionals can achieve based on their knowledge of hospice/palliative care and their educational experience.

What services do volunteers offer, and if requested, how quickly will a volunteer be available?

Volunteers can provide a variety of services, including friendly visits, light household chores, running errands, personal care, etc. If you want a hospice volunteer, be sure to ask how quickly one can be assigned and how they match volunteers to meet your needs.

Will staff come to the home if there is a crisis at any time of the day or night and on weekends? Who is available to make the home visit (nurses, doctors, social workers, chaplains)?

Hospice staff are available by phone to help you twenty-four hours a day, seven days a week. However, some hospices offer limited in-home support on nights and weekends, while others are able to send staff out to a patient's home no matter when a crisis arises. Frequently a nurse is the best person to make a visit if it is a medical crisis; however, sometimes the crisis is best handled by a physician, social worker, chaplain or another member of the team. Ask if all members of the team are available in a crisis situation during nights and weekends.

If I need to go to a hospital or nursing home, which ones does/doesn't the hospice work with?

If you have a preferred hospital or know that you may need to go to a nursing home, it's important to find out which ones the hospice has contracts with so they can continue to provide your hospice services in this different setting.

What "extra" services does the hospice offer?

All hospices provide expert medical care, emotional and spiritual care, medicines, medical supplies and equipment, volunteers, and grief support after the death of a loved one. In addition to these services, some hospices offer specialized programs for children, people with specific diseases, "pre-hospice" care for individuals not yet medically ready for hospice care and other "extra" services that may benefit your family.

How long has the hospice been operating in the community?

Again, length of time in the community may be important to you and your family.

How many patients at any one time are assigned to each hospice staff member who will be caring for the patient?

Some hospices assign a certain number of patients to each staff member and may be willing to share that information with you. That might influence your decision to receive care from a hospice.

What screening and type of training do hospice volunteers receive before they are placed with patients and families?

All volunteers must receive training or orientation on hospice care. Some hospices provide specialized training related to bereavement, pediatric care, nursing home care, etc.

How quickly can the intake/admissions staff come to begin the admissions process? Is someone available at nights or on weekends?

Some hospices are able to begin the admissions process and have someone begin hospice services at night or on weekends. If you are referred to hospice late in the day or on the weekend, a hospice's ability to start services quickly may be very important.

What is the organization's governance structure?

Whether or not the organization is a nonprofit, for-profit, government, faith-based, or part of a larger healthcare organization may be important to you and your family.

Is the hospice a We Honor Veterans Partner?

We Honor Veterans partners have demonstrated their commitment to improving the care they provide to veterans and their family members.

CPSIA information can be obtained
at www.ICGtesting.com
Printed in the USA
JSHW041110120722
PP11763900001B/1

'Perfect for the poolside or curled up by the fireplace.'

'I have read all of Debbie's books and I'm now re-reading her older ones, I just cannot get enough of her wonderful reads!! LOVE, LOVE, LOVE her and her characters that come to life. Thank you for following your dream of writing, Debbie, and giving us all happiness through reading your books.'

'She takes you on an adventure of the heart.'

'A great book not only for entertainment but to learn ways to make life better.'

'Debbie Macomber at her unputdownable best . . . I will now need to download several of her books to take on holiday.'

'I can't remember a Debbie Macomber book I haven't liked . . . What I really like about her writing is the ability to create loving relationships, kind of like the old movies.'

'Will warm your heart as you read.'

Debbie Macomber

Merry and Bright

arrow books

1 3 5 7 9 10 8 6 4 2

Arrow Books
20 Vauxhall Bridge Road
London SW1V 2SA

Arrow Books is part of the Penguin Random House group of companies
whose addresses can be found at global.penguinrandomhouse.com.

Penguin
Random House
UK

First published in Great Britain by Arrow Books in 2017

www.penguin.co.uk

A CIP catalogue record for this book is available from the British Library.

ISBN 9781784758738

Printed and bound in Great Britain by Clays Ltd, St Ives Plc

Penguin Random House is committed to a
sustainable future for our business, our readers
and our planet. This book is made from Forest
Stewardship Council® certified paper.

To Barbara and Don Gervais
Wishing you many happy years
in your Vero Beach, Florida, home

Debbie

Christmas 2017

Dear Friends,

After all these years, you, my readers, have come to expect a Christmas story from me, and I look forward to supplying one. It's one of the many joys I have as a writer. I've always been a Christmas kind of girl. I seem to go overboard every December with multiple lights, decorations, and nativity scenes all around the house. I can't help myself. (Wayne is a tolerant husband.)

This book is dedicated to the couple who purchased our Florida home, with the hopes that they will enjoy it as much as Wayne and I did. It was hard to let it go, but we feel we left this special home in good hands. This last winter Wayne and I decided that instead of wintering in one location, it was time for us to spend part of our winters traveling around the world. We call it our *adventure before dementia*. We already have our trip planned for this winter. We're off to explore the Great Wall of China.

Merry and Bright is a fun story. I hope you have the chance to sit back, prop up your feet, and take a break from the holiday craziness to read it. My wish is that you will smile and it will bring a bit of light and warmth to your winter.

From the time I published my first book, I looked forward to getting mail from my readers. That hasn't changed. You can reach me through my website at debbiemacomber.com or on Facebook, Twitter, or Instagram. Or you can write me at P.O. Box 1458, Port Orchard, WA 98366.

I'll close this by sending you the warmest of holiday greetings.

Merry Christmas.

Debbie x

CHAPTER ONE

＊

Merry

"Mom, I need to work overtime, so I won't be home to help with dinner."

"Again?" her mother moaned into the phone.

"Yes, sorry." Merry hated leaving her mother with the task of cooking dinner. Robin Knight struggled with mobility issues due to complications with multiple sclerosis. As much as Merry hated the thought of it, her mother would soon be confined to a wheelchair.

"That's three nights this week."

Merry didn't need the reminder. Three nights out of four. Matterson Consulting, the firm where she worked as a temp, was involved in a huge project, its biggest one to date, for the Boeing Company. With the time crunch, everyone on staff was putting in mandatory overtime. Normally, few would object to the extra hours, but the holiday season was right around the corner. People were busy planning parties, shopping for gifts, decorating, baking, and making holiday plans to visit families. All the normal, fun things that were part of this time of year, but for those employed by Matterson, it didn't matter. Christmas might as well be blocked off the calendar.

"Don't worry, dear," Merry's mother assured her gently. "Patrick will help me with dinner."

Merry closed her eyes and let her shoulders sag. Patrick was a dear boy, but he tended to dirty every dish in the house when he cooked. Her eighteen-year-old Down syndrome brother was the light of her life, but his help in the kitchen was questionable at best.

"Heat up soup and have Patrick make sandwiches," Merry suggested.

"We can do that, but you should know Bogie is out of dog food."

Bogie was Patrick's golden retriever, who had an appetite that rivaled that of an entire high school football squad. Grocery shopping was a task Merry had taken on as her mother's illness progressed. However, working the hours she did made it nearly impossible to find the time needed. "Oh Mom, I'm sorry. Poor Bogie. I'll stop off at the store on my way home and pick some up." While she was there she'd grab a few other essentials, too, like milk and bread. They were running low on both. And maybe some ice cream for Patrick, who never complained about the need to help his mother.

"Your father can do that on his way home—"

"Don't ask Dad," Merry interrupted. Her father was in pharmaceutical sales and traveled extensively around the Pacific Northwest and was often on the road. He carried a heavy enough load as it was. By the time he got home from driving across the state, he'd be exhausted. Merry didn't want to burden him with any extra chores. Buying the groceries was her responsibility.

Everyone worked together in the Knight family. They were a tight-knit group by necessity and by love. Merry had taken the twelve-month temp job with Matterson Consulting to save tuition money for college. Her educational expenses were more than their family budget could manage. She'd been hired by Matterson Consulting specifically for this Boeing project and had worked extensively on inputting the data. It'd taken months to accumulate all the necessary information. It was all winding down now. December 23 would be her last day on the job.

After working with the company for nearly a year, she'd made friends with the other two women working in data entry. They considered her part of the team and often turned to her with questions, as she had replaced the department head. Although she was only a temporary employee, her skill level was above those currently assigned to the project.

Merry took another bite of the peanut-butter sandwich she'd brought for lunch. She usually ate at her desk and worked through her lunch break. Most everyone else went to a local café around the corner, where the food was fast, cheap, and tasty. All three were necessary if Merry was going to splurge and eat out. She treated herself once a week, but more often than that would play havoc with her budget. Most days she brown-bagged it.

"When was the last time you went out, Merry?" her mother asked.

"I go out every day," she answered, sidestepping the question.

"On a date."

"Mom! When do I have time to date?" Merry had a fairly good idea what had prompted the question. Her best friend from high school had recently announced she was pregnant.

"That's exactly my point. You're twenty-four years old and you're living the life of a nun."

"Mom!"

"Patrick dates more than you do."

Merry had to smile, even though her mother was right. Her younger brother was involved with a special group that held dances and other events that allowed him to socialize with other teens who had Down syndrome. As a high school senior, he was active in drama and part of the football team. He had a girlfriend as well.

"It's time you stopped worrying about your family and had some fun."

"I have fun," Merry countered. She had friends, and while she didn't see them often, they were in touch via social media, email, and texting. If Merry was busy, which she tended to be, then she communicated with emojis. It was fun to see how much she could say with a simple symbol or two.

"Have you ever thought about joining one of those online matchmaking sites?" her mother asked, sounding thoughtful.

"No," Merry returned emphatically, rolling her eyes. She hoped the state of her social life would change once she could afford to return to school. It wasn't like she was a martyr, but at times she struggled with the weight of family obligations. She tried not to think about everything she was missing that her friends enjoyed. It was what it was, and it didn't do any good to feel sorry for herself. Her family needed her.

"Why don't you try it? It'd be fun."

"Mom, have you seen all the forms and questionnaires that need to be filled out for those dating sites? I don't have time for that." *Especially now, with the demands of my job,* she thought to herself.

"Make time."

"I will someday," she said, hoping that would appease her mother.

"*Someday,* Merry? Failing to plan is planning to fail."

"Mom. You sound like Anthony Robbins." Although she complained, her mother was right. The timing, however, was all wrong.

"I'll think about it after the first of the year," she promised.

Her best friend Dakota had met the love of her life online at Mix & Mingle. Inspired by Dakota's success, Merry had checked out the site, but she became bogged down with the page upon page of questions that needed to be completed. She started filling out the forms but quickly gave up, exasperated by all the busywork.

"You need to get out more, enjoy life," her mother continued. "There's more to life than work and more work."

"I agree. After the holidays. Let me finish this temp job first."

"It worked for Dakota."

"Mom, please. I have plenty of time to get out there." Merry didn't need the reminder about her friend's happy ending. After Dakota met Michael on the site, she had sung the website's praises to Merry like a wolf howling at the moon. She wouldn't stop bugging Merry about it until she'd promised to give it a try.

"I heard from her mother this morning. Did you know Dakota and Michael are expecting?"

"Yes, Mom, I heard." Merry reached for her sandwich and was about to take another bite when the vice president of the company, Jayson Bright, walked past her desk. He had to be one of the most serious-minded men Merry had ever met. To the best of her memory she had never seen the man smile. Not once. He looked about as happy as someone scheduled for a root canal.

Jayson Bright paused and stared at Merry. His eyes fell to the nameplate on her desk. MARY KNIGHT. She'd asked HR to correct the spelling of her first name twice, with no success, and then gave up. Seeing that she was a temp, they hadn't shown that much interest. Her boss's gaze landed on the sandwich she had on her desk, and for a moment she toyed with the idea of offering him half, but as she doubted he'd find any humor in it, she restrained herself. He arched his brows before he walked away.

"Merry, did you hear me?" her mother asked.

"Sorry, no, I was distracted." From Mr. Bright's look, Merry had to wonder if there was something written in the employee handbook about eating at her desk. She'd been doing it for almost a full year now, and no one had mentioned that it was frowned upon before.

"Merry?"

"Mom. I need to get off the phone. I'll call you before I leave the office."

"Okay, but think about what I said, all right?"

"I will, Mom." Merry's mind filled with visions of meeting her own Prince Charming. Of one thing she was certain: It wouldn't be someone as dour as Jayson Bright.

Sure enough, just as Merry suspected, at three that same afternoon, a notice was sent around the office.

It is preferred that all staff refrain from eating at their desks. For those who choose to remain in the office for lunch, a designated room is provided. Thank you.

Jayson Bright
Vice President
Matterson Consulting

Merry read the email and instinctively knew that this edict was directed at her. She preferred to avoid the lunchroom, and with good reason. The space was often crowded and it was uncomfortable bumbling around, scooting between those at the tables and those waiting in line for a turn at the microwave. Besides, it was more efficient to eat at her desk. Not that Mr. Bright seemed to notice or care.

What a shame—the company vice president was such a curmudgeon. Merry had heard women in the office claim he was hot. She agreed. Jayson Bright was hot, all right. Hotheaded! He was young for his position as vice president. The rumor mill in the office said he was related to the Matterson family; the company president was his uncle. Bright would assume the role when it came time for his uncle to retire. His uncle would continue as chairman of the board.

Merry's thoughts drifted to Jayson Bright and she mused at how attractive he would be if he smiled. He was about six feet tall, several inches taller than her five-five, with dark brown hair and eyes. He kept his hair cut in a crisp professional style. Wanting to be generous in spirit, Merry supposed he carried a heavy responsibility. Word was that Jayson Bright was the one responsible for obtaining this Boeing contract. A lot weighed in the balance for him with his job. Merry knew that he put in as many hours, or more, than the rest of the staff.

By the time Merry arrived at home, hauling a ten-pound bag of Bogie's favorite dog food, it was after eight o'clock. As soon as she walked in the door, Patrick rushed to help her with the heavy sack.

His sweet, boyish face was bright with enthusiasm. "Merry's home," he shouted, taking the dog food out of her hands and carting it to the kitchen pantry.

"Hi, sweetheart," her mother called. Her mom leaned heavily on her walker, now exhausted and fatigued, because she grew tired at the end of each day.

"Can I tell her?" Patrick asked excitedly.

"In a minute," her mother said. Merry noticed that her lips quirked in an effort to hold in a smile.

"Tell me what?"

"We got you an early birthday gift this afternoon and it's the best one ever." Patrick rubbed his hands together, unable to disguise his eagerness.

"You did?" Knowing the family budget was tight, Merry wasn't expecting much. Born on December 26, the day after Christmas, Merry had felt cheated as a child when it came to her birthday gifts. Her parents had done their best to make her birthday special, but it being so soon after Christmas made that difficult. It wasn't unusual for Merry to get her birthday gifts early because of it.

"And you're going to be so happy," Patrick assured her. "I helped Mom with everything."

"You helped pick it out?" Merry asked. The two of them must have ordered something off the Internet, because her mother was no longer able to drive and Patrick couldn't. Those with Down syndrome could legally drive in Washington State, but the family couldn't afford a second car. The family had only the one car, which her father used for work. Merry used public transportation to and from her job.

"Well, this isn't something we picked out. You need to do the picking."

"Patrick," his mother chastised. "You're going to give it away."

"You can show me after you feed Bogie," Merry suggested, as Bogie eyed the pantry door.

"We can't really give it to you yet," Patrick told her. "You get to pick for yourself, but I'll help if you want." From the way his eyes lit up, Merry knew he'd be terribly disappointed if he didn't get a say in this.

Okay, now Merry was willing to admit she was intrigued. It was still November, over Thanksgiving weekend. Her brother was barely able to contain himself and rushed to grab Bogie's food dish. She enjoyed his enthusiasm. Seeing the happy anticipation in him piqued her own. She couldn't imagine what this special birthday gift could possibly be.

Bogie pranced around in his eagerness for Patrick to fill the dish so he could eat.

"Now, Mom, now?" Patrick asked, jumping up and

down after he poured the dog food into the bowl. Between the dog and her brother, the two looked like they were doing a square dance.

"Let me eat dinner first," Merry said, teasing her brother.

Patrick's eyes rounded. "Merry, no, please. I've been waiting and waiting to tell you. I don't think I can wait any longer." Merry and her mother shared a smile.

"Have pity on the boy," her mother urged.

Holding back a smile would have been impossible. "Okay, Patrick, you can tell me about my birthday gift."

Her brother's eyes lit up like Fourth of July sparklers. Whatever this early birthday present was must be special. Merry hugged her brother and, wrapping her arms around his torso, she gave him a gentle squeeze.

Patrick took hold of her hand while their mother opened the laptop and pulled out a chair to sit down. Merry joined her mother.

"You ready?" Robin Knight asked, turning on the computer.

"I can hardly wait," Merry answered.

Tucking his arm around her elbow, Patrick scooted close to Merry.

She looked at the blank computer screen, getting more curious by the second. They both seemed to be squirming with anticipation. "What did you two order me?"

Patrick laughed and pointed to the computer, crying out, "We got you a *man* for your birthday!"

"What?" Merry asked, certain there was some misunderstanding. "I don't think it's possible to buy me a man."

"Not exactly buy," her mother explained. "Patrick and I spent the afternoon online answering the questionnaire for Mix & Mingle. We filled in your profile and signed you up for the next six months."

Merry was speechless for several moments. *"You did what?"*

"We got you a date," Patrick answered, beaming her a huge smile.

If she wasn't already sitting, Merry would have needed to take a seat. Her immediate thought was how best not to disappoint her mother and brother by telling them this wasn't anything she wanted. That thought was quickly followed by a question. "What photo did you use?" She hoped it was a recent one and not some high school prom picture. She'd changed a lot since her teen years. She wore contacts now instead of glasses, which showed off her deep brown eyes; her hair was longer now, shoulder length, parted in the middle. She'd be mortified if they'd used the photo on her employee badge for Matterson Consulting, where she looked like a deer caught in the headlights. Actually, it resembled more of a mug shot.

"That's the best part," Patrick told her, looking well pleased with himself. "We didn't use a photo of you."

Now Merry was totally baffled. "You mean to say you posted a picture of someone else?"

"Don't be silly," her mother responded.

"Well, if it isn't me, then whose photo did you use?"

Patrick's glee couldn't be contained. "We used Bogie's."

"You made me a dog?" Merry cried, resisting the urge to cover her face. "Why?"

"Two reasons," her mother explained.

"One," Patrick intervened, thrusting his index finger into the air, ready to show his reasoning. "You love dogs."

"Ah . . . I guess," Merry admitted. Bogie was as much her dog as Patrick's. He often slept on her bed. She took him for walks on the days Patrick couldn't. Bogie was considered part of the Knight family.

"And second, and most important," her mother continued, "You're a beautiful young woman. Too many potential dates would judge you purely on your looks. That didn't sit right with me. I wanted them to get to know you as a person, as the generous, kindhearted, loving woman you are. They will need to dig deeper into your profile rather than to simply gaze at a photograph. And," she added, "We weren't sure how you'd feel about all of this, so we chose a pseudonym for your name. You are now Merry Smith."

"Merry Smith," she repeated slowly, still having trouble taking all this in. Looking at her profile as it came up on the screen, she withheld a groan. Seeing Bogie with her pseudonym listed below, she figured it was highly unlikely anyone would send her a Mix & Mingle message. Anyone looking at the photo would think her profile was all one big joke. No one wanted to date a dog.

CHAPTER TWO

＊

Jayson

Jayson Bright walked into his penthouse condo, which had a sweeping view of Puget Sound, and headed directly to his liquor cabinet. It'd been a hellish day. His uncle had been on Jayson's back about this Boeing contract from the moment he stepped into the office that morning. For the thousandth time, Jayson assured his uncle Matt that all was well and that the report would be on time before the Christmas deadline. All he could do was hope that he wasn't blowing smoke. It felt as if his entire future with the company hung in the balance.

Jayson poured himself a glass of his favorite Malbec and sank onto the sofa, resting his head against the back cushion. He took in several deep breaths, doing his best to ease the tension between his shoulder blades. With pressure mounting, he'd been at the office for twelve straight hours and had skipped lunch. By six-thirty he was ravenous. Rather than wait until he was home, he grabbed a sandwich and a latte on his way out of the Fourth Avenue high-rise. This wasn't how he intended to live the rest of his life, and yet it was all he'd known since he'd accepted this position with his uncle's company.

His phone vibrated inside his suit jacket, reminding him that he'd turned off the ringer for the last meeting of the day.

"Yeah," he said, exhausted. It was Cooper, his cousin on his mother's side.

"Hey Jay, is that any way to greet me?"

Despite how tired he was, Jayson grinned. "Where are you, man?" Cooper lived in the San Francisco Bay area. They got together when they could, which wasn't nearly enough to suit either of them. They were the same age and had always been close. Cooper was as close as a brother to Jayson.

"I'm in town."

Jayson sat up straight. "Seattle?"

"Yeah. Technically, the airport. I just stepped off the flight. I'm on my way back from a business trip and got a layover in Seattle."

This was a shock. Had Jayson known, he would have sent a car to get Cooper. "You should have told me you were coming."

"I did. I sent you two texts and left a voice mail. What more do you want?" Cooper razzed.

Jayson set his wineglass aside and wiped his face. "I was in a meeting and had my phone on vibrate."

"I'll get a cab and be to your place in thirty."

"Perfect." As tired as he'd been, Jayson felt refreshed and eager to see his best friend. It'd been three months since they'd last seen each other, and it felt like a year or longer.

Sure enough, a half-hour later, Jayson let his cousin into the condo. The two pumped fists and then hugged, slapping each other across the back.

After their greeting, Cooper paused and stared out at the sweeping view of the waterfront, lit up with sparkling lights. All too familiar with the view, Jayson barely noticed the scene. The white-and-green ferry gliding across the dark waters of Puget Sound looked like a beacon steering toward Bremerton. The entire Seattle waterfront was lit up in a festive holiday scene.

"I got to tell you, bro, this view gets me every time. It's even more breathtaking with all the Christmas lights."

Christmas.

Jayson didn't want to think about it. It was a month away now, and the pressure was on. Not for the holidays, but for this report the CEO of Boeing was expecting on his desk before the holidays.

Jayson frowned and stared at it himself, then shrugged. "It's okay."

"What?" Cooper cried. "You have one of the most fantastic views in the world and you show no appreciation."

Jayson shrugged. "By the time I get home, I'm too tired to give a damn. Too tired to even notice." It'd been this way ever since his move to Seattle.

His cousin shook his head as though he couldn't believe what he was hearing. "Jay, listen, it's time to stop and smell the roses."

Jayson cracked a smile. "Someday." Frankly, he didn't see any roses, and even if he did, he wasn't about to stop and take a whiff. His life was busy. He was in the middle of an important assignment and he didn't have time to enjoy the view—or anything else, for that matter.

"Wine?" Jayson asked, diverting Cooper's attention away from the nighttime panorama.

"Sure."

Jayson poured a glass of the rich red Malbec and handed it to his best friend. They clicked glasses and each took a sip.

"Hey, this is good. California?" Cooper asked.

"No, this is from Argentina. The Mendoza area."

Cooper took another sip and said, "I should have known."

Jayson and Cooper were wine snobs and tried to best each other with their out-of-the-way finds. Jayson enjoyed finding small boutique wineries from around the world. It wasn't uncommon for him to order wine for himself and for his cousin and have a case delivered to Cooper's California home. Jayson's biggest coup came when he found a sauvignon blanc at a winery that was practically in Cooper's backyard.

"So what brings you to town?" Jayson asked, taking a seat on his sofa.

His cousin sat on the edge of the cushion on the recliner next to the fireplace. "I'm in love."

Jayson nearly spewed his wine back into the glass. For a long moment, he stared at his cousin to be sure this wasn't a joke. "What? You're in love? I know you said you were dating a new girl, but love? How did this happen?"

"How?" Cooper repeated, grinning like a schoolboy. "You're acting like I caught some sort of infectious disease."

Years ago, they had made a promise to each other not to marry before they were forty. If then. Both sets of their parents had been through multiple marriages. They decided they'd be smarter than their parents. If and when they ever *did* fall in love, it would be when they were mature enough to know what they wanted.

"Are you sure it's love?" Jayson found it hard to believe. He could tell this wasn't a joke. Cooper was as serious as an undertaker.

"She's got me—hook, line, and sinker."

Jayson rolled his eyes. "I can't believe this. Next thing I know you're going to tell me you're getting married."

In response, Cooper arched his brows.

Jayson froze. "You kidding me, man."

"No. Flew here to ask you to be my best man at the wedding."

Too stunned to react, Jayson remained speechless as his mind whirled with the question. "You're serious? You're really going to do it?"

"Yup."

"This girl's family's not blackmailing you? This is completely voluntary?"

"Completely voluntary," Cooper repeated, grinning at the question. "Fact is, I can't wait to make Maddy my wife."

Jayson slouched against the sofa in disbelief. Something was up. This wasn't the Cooper he knew as well as he knew himself. There had to be a catch to all this. Frowning, he said, "I've got to meet this woman. This Maddy must really be something to knock you off your feet."

"You have met her. Remember Maddy Baldwin? She attended boarding school and camp with us."

Jayson bolted to his feet and brushed the hair from his forehead. "Maddy Baldwin? The girl who was a major pain in the butt?"

"Yup, her."

Jayson knew exactly who Maddy was. He'd spent one entire summer with her at an East Coast camp. Both Jayson and Cooper were more of an inconvenience to their parents, so as soon as they were old enough to be shipped to boarding school, off they went. During the summers, it was camp. They rarely had any contact with their parents. When they did, it was a disappointment. The cousins had each other, and they became their own family.

"Man, you've got to be kidding me. The Maddy I remember had red hair and braces on her buck teeth. She drove us both nuts."

"That she did."

"I thought she moved to California after her sophomore year?"

"She did."

"You kept in touch with her?" Surely Cooper would have mentioned it before now if he had. As a twelve-year-old, she'd been a major pest. She was a tomboy and always wanted to join in on their fun. Despite everything the two had done to ditch her, Maddy would inevitably find them. That entire summer she'd been a constant thorn in their side. The girl simply wouldn't take no for an answer.

"We found each other six months ago and hit it off. It didn't take long for me to realize she's the one. Trust me, the buck teeth are gone. You wouldn't recognize her these days. I'm telling you, Maddy's a knockout." Cooper reached for his phone and brought up a current photo.

His cousin wasn't exaggerating. Maddy was a looker, all right. Jayson blinked a couple times, hardly able to believe this was the same Maddy who'd plagued them all those years ago. "That's Maddy?"

"Yup. I gotta tell you, cuz, the minute we connected, I felt something right here." He pressed his hand over his heart and patted it several times. "I never told you, but back at camp she was my first kiss and I was hers."

"You kissed her? No way." Jayson shook his head, finding this confession more than a little shocking.

"It was after you left camp. Maddy offered to pay me."

Jayson burst out laughing.

"No joke. She wanted to know what it was like to be kissed and offered me five bucks. I'm no fool—I took it. I mean, it wasn't going to hurt any, and frankly, I was a little curious myself. We did the deed and then she demanded a refund because, in her words, it was gross."

"Did you return her money?"

"No way. I fulfilled my part of the bargain. I told her if she felt cheated she could take it up with an attorney."

Jayson rubbed his hand down his face. He found it difficult to believe his closest friend and cousin loved a woman enough to marry her. "How did you two reconnect?"

"You aren't going to believe this."

At this point, Jayson was ready to believe just about anything. "Tell me."

"I saw her on Mix & Mingle."

The last thing his cousin needed was help finding dates. Cooper was a magnet when it came to attractive women. "Mix & Mingle? Isn't that an online dating site? What were *you* doing on a dating site?"

"No, not me. One of the guys from the office was on the site and looking at profiles. He asked me to look with him. You remember Doug, don't you? Nerdy guy, thick glasses. A computer genius, but when it comes to women he was a total loser. He signed up, and once he had all these women's profiles to review, he got overwhelmed. I told him I'd help him find the perfect woman for him. Finding Maddy on that site was my destiny."

"You stumbled upon Maddy's profile?"

"I saw the name before I saw the photo. Couldn't believe it when I realized this was Maddy. Our Maddy. Then I found the woman I thought Doug would like, and as a thank-you, he let me send Maddy a message. She remembered me, too, and answered back. As they say, the rest is history."

Jayson remained suspicious. "If Maddy's so hot, why'd she resort to an online dating site?"

"I asked her the same thing. She'd been batting zero in the romance department. No time, working crazy hours, but then a friend talked her into it. Naturally, she was skeptical, but she decided to give it a try."

"What does she do?"

"Maddy's a doctor."

"A doctor. Maddy?"

"Yes, and she's amazing. I can't wait for you two to talk. The minute you see her, you'll know why I decided she's the one."

Jayson raised his glass for a toast and Cooper touched the rim of the wineglass with his own. "To craziness, marriage, and finding love when least expected."

"Hear, hear."

They both took a healthy swallow of the wine.

"When's the wedding?"

"Not until September. Maddy thought we'd get married in a vineyard, seeing how we both share a love of wine."

"Great idea." He could picture the scene in his mind, with the rolling hills of vines in the background. Any number of beautiful spots in California wine country would be a great setting for a wedding.

"In New Zealand."

Jayson laughed. "A destination wedding."

"You'll make it, won't you? Clear your schedule now."

No question Jayson would be there. If need be, he'd willingly fly to the moon for this wedding. "I wouldn't miss it for the world."

"Great. Then you'll agree to serve as my best man?"

"I'll consider it an honor."

Cooper spent the night and then took an early-morning flight back to San Francisco the following day. It was a good thing Jayson's cousin had delivered the news in person. If Cooper had told him over the phone, Jayson would never have believed him. He would have been convinced it was a hoax.

As Jayson dressed in his usual suit and tie for work the next morning, he realized he'd been so caught up in work that he hadn't gone out socially in several weeks. His relationships were nonexistent, especially since he started working for his uncle. He rarely dated the same woman more than a few times.

Like his cousin, he'd never had trouble connecting with women. Six feet, broad shoulders, dark hair and eyes. No one needed to tell him he stood out in a crowd. The problem was that most women were attracted to his name and his wealth. He was continually left in doubt if their feelings for him were genuine. He was considered a prize catch. He wasn't being vain; it was just the plain truth. Humility had nothing to do with it.

Out of curiosity and more than any need or desire to date, Jayson decided to log on to the website for Mix & Mingle and searched for the photos of women who'd signed up in the Seattle area.

Immediately he saw row upon row of photos. He was ready to exit the site when something different caught his eye. Instead of a woman, there was a picture of a dog.

A golden retriever.

He looked again to be sure he wasn't seeing things. Yup, it was a dog.

He couldn't imagine why someone would put up a photo of a dog. For several moments, he mulled it over and was unable to come up with an answer. He figured he'd wasted enough time, shut down his laptop, and headed for the office.

Friday finally arrived and Jayson should have been thinking about something other than work. His friends, few of them as there were, would be going out, enjoying themselves. But anything social wasn't in the cards for him.

Later in the afternoon as the workday was winding down, his scheduled conference call was canceled. He had a few minutes, and for no reason he could name, he went back to the Mix & Mingle website.

The photo of the dog was still up. Again, he stared at it, and as he did, the thought came to him that maybe the woman who'd posted it was like him. A woman who put more stock in character than in looks or position.

Her profile listed her name.

Merry Smith.

Clearly that was made up, and he suspected her first name referenced Christmas, which was interesting.

The dog in the photo was cute. Jayson had a dog once. Rocky had been a golden retriever like this one. His dad had bought Rocky for him when Jayson briefly lived with him. During his junior year, his mother had a fit of guilt and insisted he finish high school living with her rather than his father. Unfortunately, Jayson didn't get along with his new stepdad, so his mother had shipped him back to live with his father. It wouldn't have been so bad, except his stepmother wasn't that keen on him, either. Jayson spent a miserable two years with his father. The only thing that helped him through that time was Rockefeller, or

Rocky, his dog. He stared at the photo for several minutes and then closed the site.

By the time he left the office, Jayson discovered only a few staff voluntarily stayed behind to work the overtime hours that had been approved to finish this Boeing contract on time. It wasn't mandatory on Friday night, and Jayson appreciated those who were willing to work when it wasn't required.

As he headed toward his condo, Jayson couldn't help but think back to the website and to the woman behind the dog. He wanted to know more. His curiosity got the best of him and he spent an hour filling out the questionnaire. Even as he filled in the answers, he suspected it would be a complete waste of time. When it came to inserting his photograph, he found an old photo of Rocky and posted it.

Pleased with himself, he shut down his laptop. Maybe later, if he felt like it, he'd send Merry Smith a message and see how it played out.

CHAPTER THREE

*

Merry

It was after seven by the time Merry arrived home from work the following Monday. As soon as she walked into the kitchen, Patrick looked up from the laptop on the table and shot her a wide, happy grin.

"Merry, you got a wink on Mix & Mingle! His name is Jay and he likes you."

Not wanting to disappoint her brother, Merry swallowed a groan. As a matter of fact, she'd received several "winks" on the dating website, most of which told humorous tales of having dated other dogs. But in the end, the winks told Merry they weren't interested in actually meeting her. Why these men even bothered to contact her remained a mystery—one she would rather not explore. In a way, her mother had been right. Putting up the photo of Bogie helped filter out those who would be a poor match. Those heartless winks told her as much.

Robin Knight sat in the family room. "This guy looks promising," she called out in a happy, singsong voice.

Patrick nodded enthusiastically. "If you look at his photo, you'll like him, too," her brother insisted, his eyes twinkling with delight. Bogie, his faithful companion, was at his side and stared up at the computer screen alongside Patrick. Bogie cocked his head to one side as if intrigued himself.

"Give me a minute to unwind," Merry pleaded.

"You need to answer him," Patrick insisted.

"Later . . . okay?"

"Do it now," her brother tried again, his eyes wide and hopeful. "Just look at his picture."

Merry glanced over and blinked. Twice. "He sent the picture of a dog?"

"It's a handsome dog. A golden retriever like Bogie."

Her mother gave her the look. It was one Merry had learned to recognize—the look that said if Merry didn't follow through, then she would be disappointing Patrick.

"I like Jay," Patrick said.

"Okay, okay," Merry muttered, giving in. No wonder her family was intrigued, and she had to admit that now she was, too.

After heating up leftover meatloaf and scalloped potatoes, Merry sat down next to Patrick, prepared to send her first message.

"What should I say?" she asked her brother, seeking inspiration.

Patrick mulled over the question. "Tell him you like his photo."

Merry grinned and set her fingers on the keyboard and typed.

Bow wow.

Along with her message, the picture of Bogie showed up on the screen so he'd know it was her.

Patrick read Merry's message and laughed.

Almost right away a response came through, as if he'd been sitting in front of his computer, waiting for her.

Bow wow back.

You have a dog, too?

Not anymore. The photo is of Rocky. Had him as a teenager. He died while I was away at college. Still miss him.

You didn't get another dog?

No. Hate to leave one cooped up in a condo all day. Not fair to him.

I agree. Bogie is a family dog.

You done this dating-website thing before?

Never. A first for me. You?

Me, neither. Feeling a little foolish, actually.

Understand. Me, too.

Patrick continued to sit at Merry's side and read their exchange. "Tell him that Mom and I signed you up for your birthday gift."

"Okay."

My teenage brother signed me up for this as a birthday gift.

Something you wanted?

Yes and no. Busy with work. Don't have time for a social life.

Same here.

What prompted you to sign up on Mix & Mingle?

Best friend met the love of his life on here. Curiosity got the better of me. Figured it'd be a waste of time.

Then what made you go through with it?

You.

Me?

The answer made Merry sit up and take notice.

Delighted, Patrick clapped his hands. "Mom and I did good, didn't we?"

"Looks that way," Merry agreed.

You and the photo of your dog. Reminded me of Rocky.

Merry paused to take a bite of her dinner. Before she could respond, Jay sent another note.

Your profile intrigued me.

Remember, my brother is the one who filled it out. I have to admit, I didn't read it over.

You don't know if it's true or not?

Oh, I'm sure it is true. Patrick is honest to a fault.

"Tell him I'm special," her brother said, leaning forward and balancing his elbows on the tabletop.

"Okay, okay."

Patrick wants me to tell you he's "special," if you know what I mean. He's a great kid and works at a local grocery store.

A pause followed, as if Jay was trying to read between the lines.

How old is Patrick?

He's eighteen/twelve.

Gotcha.

Worked ten hours today. It's time for a hot bath and bed.

Hear you. Would you like to chat again?

Merry read the line twice.

"Tell him yes," Patrick urged. "He didn't make any bad jokes about you being a dog or anything."

Bogie seemed to agree. He rested his chin on Merry's thigh as though to urge her.

Sure. When?

Tomorrow night. Same time?

Okay.

Merry closed the computer and leaned back in the chair.

"Well, what do you think?" her mother asked.

Merry was surprised to realize she was interested in getting to know Jay better. When she'd learned what her mother and Patrick had done, she'd been convinced it had been a waste of time and their limited funds. She never expected anything to come of it. And it very well might not. She'd chatted with one guy. Just one. The other "winks" were from men she wouldn't seriously consider meeting.

Merry got out of the office later than normal on Tuesday night. She'd told her new Mix & Mingle friend, Jay, that they could connect around the same time, and she was thirty minutes behind schedule. Being on time had been drilled into her from when she was young, and she hated the thought of being late. For Jay. For anyone.

Rushing in the front door, she shucked off her coat and headed to the kitchen to find both her mother and Patrick leaning over the laptop set up on the round table.

"I need to log on for Jay," she said, anxious now.

"Patrick and I are talking to him," her mother said, looking pleased with herself.

"What?" Her fear was that they were pretending to be her, which would be disastrous. She could only imagine what they would say, and she inwardly groaned.

"No, no—Patrick and I let Jay know it was us. We didn't want to keep him waiting," her mother explained, as if she was only doing what was necessary. "Otherwise he might think you aren't interested, and you are."

Merry was anxious to chat with Jay again. "What did you tell him?"

"Nothing much. Just that you had texted to say that you were late getting out of the office."

Her heart was pounding as Patrick slid out of his chair for her to get in front of the computer. "You can take over now."

"Thanks."

"I like him, Merry," her mother said. "He seems polite and nice."

Having her mother and Patrick's seal of approval went a long way toward making her more comfortable with Jay.

I just stepped in the door. So sorry to be late.

Enjoyed the chat with your mom and Patrick. They sang your praises.

Don't believe everything they said. On second thought, please do. I'm tall, thin, and gorgeous. That's what they said, right?

Close. Were you out Christmas shopping?

No, work again. Mandatory overtime.

Same. I'm still at the office.

Oh no. Hope you don't have a long commute.

Not at all.

Good.

Good day for you?

Fairly good. Not a fan of my boss and grateful I didn't see him today. I think he might be out of the office. How about you?

Meetings all day. Found my thoughts drifting a few times, thinking about our chat. Gave me something to look forward to this evening.

I felt the same way.

Merry sat at her computer for an hour as they typed messages back and forth. He asked and answered question after question. From his responses, she could see that he was becoming more relaxed with her. She was beginning to be more at ease with him, too.

Wednesday night Merry spent another hour online with Jay. This time she took the laptop into her bedroom and sat on her bed with her back against her headboard and the computer balanced on her lap as she typed away. About thirty minutes into their exchange, Patrick knocked on her bedroom door.

"Yeah?"

Her brother stuck his head into her room. "Tell Jay I said hello. Okay?"

"Okay." Her fingers flew across the keys.

Patrick wants me to tell you hello. Of all the men who winked at me, he likes you the best.

You got a lot of winks?

A few. She didn't mention they were mostly making fun of her dog picture with no real interest in her. You?

A few.

More than three?

Way more.

Really. How many is way more? Four?

Ha, ha.

Okay, I give up. How many?

A dozen.

That's a joke, right?

Hey, a handsome guy like myself is a real find.

Merry couldn't keep the smile off her face.

After an hour had passed, they set an earlier time for Friday to chat again.

All day Friday Merry found herself glancing at the clock every few minutes as it neared five o'clock. She didn't want to be late the way she had been on Tuesday. Thankfully, her boss had made Fridays an exception to the mandatory overtime. The minute it was five o'clock, Merry started clearing off her desk, eager to escape.

Kylie, one of the other data entry workers, was in an even bigger rush to get out of the office.

"How's Palmer today?" Merry asked.

Kylie's three-year-old, Palmer, had come down with the flu and she'd been up half the night with him. She'd phoned in sick, but when Jayson Bright got wind that the department was one person short, he'd come unglued. Not that he'd shouted or made a scene. That wasn't his way. He'd personally contacted Kylie and explained that it was vital that this report be finished before Christmas. She was needed at the office and he wasn't willing to accept excuses. Her son would be perfectly fine with a babysitter.

Kylie had tried to argue, but the heartless Mr. Bright had given her the choice: a babysitter for her son or her job. Fortunately, at the last minute Kylie's mother had been able to look after the little boy.

Merry had been angry on Kylie's behalf. As far as she was concerned, the man was heartless and unreasonable and had his priorities askew. Even worse, he wouldn't allow personal phone calls on company time. While that was standard for most workplaces, extenuating circumstances did occur, like a sick three-year-old.

Kylie had her phone pressed to her ear, checking up on

her son, as she raced toward the elevator ahead of Merry and Lauren, who sat at the desk closest to Merry.

For that matter, Merry was in a hurry to get away herself.

"Hey, what's the big rush?" Lauren asked. "You got a hot Friday-night date?"

"Sort of." Merry grabbed her purse from beneath her desk and slung the strap over her shoulder.

"How do you *sort of* have a hot date?"

"I'm talking to a guy I met online."

Lauren whistled softly. "Oh yeah. Where's all that complaining and grumbling you did after your mom and Patrick signed you up for that dating site? I see you're singing a different tune now."

"This guy sounds great."

Lauren had yet to be convinced this was a good way to meet somebody. At forty-five, she'd been divorced ten years and had given up on men and romance. "*Sounds* great?"

"Yeah, his profile picture was a golden retriever, too."

"You mean to say you don't know what he looks like?"

"No," Merry said, unruffled by her friend's concern. "Remember, he doesn't know what I look like, either, so we're both taking a chance."

Lauren remained skeptical. "He could be fat and fifty."

"He isn't." Merry wasn't sure why she was so confident

of this. Jay sounded young, and he hit all the right notes with her. She chose to believe he was everything he said he was.

Lauren squinted her eyes. "How do you know?"

Unable to explain her gut feeling, Merry shrugged. "I can tell."

"Has he suggested you meet yet?" Lauren asked as they walked to the elevator.

"No." But she hadn't, either. They were in the getting-to-know-you stage. No need to rush this, especially when they both seemed to be heavily involved with work.

Lauren arched her finely trimmed eyebrows as if that said it all.

"You're far too skeptical," Merry complained as she pressed the down button. "We've only messaged a few times. It's too early. I want to know more about him before I'm willing to do a face-to-face." Although he hadn't said it, Merry was sure Jay felt the same way. It was far too soon in their relationship.

The elevator door slipped open and Merry and Lauren stepped inside. Lauren pushed the button for the lobby.

"Hold that door," Jayson Bright shouted as he raced across the floor, weaving his way around desks while shoving his arm into the sleeve of his three-quarter-length raincoat.

This was the man who had been unrelenting when it came to these long mandatory hours of overtime. He'd been unwilling to listen to excuses for time off. Even for a sick child.

Heartless.

Demanding.

Unreasonable.

If it was up to Merry she would have let the elevator door close in his face.

Lauren apparently didn't share her dislike of their boss. She thrust out her arm, which caused the automatic door to glide back open.

"Thanks." Jayson Bright joined them.

Standing behind him, Merry made a face. She put her thumbs in her ears and wiggled them back and forth while sticking out her tongue at him.

Stifling a giggle, Lauren cupped her hand over her mouth.

One floor down, the elevator stopped again. Jayson stepped aside to allow more employees to get on, and then impatiently pushed the button for the lobby.

Merry arched her brows at her friend. He seemed to be in an almighty hurry.

As soon as the elevator hit the floor, Jayson shot out like he was being chased.

"Maybe he's got a hot date tonight," Lauren commented as they walked out of the building and toward the bus stop.

"Doubt it," Merry murmured. "I can't imagine any woman in her right mind being attracted to him."

CHAPTER FOUR

※

Jayson

Jayson couldn't get out of the office fast enough. He'd enjoyed every minute he'd spent messaging with Merry this week. He had yet to even ask for her real name. For that matter, he hadn't divulged his full name, either.

Not important.

Not necessary.

He preferred she have no idea who he was. To Merry, he was just an overworked office employee not unlike herself. They'd exchanged a lot of personal information, including memories of their childhoods. He'd learned Merry lived with her parents and brother and that she worked in downtown Seattle, the same as he did. She was about as apple-pie as she could be, and he appreciated that. Her youth had been vastly different from his own.

She'd had stability and love. Both she and her brother were cherished by their parents.

By contrast, Jayson had been used by his mother to manipulate his father. Precious little love had ever existed between them, and not near enough was left over to nurture him. He'd spent much of his childhood in boarding schools and summer camps with Cooper. For most of his childhood, when he was with family, he'd been shuffled around between his parents. Neither one wanted him. Neither one showed much interest in his emotional well-being. If it wasn't for caring teachers and a few good friends, he wondered what might have become of him.

His uncle, for whatever reason, had never married and had no children. All Matthew Matterson's energy had gone into building his consulting firm. He realized Jayson possessed the same drive and ambition, so he'd taken his nephew under his wing after college. Looking to prove his worth, Jayson had approached the job with an all-consuming passion that allowed him to climb to the position of vice president of the firm.

Merry was his first distraction in a long time. He should be thinking more about this contract with Boeing than spending time online chatting with her, but at this point his work hadn't suffered due to their budding relationship. He had to say, though, he found himself looking at the clock far more often than he ever had before, calculating how many hours it would be until they could chat again.

Speed-walking toward his condo building, Jayson stopped off at the Corner Deli, where he collected a pastrami sandwich for his dinner along with a mixed green salad. He was a regular patron and was greeted by name by the owner.

"Hey, Jayson."

"Cyrus," Jayson responded, but he had no time for small talk.

Jayson walked past the woman ringing the bell for the red bucket, collecting for charity. He gave at the office. As he neared his condo, he noticed a homeless man had set up his bed for the night against the side of the building where Jayson lived. Much more of this and property values would be affected. Not good.

He pointed out the homeless guy to the doorman. "See what you can do about that," he instructed.

"Will do."

Peter, the evening doorman, was looking for a Christmas bonus. Jayson was one who appreciated excellent service and rewarded it generously. He was heading for the elevator that would take him to his condo when his phone pinged, indicating he had gotten a text.

While he waited, he reached for his phone. For one wild moment, he thought it might be Merry, then realized that would be impossible, as she didn't have his personal number. Only a select few did.

The text was from his father.

In town.

Jayson groaned. That meant Alex Bright was going to want to see him. Jayson had no desire to connect with him. He ignored the text and shoved his phone back into his suit jacket as the elevator arrived.

As he entered his condo, his phone rang. Irritated by now, he grabbed it and saw his father's face appear on the screen. Tightening his jaw, he was inclined to let the call go to voice mail. It would do no good, though. Knowing how persistent Alex could be, delaying the inevitable would serve no useful purpose.

"Yes," Jayson answered, revealing no warmth or welcome.

"Is that any way to speak to your father?"

"How long are you going to be in town?" he asked Alex, avoiding his father's remark. If it was up to him he would gladly cut off all ties with both parents. Unfortunately, that wasn't an option, because his uncle was his mother's brother, as well as his father's best friend. All he could do was maintain a safe distance from their toxic lives.

"I came to see you," his father insisted.

"I'm busy." Jayson made sure he was always busy when either parent was in town.

"How about dinner tonight?"

"I have a date." A slight exaggeration, as his date consisted of messaging Merry. He was determined not to give up this one small pleasure because his father just happened to be in town.

"A date," his father repeated slowly. "That's wonderful. Bring her along."

"No thanks." If he did have an actual dinner date, no doubt his father would spend the entire evening flirting with her. No way. Not happening. The thought of Merry meeting his father made him cringe.

"You serious about this girl?"

Jayson hated these conversations. "Maybe." He was elusive, as that worked best with his father. The less either parent knew of his personal life, the better.

"It's time you thought about marriage," his father advised, as if Jayson would listen to any marital advice from the man who had sported four wives and an equal number of stepchildren, although Jayson was his only son.

"Perhaps," he replied, hoping that would satisfy his father.

"This girl you're seeing. Is she the one?"

It seemed Alex wasn't going to willingly drop the subject. "It's too early to tell."

"But you like her."

"I wouldn't be dating her if I didn't." He did like Merry.

She interested him more than any woman he'd known to this point. The anonymity between them suited him and his purposes for now. One day they would meet, and most likely it'd be relatively soon. At this point, however, he was content with their messaging. Which reminded him . . .

Jayson glanced at his wrist. "I need to go."

"Not before we set a time to get together."

"Tomorrow." He would agree to just about anything if it meant he could get off the phone.

"Good. Dinner tomorrow. Don't disappoint me the way you have the last two times I've been in town."

Jayson had used several convenient excuses to get out of seeing his father. Meals with Alex could drag on for hours. Besides, it was highly probable that his father was romantically involved with some poor, unsuspecting woman who had no clue what she was getting herself into, and his dad usually brought her along. Jayson wanted no part of that.

This was a pattern. His father, showing his age now, would use younger women to boost his ego. In a sad attempt to prove what a fine catch he was, he would involve Jayson. Having a successful, handsome son was a credit to him.

"Make it lunch," Jayson suggested. "I have a date tomorrow night as well."

"Same girl?"

"Don't know yet."

He heard his father's sigh. "It's time to stop playing the field, Jayson. Find the right woman and settle down."

This was an interesting tip, coming from his father.

"Yes. You're getting to the age when the right marriage to the right woman can be an asset to your career. Take my advice, find a woman who will look good on your arm and provide the right kind of business connections."

"I'll do that," he said, trying his best to hide his sarcasm. Then, unable to resist, he added, "Especially since marrying for money and connection has made you so happy and successful."

His father ignored the slight. "See you tomorrow."

Eager to get off the phone, he quickly agreed to a time and restaurant. Jayson ended the call without bidding his father farewell. Good riddance. He didn't know how long Alex Bright intended to stay in town. Hopefully it wouldn't be for long. Here today. Gone tomorrow. That was what he remembered about his father from his childhood.

Anxious now to get online with Merry, he went into his home office and logged on to the Mix & Mingle website and waited for Merry to do the same. In his rush, he'd left his dinner downstairs. He returned to the lobby to retrieve it, collecting a plate and fork in his kitchen along the way. He took everything into his home office with him.

As he began eating, he remembered seeing the data-entry temp eating her lunch at her desk and how it had annoyed him. He'd frowned upon the practice, and yet here he was doing the same thing. In retrospect, he should have commended her for being committed to her work. Too late now. The memo had already been issued. No eating at one's desk.

His computer dinged, indicating that Merry was online. Right away he started typing.

Wonder what it means that we're both home on a Friday night? he wrote.

Jayson thought about his dad in a downtown motel. Likely he was living it up, drinking too much and working hard to impress his latest conquest.

It says a lot, doesn't it? Merry typed.

Thing is, I wouldn't want to be anyplace else than right here, right now, chatting with you.

Are you sweet-talking me?

And if I was?

Then keep talking.

Jayson leaned back in his chair and smiled. He'd smiled more in the last week than he had in the last year, and it was all due to Merry. Involved as he was in this current work project, he hadn't realized how lonely he'd become.

Hope your day was good, Jay.

Kept looking at the clock, wondering how long it would be

before we could chat. He wasn't sure he should admit this, but he did it anyway.

I did the same thing. My life is busy. I assumed there wasn't room for anything or anyone else, and then I connected with you, and, well . . .

Well what?

I'm not sure I should admit this.

Tell me.

My life is full and yet it's empty. I assumed all this time that I was content, but talking to you has proven that there's a part of me that hungers for an emotional connection. When I learned that Patrick and my mother had signed me up for Mix & Mingle, I brushed it off as something I didn't need or want. Messaging with you has opened my eyes.

Jayson read her note twice before he replied. Mine, too.

My friends are skeptical.

You mean because we haven't set a time to meet?

Yes.

Is that what you want?

He waited several moments for her reply as if she was mulling over her answer. It could be she was typing a lengthy reply, too.

Yes but not yet. Would you mind if we waited awhile longer? I'm finding just talking to you online is enough for now. It gives us both a chance to feel comfortable with each other.

Are you afraid meeting me will disappoint you?

Not at all. But I'd feel more comfortable about setting a time once I got to know more about you. It's more important to know who you are deep inside than what you look like. Besides, I have a small problem.

What kind of problem?

I'm working long hours now and have family obligations. And it's getting close to Christmas and I have a zillion things I need to do.

Like?

Baking. Mom, Patrick, and I bake for friends and family. It's our gift. Mom takes the baked goods to her friends whose MS is more advanced than her own. Then there's all the wonderful people in our lives who help us. Giving them something we've baked ourselves is our way of letting them know how grateful we are for what they do.

Service people?

Yes, but they're friends, too.

Like who?

There's a visiting home health aide who comes in and helps Mom two days a week, the postman, the newspaper boy, the teacher at Patrick's school. Those kinds of people.

In all his life, Jayson had never thought to gift anyone other than his doorman, and he did that with cash. Totally impersonal. Easier for sure. Merry and her family gave of themselves. This was a completely foreign idea that left him wondering if this was something other families did.

Without Mix & Mingle, he would never have had the chance to meet someone like Merry. To be fair, he might have met her, but he wouldn't have given her a second thought. It made him aware of how narrow-minded he'd been when it came to his dating options, and what had been important to him in a woman.

He wanted to tell her about his father's visit and get her opinion.

Don't mind waiting to meet you. I'm busy with work, too. Plus, my father is in town. Not happy about that.

You don't get along with your father?

Not particularly. He didn't have much to do with me when I was younger and now he wants a relationship. Far as I'm concerned, I'm not interested.

Better late than never.

Thought you'd say that. From what he knew of Merry and her family, he wouldn't have expected anything less.

I love my dad.

He grinned, not surprised. You're lucky to have a decent father.

I agree. You might want to give your own dad another shot. Perhaps he's looking for a second chance with his son.

Don't think that will work.

It won't if you don't try.

I'll think about it.

From Merry's profile, Jayson knew she was in her mid-twenties. He had to wonder how it was that a woman this young could be so wise.

They typed back and forth for two hours. It was only when Merry had to leave to pick up her brother from his job at the Kroger grocery store that she needed to close. Otherwise, Jayson was convinced they could have continued into the wee hours of the morning.

After they'd logged off, he thought about what Merry had written about her father, who sacrificed and supported her family. Jayson considered his own father to be a failure on every level. He'd been a cheating husband; a piss-poor father; a shrewd, heartless businessman; and, for the most part, a lousy friend.

Jayson could count on his right hand the number of times his father had taken advantage of his visitation rights and spent time with Jayson. For all of Jayson's life, Alex Bright had considered his son a nuisance who was best ignored in the hopes that he would go away.

The following afternoon, father and son met in the dining room of the best steakhouse in town. Alex came alone, which was a surprise. Jayson noticed that his father had added on a few pounds around his middle, which told him the older man's lifestyle was catching up with him fast.

Alex Bright grinned and slapped Jayson across the back. "I'm glad you could squeeze me into your tight dating schedule."

Jayson slid into the plush steakhouse booth. "Like father, like son."

His father laughed and took the seat across from him. "So tell me, how is it you found time to meet me for lunch? I figured you'd cancel again."

That was the million-dollar question. Jayson released a long, slow sigh as he considered his answer.

"A friend said something that made me reconsider."

"A friend? What did he say?"

"She."

His father arched his brows. "What did she say? Don't suppose it happens to be that girl you're dating."

Jayson preferred to leave the answer to speculation and ignored the question. "She said I should give you a chance. So, Dad, this is your chance."

Alex's eyes widened and, flustered now, he reached for the menu and avoided eye contact. "Thank her for me," he murmured.

Jayson stared at his father for a long time, not knowing what to think.

*

CHAPTER FIVE

Merry

Merry spent the entire weekend decorating the house for Christmas. Shopping for the perfect Christmas tree had always been a family tradition. Patrick got so excited that once they reached the Christmas tree lot, he bounced from tree to tree like a jackrabbit, extolling the virtues of each one. Her brother simply loved the holiday season and was never happier than he was in the weeks leading up to Christmas morning.

It took hours to get the chosen tree home, up, and decorated. Christmas music played in the background as they strung the lights and added their special ornaments, many of which Patrick had made over the years. There were more than a few of her own. It was truly a Charlie Brown tree except when it came to the ornaments, but Merry loved that her mother had kept them and insisted on using them year after year.

On Sunday following church, Merry and her mother baked cookies, and Patrick decorated the eggnog cookies with frosting and sprinkles. While Merry was busy placing the cutouts on the cookie sheets, her thoughts drifted toward Jay.

During last night's chat, Jay shared that he'd gone to lunch with his father, and apparently their visit together had gone relatively well. Not great. But better than Jay had expected. It sounded like father and son would never be "buddy-buddy," but they'd been able to have a decent conversation about each other's lives.

Merry had shared that she was going to spend Sunday afternoon baking cookies. Jay told her he couldn't remember the last time he'd tasted homemade cookies. Merry wanted in the worst way to give him a box and decided that when they met for the first time, she'd bring him a batch.

Monday morning, Merry arrived at the office thirty minutes early. Once there, she set up a tiny flower pot–size Christmas tree on the corner of her desk. Then she looped a silver garland around three sides of each office desk and hung glass ornaments strategically on each garland. When she finished, she stepped back to examine her work and felt good about what she'd accomplished. These few decorations added a bit of holiday cheer to their small department and brightened the area. They'd all been working extra-hard, putting in countless hours of overtime. This was her way of adding a little fun to their day and acknowledging the season.

Lauren was the first to arrive, and when she saw Merry's handiwork, her eyes lit up. "Cool."

"You like it?"

"Love it. I've been feeling down lately. It seems like I can't keep up with everything. This mandatory overtime is killing me."

Kylie added her voice to Lauren's once she arrived. "Me, too." When she saw the decorations Merry had arranged around each of their desks, she clapped her hands. "This is great."

"I downloaded a few Christmas songs, too. Thought we could softly play those while we work."

"Super."

Kylie grinned. "I adore Christmas music."

"Just don't be tempted to sing along," Merry advised. "Someone might hear." By *someone,* she meant their annoying boss. Even a hint that they might be enjoying themselves was sure to upset him. It was all work, work, work for Bright. The man was a real Grinch.

"Mr. Bright," Kylie said, ending with a moan of displeasure.

"He doesn't know the meaning of the word *fun*." Merry struggled with negative feelings when it came to her boss. He looked like he was in a perpetual bad mood. His entire focus was on the business, as if this job was the meaning of life.

Merry knew this current project was important to the company and the reports had to be in before Christmas. She also understood that Mr. Bright held hope that if the report proved useful, the aircraft company would become a major client. Then Matterson Consulting would be able to expand and add more offices, and thus accumulate a higher profit. To Merry's way of thinking, bigger wasn't always better, but no one had sought out her opinion, least of all her boss.

They started work, typing in the data, listening to the Christmas carols as their fingers tapped against the computer keys. It was the best Monday Merry could remember having in weeks. Even knowing her workday would last for a long ten hours, her mood was good.

She thought about Jay and was eager to chat with him that evening. They hadn't been online nearly as long Sunday night as they had been earlier in the weekend because both had to be at work early on Monday. For her part

Merry was tired from all the decorating and baking. Her weekend had been full of family activities.

Patrick seemed to realize how important Jay had become to his sister in this short amount of time. Her brother wanted to leave Jay a message, so she'd let him type a few lines to him on Sunday. It made her nervous wondering how Jay would respond to him. It pleased her with how patient he'd been with her brother to this point. He'd treated Patrick like he would anyone, and had been thoughtful and kind.

This alone comforted Merry in their growing relationship. Once, in high school, a date had made a joke about her brother, which had infuriated Merry. She never went out with him again, although he'd insisted it had all been in fun. Clearly, she couldn't take a joke, her date had told her. Jay had been wonderful, though, and that endeared him to her even more. After their Sunday night chat, she toyed with the idea of meeting Jay sooner rather than later. This evening when they went online, she was willing to approach him with the suggestion and see how he felt.

The afternoon was progressing smoothly until Mr. Bright happened to walk through their department. He paused when his gaze landed on the holiday decorations.

Merry looked up from her computer screen and glared at him, daring him to comment.

He regarded the three of them steadily before he asked, "Who did this?"

Merry stood ready to face him head-on. "Me."

"It's nice, but unfortunately, I have to ask you to take all this down."

"But why?" she asked, doing her best to hide her irritation. "It isn't disrupting our work. Ask Lauren and Kylie if you don't believe me. In fact, the music relaxes us so we work faster and more efficiently."

"I don't mean to—"

"What could you possibly have against Christmas?"

"I don't dislike Christmas," he insisted. "The employee manual clearly states—"

"The employee manual?" she repeated.

"It's required reading for all employees, Miss . . ." He paused and glanced at the nameplate on her desk. "Knight."

"I'm a temp and no one gave me an employee manual," she told him.

"Which explains why you were unaware of the rules. I can't let you keep these decorations up because that would encourage others to ignore company policy."

"I see," she said, biting into her lower lip. Far be it for anyone to enhance their work area or show a bit of cheer for the season.

As if reading her mind, Mr. Bright added, "The handbook specifically states there are to be no decorations for holidays. No displays on desks or floors. I apologize that HR didn't give you a handbook. I'll see to it that you receive one. Please read it."

"I will," she murmured, although it was a little late, seeing that her last day working as a temp would be right before Christmas. Finding the time to read the manual, especially now, would be difficult.

"I suggest you start with page twenty, third paragraph from the bottom," Bright told her, as if knowing her intentions.

Naturally, he would know the handbook by chapter and verse.

"This has long been the company policy," he said defensively. "I didn't make the rules, Ms. Knight, but it is what it is. Can I count on you to remove these decorations?"

Merry expelled her breath and slowly nodded. "Yes."

"Thank you." He looked over her desk, and for one moment she was convinced he showed regret, but then she was probably mistaken.

"I'll make sure not to do it on company time," she assured him. "You should know I came in early and arranged all this before starting work."

"That's appreciated. Thank you."

He left then. The entire time they'd been talking, both

Lauren and Kylie continued to work, doing their best to pretend not to notice their conversation.

Once he was out of sight, they stopped work and turned to Merry.

"You okay?" Lauren asked.

"Of course. I didn't know holiday decorations were against company policy," Merry said, biting the inside of her cheek. Her other team members apparently didn't, either, or they would have said something earlier.

"We'll help you take everything down," Kylie offered.

"No. It's fine," she assured her friends. "I was the one who put them up and I'll be the one to take them down." It took Merry several minutes to settle her nerves. She didn't know what it was about their boss. It went without saying that he was under pressure. They all were. At times, it seemed he went out of his way to find fault with her. The truth was Merry thought Bright and the employee manual were all a bit ridiculous, yet she had the impression he hadn't been happy about asking her to remove the decorations. He'd simply been doing his job.

Thankfully, this was a temporary situation, and in a short time she'd have completed her contract with Matterson Consulting.

———

Once home, Merry's mother noticed her slumped shoulders. Or she may have noticed the way Merry closed the microwave door with more force than was necessary.

"Hard day, sweetie?"

"The worst," Merry said, whirling around to face her mother. "Mr. Bright made me take down the holiday decorations and then at lunch I spilled tomato soup on my white blouse and if that wasn't bad enough I made a mistake and entered data in the wrong file and had to redo it all, wasting time when we're already on such a tight schedule."

Her mother, who was a salt-of-the-earth kind of person, frowned. "I'm sorry."

"Mom, you have nothing to be sorry about. This is all on me."

"Why would your boss make you remove the Christmas decorations?"

"Company policy," she reported, holding back a smile. "Page twenty of the employee handbook. Third paragraph from the bottom."

"Did your boss tell you that?"

"He did."

"It sounds like he wrote the handbook."

"I don't think so, although he must have the entire thing memorized." She wanted to blame Bright for her bad mood. It was easy to lay the fault on him, but she was the one who'd spilled her soup and the one who'd entered the data incorrectly. Still, it had all started with him.

Later that night, once she'd settled her nerves, Merry went online with Jay. Within only a few minutes he sensed something had upset her, and asked what was wrong.

I had a truly terrible, awful, no good Monday. Hope yours was better than mine.

Want to talk about it? I'm a good listener.

No, but thanks. If I reiterate everything that went wrong, that will only upset me again, and I don't want to waste another minute dwelling on the negative. Bottom line, I had a run-in with my boss. I'm over it and want to move on.

I hate the thought of you being upset.

Talking to you helps. And it did. Already Merry could feel her spirits rising. Chatting with Jay was exactly what she needed to help her deal with her horrible Monday.

I'd give anything to comfort you with a hug right now.

Merry hesitated. She'd give anything to get a hug from him. They'd decided to wait to meet, but maybe they were overthinking this. If they waited too long it could become an issue.

Are you thinking what I'm thinking? she asked.

What keeps going through my mind is seeing you in person, talking face-to-face instead of through a computer, having coffee together, laughing together, reaching over to hold your hand . . . What do you say?

Although this was what she wanted, Merry hesitated. What made you change your mind?

I'm not entirely sure. Think it might be what happened this last weekend. Things changed between us.

She felt it, too. There had been a slight shift in their relationship, a deeper understanding. Jay had chatted with Patrick, and afterward it was as if she'd lowered a wall she didn't even know was there. He had, too. Their discussion, although shorter than usual, had grown deeper, more intimate.

I appreciated the advice you gave me regarding my dad. What you said made a difference. You helped me to see him in a different light. He seems to regret much of what's taken place in his life, the kind of father he's been. I had the feeling he's looking to make up for lost time. We'll never be bosom buddies, but I could talk to him without resentment and I thank you for that. After the lunch with my dad, I had the strongest desire to meet you. Are you ready for that?

You're serious? You want to meet?

I do, and the sooner the better.

It'll have to be next Sunday. I'm working late every night this week, and Saturday I promised to go with Patrick and a group of his friends over to Leavenworth on the Christmas train. I won't be back until late.

Then Sunday it is. What time?

You're sure about this?

Positive. More so every minute.

How about three? I like the idea of us having coffee together.

After trading several messages back and forth, they decided on a meeting location: Starbucks in Pacific Place, a downtown mall. It was convenient to them both, although she'd need to take the bus. To be able to recognize each other, they agreed that he would wear a blue dress shirt and she would have on a beige coat with a brown-and-black plaid scarf.

Lauren and Kylie noticed Merry's upbeat mood first thing the following morning.

"Hey, what's up with you?" Lauren asked. "Did you win the lottery or something?"

Merry could hardly contain her excitement. "Jay and I decided to meet this Sunday."

"Jay, that guy you met over the Internet?" Lauren asked, picking up on the conversation. "You do realize he could be a serial killer, right?"

"Would you stop?" Kylie teased. "This is the way women meet men these days. And who else could Merry mean? She's been loopy ever since she started messaging with this guy."

"Don't do it," Lauren advised. "Trust me, no good will come of this."

Merry suspected that was what her friend would say. "Don't worry, we're only having coffee."

"In a public place?"

"Yes, of course."

"This is so romantic," Kylie murmured dreamily. "You know I'm living vicariously through you."

Lauren didn't agree. "You'll be disappointed. Mark my words."

"Lauren," Kylie chastised. "Don't say that. You need to let this play out."

Their coworker was having none of it. "Bet he's as ugly as sin and that's the reason he's waited this long to suggest you meet."

"Will you stop," Kylie said, and wagged her index finger at her coworker.

At this point, Jay's looks didn't matter to Merry. She enjoyed chatting with him, getting to know him. Over the last couple weeks, she'd discovered how much they had in common. While there was a lot about him that she didn't know, he'd opened a whole new world to her. They were kindred spirits, lonely souls, caught up in duty and commitment. It wasn't until they started talking that Merry realized how isolated she'd become. Her life consisted of home and work, with few social outlets.

That evening, when Merry logged on, Jay was waiting for her.

Well, did your coworkers talk you out of meeting me?

No. How did you know they would even try? His question was uncanny. It was almost as if he knew what Lauren had said. Did *your* friends try to talk you out of meeting me?

My friends are few and far between, Merry. My best friends live in other parts of the country. It's been all work and little play for me until I met you.

My dearest friend married a guy in the Navy and moved away. It's a lot of work and little play for me as well, which is why Mom and Patrick signed me up.

I'm grateful they did.

Me, too.

Patrick came into her room and sat down on the corner of her bed. "You talking to Jay?"

She sat crisscross style with her laptop balanced on her knees. "Yeah."

"Can I talk to him again, too?"

Seeing how patient Jay had been earlier, she let him.

Hi Jay. It's me. I'm Patrick. Sissy said I could type.

Did she tell you we're going on our first date?

Yes, and she said she was going to bring you cookies we baked as a surprise. I frosted them and put on the sprinkles, but there are more than eggnog cookies. You like cookies? I do.

I love cookies.

I like baking and eating. Sissy says she wants you back now.

K. Nice talking to you.

Merry rotated the laptop so she was in control of the keyboard. Patrick had no idea he had ruined her small surprise and she wasn't about to tell him.

I'm back.

Cookies? Did someone mention cookies?

Well, you know what they say, don't you? The way to a man's heart is through his stomach.

The thing is, Merry, you won't need cookies to find your way there.

Merry read that line twice. It was too soon. He shouldn't be saying things like this. Too soon or not, she felt like she was walking two feet off the ground, happier than she could remember being in a long time.

Sunday couldn't come fast enough for Merry.

CHAPTER SIX

✳

Jayson

Sunday couldn't come fast enough for Jayson.

He was excited to finally have the chance to meet Merry. He didn't know the details of what had upset her at work this past week. She'd briefly mentioned her boss; the two apparently had a run-in earlier. Merry hadn't wanted to talk about it. He wished she would. Unfamiliar emotion rocked him and he was ready to punch whoever had upset her. He wasn't violent by any stretch of the imagination, and this overwhelming protective urge was foreign to him. Merry was a beautiful soul. Anyone who mistreated her should be made to regret it. His reaction told him how strong his attraction for her was.

The fact that Merry had been unwilling to discuss the negative gave him insight into her character. Merry wasn't one to linger on adversity. She wasn't looking for sympathy or reassurance. Whatever had happened, she'd handled it herself and didn't want to burden him or anyone else with her troubles. She did mention that she was tempted to not renew her contract with the company if they asked, but that was the extent of what she'd said. His admiration for her grew each day.

They'd chatted until almost midnight nearly every night. It was hard for them to stop talking. He'd had no idea he would have that much to say to anyone, let alone a woman he had yet to meet. She'd written about the Christmases of her youth and how her parents had worked hard to make them special, even with their limited finances.

The Christmases of Jayson's childhood had been hellish. There were always gifts—plenty of those for sure—but gifts meant little when only strife existed between the two most important people in his world: his parents. The one tradition his family had was heated battles, leaving him feeling unloved and unwanted.

The contrast between Merry's home life and his own was striking. Afterward he had a hard time sleeping, as his mind wandered and he imagined what Christmas would be like with Merry.

Naturally, there'd be a tall Christmas tree with handmade ornaments made by Patrick and their own children.

Wait.

Children?

Him with a family? No way.

The thought shook him to the point he sat up in bed. *What am I thinking?*

A couple weeks of chatting online with this girl and all at once he was walking through a field of daisies with a rainbow overhead and unicorns prancing close by. This wasn't like him.

Lying back down, he closed his eyes and tried to ease the tension from his limbs. As soon as he was half asleep once more, the same picturesque scene returned. The eight-foot Christmas tree filled the living room and the scent of freshly baked eggnog cookies stirred his senses to the point he could almost taste the frosting. Oddly, no gifts were under the tree in his daydream. Presents weren't the point, after all; besides, Santa had yet to arrive.

Santa?

Even as a young boy, Jayson had never believed in Santa. How could he? As far as he was concerned, he'd never had a childhood. It wasn't that he was filled with self-pity. Other children had it far worse than he ever did. He'd always had a place to sleep and food to fill his stomach. What he'd craved was love, and that had been in shockingly short supply.

———

The following morning, Jayson made a point of walking past Mary Knight's desk. He'd felt bad about needing to ask her to remove the decorations. It was a role he disliked, but unfortunately it was necessary. He'd done his best to explain, and he hoped she hadn't taken it personally.

As Jayson strolled past the data-entry area, he noticed that the miniature Christmas tree was gone as well as the silver garlands around the cubicles. He'd run into Mary before, he remembered, when he'd found her eating at her desk. The company had a perfectly decent lunchroom, and he didn't like the idea of Mary working through her lunch hour. He thought that perhaps she'd been in a rush to finish for the day because she had a date that night. That didn't set right with him, which was completely unreasonable. It made no sense that he should care. Mary was young and attractive, so there was every likelihood that she was romantically involved. Not that it was any of his business.

The fact was he liked Mary. She had a lot of spirit and wasn't afraid to share her opinions. He found himself thinking about her and instantly was filled with guilt. He was set to meet Merry soon and she was the one who held his interest.

He noticed Mary wasn't at her desk. Surprised, he checked his watch. He'd never known her to be late, and it was four minutes past eight. As the thought flittered through his mind, Mary came rushing toward her desk, carting a tray with three take-out cups. Apparently, this was some fancy coffee drink for her team, neither of whom had arrived yet, either.

Smiling and in a good mood, she placed the cups on each of their desks and hummed a Christmas carol as she agilely moved from desk to desk. When she glanced up, she must have caught sight of him, because she paused, frozen in place for several seconds, as if awaiting his reprimand.

"We're allowed to drink at our desks," Mary reminded Jayson, as if he wasn't already aware of it. "I didn't see anything in the employee manual that said otherwise."

"You actually read it?"

She hesitated. "Ah, no, but I will."

He smiled and she smiled back. Then, feeling foolish at having been caught watching her, he glanced at his wrist and commented, "You're late."

Her smile disappeared. "Mr. Bright, if you're looking for an excuse to fire me, then all I ask is that you wait until just before Christmas."

The last thing he intended was for Mary to feel threatened. "Your position is secure, Ms. Knight."

"Thank you, but I realize it's only because you need me until this project is completed."

He opened his mouth to contradict her and stopped. This was getting awkward, and the last thing he wanted was to start his morning off with a verbal confrontation with a temp.

"I won't keep you any longer," he said, and headed toward his own office. Jayson felt uneasy with the way he'd handled the situation. He wished he knew what it was about Mary Knight that lingered in his mind.

Later that morning, when he was between meetings, Jayson's personal phone rang. He smiled when he saw Cooper's name come up on the caller ID.

"Hey, Jay," Cooper greeted in the same cheerful voice that was his signature. "What's going on?"

"Work, what else? What's on your mind?" He didn't have time for idle chatter. The project deadline was looming.

"Actually, Maddy wanted me to ask if you'll be bringing anyone with you to the wedding."

"The wedding isn't for months yet."

Cooper sighed, as if that was exactly the response he'd expected. "What can I say, the woman likes to plan ahead."

Jayson was about to tell him he would attend alone, but before the words could leave his mouth he hesitated. "I might."

"What?" Cooper sounded shocked. "I told Maddy I'd ask, but you've always been a lone ranger. You meet someone special since the last time we talked?"

"Yeah. Sort of."

"How do you 'sort of' meet someone?"

Jayson decided he might as well fess up, as Cooper would eventually find out anyway. "After you stopped by and told me about you and Maddy, I logged on to that website you mentioned."

"Mix & Mingle. Really?"

"Yeah, I know. I saw this photograph of a dog . . ."

"You're dating a dog?"

"No, Coop, I'm not dating a dog. And stop your snickering, I'm being serious."

"Okay, sorry."

"I saw the photograph and figured she was probably someone like me who wanted to be liked for herself."

"Are you telling me you signed up and messaged her?"

"Yup." He couldn't seem to wipe the grin off his face as he imagined the shocked look from his cousin.

"So, you haven't actually met face-to-face?"

"Not yet." He thought about their date for coffee on Sunday. "We've been talking online and I like her. A lot."

"Do you have any clue what she looks like?"

"Nope."

"That doesn't bother you?"

"Nope." It didn't. It really didn't.

"What if she's, you know, weird? For all you know you could be chatting with a fifty-year-old cougar."

Jayson barked a laugh. It had been easy for Cooper; he'd known Maddy from their childhood. "She is taking a risk same as I am. For all she knows, I could be a sixty-year-old pervert." That was what Merry's coworker had warned her; she'd shared that a week or so ago. He'd smiled when he read that and assured her she had no worries—he was exactly what he claimed to be. She'd believed him, and it sort of worried him that she would be so utterly trusting.

"You mean to say you didn't post your photo, either?"

"No, I put up one of Rocky."

"You didn't!"

He chuckled softly. "You wouldn't believe the 'winks' I got. But no one interested me more than this girl. She said her name is Merry, spelled M-E-R-R-Y. I figured she made it up, seeing how close it is to the holidays."

"Bro, listen, I'm glad to hear you've taken the leap. Just be careful. The fact she didn't put up a photo worries me."

"Why are you concerned? It's going to be great. I like this girl. I haven't felt this way about anyone." *Ever,* he added silently.

His cousin was uncharacteristically silent and then inquired, "So you're planning to meet soon, right?"

"Sunday afternoon. We're going out for coffee. Nothing big or elaborate. I realize we've only been talking for a couple weeks, but I should tell you, I'm hooked. I've never met anyone like her. She's levelheaded, family-oriented, kind, and thoughtful." He closed his mouth before he said anything more. If this thing went south he didn't want to hand his cousin bullets to use against him.

"You do realize she could look like a dog, which is why she may have posted that photo in the first place."

Jayson had considered that. Still, it didn't matter. He was intrigued by her. *Her*. He thought about Merry almost continually. Their chats had become addictive. She made him smile, and when they said good-bye each night he felt warm and happy. Both feelings were foreign to him, and he hung on to that sensation for as long as possible after they ended their online chat.

"Bro. You still there?"

"Yes, sorry. I was thinking—"

"I hope this works out," Cooper said, cutting him off. "And when the time comes, I'd like to meet this woman who's already got you twisted around her little finger."

"She doesn't," he countered, and couldn't decide who he was trying to convince—Cooper or himself.

———

Sunday afternoon Jayson was dressed and ready well before noon. In retrospect, he wished he hadn't told her to look for a man in a blue dress shirt. That was far too stuffy. He'd opted for that because it was his daily uniform and seemed a natural choice at the time. Merry must think he was a workaholic. That wasn't the impression he wanted to give her. He wished he'd said jeans and a sweater.

He smiled to himself, thinking that it would have been fun to buy one of those ridiculous holiday sweaters, like the one he recently saw in a store window, with battery-driven reindeer ears that flapped. Another one on display had a huge Santa face with a flashing light for the red nose. He was certain Merry would get a kick out of that.

By one o'clock, he was pacing in his condo, looking at his watch every few minutes. The closer the time came, the more anxious he felt.

Pacific Place was only a few blocks from his condo; less than a fifteen-minute walk. Unable to wait any longer, he left far too early and headed in that direction, taking a leisurely route. He passed a flower shop with a window display full of holly sprigs and potted poinsettias. For several minutes, he stared at the window and toyed with the idea of bringing Merry flowers. The temptation was strong and he wavered before finally giving in.

He wasn't a flower-giving kind of guy and he wasn't sure what would be appropriate for her. Carting a potted poinsettia into Starbucks seemed ridiculous. Flowers would be a nice touch, though. Feeling self-conscious, he walked into the shop. He'd have been more comfortable in a Santa suit than he was in this place. To hide his nervousness, he stuffed his hands into his pants pockets and wandered around, seeking inspiration.

"Can I help you find something?" the salesgirl approached and asked.

Jayson hesitated. She looked like she might know a thing or two about situations such as his. Throwing caution to the wind, he mentioned his mission.

"I'm meeting a girl for the first time and was thinking it might be a nice gesture to bring her flowers."

"That's a wonderful idea. Someone you met online?"

He nodded, pleased that she understood the situation without him having to explain. "We've been chatting for a while, though."

"A bouquet of roses?" she suggested.

He shook his head instinctively, recognizing that roses were a little much. Merry was the kind of woman who enjoyed simple pleasures. He remembered how she'd once mentioned her affection for wildflowers. It was unlikely the shop carried flowers like that, but perhaps they had something close, so he asked.

"We recently got in a shipment of yellow daisies. Would those do?"

"Perfect."

The sales clerk wrapped them up beautifully and tied them together with a pretty silk ribbon. While Jayson felt silly walking into the busy shopping mall carrying yellow daisies, he couldn't wait to see Merry's face once she saw them.

He arrived early and was glad of it—otherwise he wouldn't have been able to snag a table. After standing in the fast-moving order line for two coffees, he took a seat so that he could keep an eye on the entrance.

Time crawled. Then three o'clock came and went.

At ten minutes past three, he grew restless. This didn't bode well. Being punctual himself, he usually found tardiness an irritation. Merry had never been late for their chatting sessions, well, other than the one time. Even then, her brother and mother had logged on and explained for her. If he'd been thinking, he would have given her his cell number. His mind raced with the possibilities of what might have gone wrong.

"Excuse me, are you going to need this chair?" a grandfatherly man asked.

"Yes, I'm waiting for someone."

The man thanked him and collected a chair from another table.

At three-thirty, Jayson decided not to wait any longer. He was disappointed and worried. This wasn't like Merry.

As he made his way out of the Starbucks, he paused at the garbage dispenser and tossed the daisies into the can before he headed back to his condo.

CHAPTER SEVEN

✳

Merry

Merry's mom, dad, and Patrick were anxiously waiting for her when she returned from her meeting with Jay. They were sitting in the family room with the fireplace going, writing Christmas cards while carols played softly in the background. Her mother wrote notes in each of the cards, and Patrick carefully wrote his name, leaving room for her dad and later for Merry to add their own signatures. This was the way they'd always done it. Every member of the family signed their own names.

"Merry, Merry, you're here," Patrick called out excitedly when he saw her. "Did you like Jay? Was he handsome and kind?" Patrick had been almost as excited about this meeting as Merry had been herself. Her brother leaped from his chair and rushed toward her, eagerly waiting for her to tell him everything.

Immediately, her mother sensed something was wrong. "Merry? Did something happen?"

"You look disappointed," her father added.

Defeated, Merry slumped onto the sofa, unable to find the words to explain. Wanting to hide her distress, she resisted burying her face in her hands. The entire bus ride home, her thoughts had been in utter turmoil. Even now she had a hard time accepting that Jay, the one who'd consumed her thoughts every day, was Jayson Bright, the boss she'd clashed with on more than one occasion. "I . . . I hardly know what to say."

"You met him, right?" her mother asked. "You obviously didn't spend a lot of time talking, seeing that you're back this soon."

She sadly shook her head. "I didn't introduce myself. In fact, I left without saying a word to him."

"You didn't even say hi?" Patrick frowned, as if he had a hard time understanding why she would ignore Jay.

"If you didn't introduce yourself, does that mean you left him there to wait?" Her mother was unable to hide her surprise and shared a look with her husband. "Merry Knight, that isn't like you."

"You didn't meet him, but you said you would," Patrick cried. Her brother glared at her as if he was the offended party. "You stood Jay up and that's mean. You did a rude thing, Sissy."

"I know." Her brother was right; walking away the way she had was cowardly of her. The shock of seeing Jayson Bright had thrown her off balance. Merry had been too stunned to do anything more than turn around and flee. All the way home she couldn't find a way to equate the man who insisted she remove the Christmas decorations from her desk with the charming, interesting guy she'd come to know online. The two didn't compute.

"Patrick, would you go watch TV in your room for a bit while I talk to your sister?" her mother asked.

He hesitated.

"Come on, buddy," her father encouraged, his arm around Patrick's shoulders. "Let's leave the women to sort this out."

"Okay," he agreed, "but you need to tell Merry she did wrong."

"I will."

"Good." Patrick returned his attention to his sister. "I like Jay and I know he likes you, but he won't anymore because you were mean."

"I know." In retrospect, Merry felt dreadful about leaving Jay sitting in the coffee shop, waiting. She couldn't help wondering how long he'd remained before he realized she wasn't going to show. It made her heart ache.

Patrick hung his head. "Is he special like me? Is that why you didn't like him?"

"Oh Patrick, you know better than to ask me that. I'd like him even more if he was anything like you."

Her words seemed to appease her brother, who quietly left the room with his dad so Merry and her mother could talk.

"Tell me what happened," her mother said gently.

She didn't seem to be as upset with her as Patrick was. Merry looped a strand of hair around her ear. "Jay is Jayson Bright."

It took a moment for her words to sink in.

"Your boss?" Her mother's eyes rounded as soon as she understood the significance of what Merry was telling her. "The one who wouldn't let Kylie take care of her sick son?"

Merry nodded. "One and the same."

"The one who makes overtime mandatory?"

"Yup."

"Oh dear," Robin whispered on the tail end of a sigh. "But until you saw who he was, you liked Jay and enjoyed chatting with him."

"I did . . . I do." It wasn't like Merry could deny it. Jay had quickly become a large part of her world. She couldn't stop thinking of him. She counted the hours until they could connect, rushing home at the end of the work day. The man she saw at work wasn't the same man she'd come to know online. And she wasn't the same woman he knew from online, either, and that was the crux of the problem. He would be just as shocked to discover the woman he had come to know was the very one who clashed with him at every turn. What she realized in those fleeting moments before she'd turned tail was that she was bound to be a huge disappointment to him. He had someone else set up in his mind, and that someone wasn't her. She couldn't bear to see the look in his eyes when he realized he'd been chatting with the woman whom he considered to be a major menace at work.

"He brought along a bouquet of yellow daisies," Merry whispered. It seemed impossible that Jayson Bright would bring anyone flowers, let alone her. But then he didn't know . . . just as she didn't know.

"You need to tell him, Merry," her mother said in the same understanding voice she'd used earlier.

"Tell him it's me? No way, Mom. I can't. Let me finish this contract first. It goes to the end of the year, and if we finish this report for Boeing before Christmas, we've been told we can have the week between Christmas and New Year's off. My contract will be over then." She didn't mention that the employee handbook, which Jayson had insisted she read, clearly stated, "Dating between supervisors and their subordinates is strongly discouraged."

"Honey, I know, but you can't leave him hanging. You two have been talking for weeks. He must have been worried when you didn't show, wondering what had happened."

"If he finds out it's me . . . I can't. I just can't. Can you imagine how uncomfortable it would be for us? I mean, the two of us working together. He might even think I somehow arranged all this, tricking him. I know it sounds crazy. All the way home these different scenarios kept going through my head of what Jayson Bright would say had I walked through those doors to meet him." She briefly closed her eyes, trying to imagine the scene, the big reveal. She couldn't see how any good would come from it.

"Merry, you know as well as I do that honesty is the best policy," her mother reminded her. "I'm sure Jay would be as shocked as you, but he'd get over it soon enough. Given time, I believe he'd accept you for who you are, for the woman he's come to know. But by your action today, you've taken the option away from him."

While Merry would like to think that it wouldn't matter who she was, the risk was too great. "I don't want to take the chance . . . remember, he's a stickler for the rules and practically has that employee manual memorized.

The company has a clear policy about employees fraternizing." There was a lot at stake in this, especially her heart. She was half in love with Jay already. The problem was she couldn't reconcile that her boss was Jay. Her Jay.

"No matter what you decide, you owe it to Jay or Jayson to tell him the truth," her mother said, and hesitated as though unsure. "If nothing else, you should explain why you didn't introduce yourself."

"Maybe." Merry hadn't concluded in her own mind how best to resolve this problem. Patrick was right, though. Leaving without offering an explanation had been rude. In retrospect, she should have sent someone over with a message to tell him she wouldn't be coming.

"Merry," her mother said pointedly. "Do whatever it is you do and get online and talk to him. He needs to know you're safe. Explain as best you can. You owe Jay that much."

"Okay, okay." She wasn't happy about it, but she knew her mother and Patrick were right. She owed Jay an explanation, though she didn't know what she could possibly tell him to excuse her behavior.

Once in her bedroom, she climbed onto her bed and scooted up so her back was braced against the headboard. With her laptop resting on her legs, she assumed her usual position. It was the same way she sat every night when "talking" to Jay.

As soon as she logged on, Jay was waiting. His words flashed up on the screen.

What happened? Why didn't you show? Are you all right?

I could be better.

Her cursor flashed at her for several seconds. Before she could type, Jay's next words popped up on the screen.

You're sick?

No. I was there.

You were there?

Yes . . . and I decided against introducing myself.

Again, the cursor repeatedly flashed, blaming her.

Can you tell me why?

It's complicated.

Uncomplicate.

Jay was angry and she couldn't blame him. His one-word response said as much.

I wish I could. I'm sorry, Jay, but the minute I saw you I realized it would never work between us. We're too different . . .

Don't tell me that. It's an excuse. A lie. We've talked every night for weeks and have connected on a dozen different levels. It's something else, isn't it? Something you're unwilling to tell me.

No need denying it.

Yes.

What is it? You owe me that.

Please don't ask. Just accept that a relationship between us isn't a good idea. It's better to accept that now and move on. I'm sure there are any number of women on Mix & Mingle who would be a better match for you than me.

There was that dreaded cursor again, flashing accusingly at her.

Just like that? You're willing to give up on us without giving me a single reason? Unbelievable. How could I have spent all these nights talking to you and not know you? This doesn't make sense. I can't believe you're doing this. I brought you flowers. Not once in my entire life have I given a woman flowers.

Yellow daisies.

You saw and still you refused to meet me. That says it all. I should have known better. Lesson learned. My bad.

I'm sorry.

Jay didn't reply and logged off.

For a long time afterward, Merry sat on her bed, feeling numb and sick at heart.

Patrick knocked on her bedroom door.

"It's okay, Patrick, you can come in."

Her brother stuck his head past the door and stared at her for a long moment. "Are you sad?"

Merry nodded. "Yeah." *Sad* was a good word for the way she felt. *Disappointed, discouraged,* and *upset* were also part of the emotions taking up residence in her heart. She patted the edge of her bed, urging her brother to come join her. She closed her laptop and set it aside as Patrick climbed onto the mattress and sat down beside her.

Merry wrapped her arm around his shoulders and leaned her head against his, and he said, "I'm sad, too. I liked Jay. He was nice."

"He was nice," Merry agreed. "Sometimes people aren't right for each other, and I could see that I wasn't the right person for Jay."

"That's what makes you sad?"

"Yes, real sad."

Patrick released a deep sigh. "Are you going to look at some of the other men on the website to date them?" he asked.

"Maybe."

Her brother was silent for a couple moments. "That's what Mom says when she means *no* but she doesn't want to say *no*."

Merry grinned. Her brother was smarter than she gave him credit for. The sick feeling in the pit of her stomach was sure to last a long time. She had no desire to start an online relationship with anyone else. "I might look at other possibilities, but it won't be soon."

"Can I help you pick him out?"

"Sure." Seeing that she had a six-month subscription, Merry had plenty of time to decide. Presently, her inclination was never to go on the website again.

On Monday morning, Merry walked into the office to find both her friends watching and waiting for her.

"So?" Kylie asked, venturing first. "How'd the meeting go with your handsome Prince Charming?"

Merry had thought long and hard about whether she should update her friends with the truth or not. In the end, she decided it was better that they not know her Jay was Jayson Bright, their boss.

"Well?" Lauren prompted, when Merry hesitated. "I was right, wasn't I? He's a sixty-year-old pervert."

Merry took her time removing her coat and tucking away her purse. "He isn't sixty and he isn't a pervert."

"What happened?"

She shrugged. "It didn't work out."

"Told you," Lauren said, crossing her arms. "These online dating services never do."

"Oh stop," Kylie flared. "What went wrong?"

Merry shrugged. "He just wasn't what I expected."

"What did you expect?" Kylie asked, grinning. "A Saudi prince?"

Despite herself, Merry smiled. "I guess in some ways I did, but he's not even close to royalty."

"Told you."

"Lauren!" Kylie snapped. "Enough." She returned her attention to Merry. "You're disappointed, aren't you?"

"Terribly." It was the truth. Merry was more let down than words could possibly say. She held back a yawn. She'd tossed and turned most of the night and probably had only a couple hours of uninterrupted rest. All night her mind kept going to a nightmare in which she came face-to-face with Jayson Bright. In her dream, he was as shocked and as dismayed as she'd been.

And that was the crux of the matter. She liked Jay. She was half in love with Jay. But Jayson? Not so much. And yet they were the same person. She had yet to understand how that could be possible.

Somehow Merry made it until the end of the day. As she finished and was about to head home, she happened to look up in time to see Jayson Bright walking toward the elevator.

One of the staff from another department wasn't watching where she was walking and bumped into him. Merry held her breath, waiting for him to get upset. It was what she had come to expect from him. Instead, Jayson gripped hold of the older woman's shoulders so she didn't lose her balance and then bent down and helped her gather the papers that had fallen to the floor.

When he'd finished, he started toward the elevator, his shoulders slightly hunched. Merry couldn't take her eyes off him. He looked as sad and beaten down as she felt, which left her to wonder . . .

Had she made the right decision?

Was this what she really wanted?

And why, oh why, did the night ahead feel so empty?

✳

CHAPTER EIGHT

Jayson

Thursday evening arrived, and it'd been four days since Jayson had last spoken to Merry. Over the first couple days, anger had consumed him. He'd been a fool to have anything to do with that website. With her. This whole idea of dating someone he'd never met had been crazy. *What was I thinking*? Merry had played him for a fool. He'd never needed a dating service in the past. As far as he was concerned, Mix & Mingle had been one colossal mistake, and one he had no desire to repeat.

However, as the week progressed his anger mellowed. Bored and restless, he logged on to the site, wondering if Merry had left him a message. An explanation. Anything. He'd had several other winks but none that interested him. He wanted Merry.

When he looked, he found a message waiting for him. From Merry.

His heart rate accelerated, and he blinked to be sure he wasn't imagining it. To be sure, he opened the message.

Only Merry wasn't the one who'd written him.

The note was from Patrick.

My sister is sad. She likes you a lot.

Interesting. Jayson was tempted to ignore it, but then on a whim decided to leave a message of his own.

She didn't want to meet me, Patrick. I wanted to meet her in the worst way. Can I ask you a question? Can we talk in an hour?

Jayson didn't know if Patrick would see his note, but it was worth a shot. Merry's brother must have been at the computer, because he answered right away.

I do homework then.

Can we talk now? he asked. With Patrick's help, Jayson might have a chance of learning what had happened.

Okay, but I can't talk more than an hour.

That was fine by him. Great. I'm sad, too, Patrick, because I like your sister. Finding out what she'd found so objectionable about him had almost become an obsession. He couldn't go more than an hour or two without thinking about her. What was worse was not knowing. Perhaps she was someone he'd dated in the past or someone related to a former girlfriend. The possibilities were endless.

Merry's rejection had been a bitter pill to swallow. As the days had passed, he found it harder and harder to accept her decision. That left him one option, and that was to find her and ask her face-to-face. He couldn't imagine anything worthy of the way she'd dumped him with no explanation or excuse.

I knew you would want to see her. Merry is pretty, but she doesn't date a lot.

I'll make her smile again.

She needs to smile. It's Christmas and she shouldn't be sad.

You're right, she shouldn't.

Patrick added, Don't tell her I talked to you because she might not like me doing that.

I won't say a word.

Promise?

I promise. Time to get to the nitty gritty. Can you tell me what her real name is? He was certain Merry was a name she used because she didn't want him to know her actual given name.

Patrick stopped typing as if he didn't understand the question. That's funny. Her name is Merry. You know that.

That's her real name?

That's what we call her. I don't think she has another name. Her middle name is Noelle.

Okay. Interesting. He'd go about this in a different way. What's your surname?

Is this a test? I don't do good on tests.

No test.

I need help. Patrick typed. What's a surname?

Your last name.

I know this. But I'm not supposed to tell strangers.

Jayson groaned. The only thing he could figure was that it had been pounded into Patrick not to give out his name to people his family didn't know.

Where does Merry work?

Downtown.

Jayson groaned again. Getting information out of her brother was proving more challenging than he'd hoped.

Do you know the name of the company where she works?

Yes. I need to think.

He prodded when Patrick didn't answer for several pulsing seconds. Think. It felt like a month before the youth typed in his response.

I didn't remember, so I asked her, but she told me that work is work and home is home. Don't worry, I didn't tell her I was talking to you.

Good. I want to find Merry and talk to her.

I know she takes the number-eighteen bus to work. Sometimes I meet her at the bus stop, but only in the summer, because it's dark out in the winter.

That's a nice thing to do.

She likes it. I need to go now. Mom is calling me.

Thank you for your help, Patrick.

I did good on the test, right?

Very good. Bye for now.

He was about to close his computer when another message popped up. This time it was Merry.

Are you drilling my brother with questions about me?

No need denying it, he'd been caught red-handed. Yes.

Don't. Please. It's not fair to use my brother for your selfish purposes.

Perhaps not.

Don't you care?

I'm not willing to give up on us, Merry. He says that's your real name, by the way.

It is.

And Smith is your surname?

I'm not answering that.

Figured you wouldn't. It appears you have a December birthday, Merry Noelle Smith.

Not answering that, either.

Merry might not be answering his questions, but she was talking to him, and that was all that mattered.

I miss you. I can't believe you don't miss talking to me. Be honest, Merry. Give me that.

All right, if you must know . . . yes, I miss you, too.

Then tell me what it is you find so offensive about me that makes you refuse to meet me.

The cursor blinked for several uncomfortable seconds while he awaited her reply.

I know you.

That made Jayson sit up and take notice. You know me? How?

I need to end this. All I ask is that you don't talk to my brother again.

Don't go. He swallowed his pride, and in a desperate note added, Please.

Merry didn't sign off, and he sighed with relief.

Was I rude? Unreasonable?

I'm one of the little people you choose to ignore. That's all I'm willing to tell you. As soon as I saw who you were, I realized that the man I've come to know online is a different person than the one I've met previously. I can't find a way to connect the two.

Jayson didn't know what to tell her.

I accept that I can be rude and impatient. I'm working on it.

Maybe you should work harder.

Jayson grinned. She wasn't holding back.

Will you chat with me again?

Her answer took a long time coming, but he waited, working on his patience.

I don't think that's a good idea.

He wasn't willing to accept that. **Nine tomorrow night.** He didn't wait for her to reply. As the saying goes, the ball was in her court now.

Friday afternoon, just as he was about to leave the office, Jayson got the last piece of information needed to finalize the report for Boeing. This was what he'd been waiting weeks to receive. The data would need to be entered, and he didn't want to wait until Monday morning before submitting his conclusion. Christmas was right around the corner, and his hope was to get this report into the proper hands ahead of schedule.

The mandatory overtime had ended, but he wanted this done pronto so he could review it over the weekend. He might as well work. That would keep his mind occupied until he could sort out this mess with Merry.

He was no closer to tracking her down now, although he felt encouraged. His chat with Patrick had given him a few clues, but not enough to figure out her identity. She claimed she was one of the little people. His first thought was that she worked in the service industry. Perhaps she was the barista who routinely made his morning coffee. He hoped not. From what he saw of her, she wasn't especially bright. The woman who came to clean his condo once a week was a grandmother. Perhaps Merry was someone related to her. It might even be someone in the office, but he couldn't imagine who. The little people? What did she mean by that? A housekeeper? A server? A receptionist?

He stopped off at the Corner Deli a few nights each week, so perhaps Merry worked with Cyrus. His mind mulled over the options. She could be someone he routinely saw and had never noticed.

He pulled his thoughts away from Merry and back to the project and what needed to be done. Leaving his office, he walked down to the data-entry department to find the three women diligently working.

Mary was the first one to look up, and she blinked as though shocked to see him. They'd had their minor disagreements, and Jayson regretted that. When Jayson had called HR to learn more about her, he was told that Mary was contracted for a year and had filled in for the head of the department, who had given birth to twins and requested twelve months' leave. According to what he'd learned about her, she had done a fantastic job, but the position would end at the first of the year, as the woman she replaced would return then.

Mary stopped typing, and soon the other two women followed suit. All three of them looked at him, apparently waiting for him to say something.

"I need someone to stay this evening," he said. "It will probably require a couple hours." Then, remembering his determination to be less demanding and more patient, he added, "Mary, as the head of the department, I'd like you to decide who should work the overtime."

The woman with the nameplate that said LAUREN spoke first, looking at Mary. "Sorry, I can't stay. I've got family arriving this evening from Kansas. I agreed to pick them up at the airport. They're here for the holidays."

The second woman spoke up. "Billy has his school Christmas program this evening." Her eyes were apologetic. "I can't miss that. Billy plays the role of the little drummer boy."

Mary sighed and turned to her boss. "Guess you're stuck with me."

"Will this be a problem?" he asked.

"It's Friday night and . . ."

"I realize working overtime is probably ruining your date night," he snapped, and then instantly regretted his outburst. Drawing in a calming breath, he tried again. "I would appreciate your help."

She didn't correct him, which led Jayson to realize he'd guessed right. She did have a date.

"I'll need to make a phone call."

"Thank you. I have the necessary paperwork in my office. I'll be right back."

When he returned, Mary was alone, as the other women had left for the weekend.

He handed her the report. "I want you to know I appreciate your willingness to do this."

She offered him a brief smile and a dimple appeared, just one on the right side of her mouth. This wasn't the first time he'd noticed it. The dimple mesmerized him. She seemed to realize he was staring at her, which flustered him. To cover his discomfort, Jayson pulled up a chair and sat down before spreading out a large sheet with the necessary statistics listed.

CHAPTER NINE

*

Merry

They worked together, side by side, and with every moment Merry grew more aware of the man sitting next to her. Jayson gave her the necessary information and Merry entered it into the computer. She tried to do her best to keep her mind on track. She'd never been this close to Jayson before, and had never noticed the spicy scent of his cologne. It swamped her senses as she breathed it in. About ninety minutes later, when they were halfway through the report, Merry needed a break. She'd made a few mistakes, something she rarely did. Being this close to Jayson distracted her. When he paused, she straightened and rubbed her hand along the back of her neck.

Jayson noticed and set the papers down. "Let's take a ten-minute breather."

"Good idea." She stood and stretched. Determined to take a mental break, she made an excuse and headed to the ladies' room. When she returned, Jayson was nowhere in sight.

What? Maybe he thought it would be best if she finished on her own? Merry felt an immediate sense of loss. *Well, so be it,* she thought. Feeling let down, she started again on her own.

Being alone left her feeling bereft. This was the first time it'd been just the two of them. These ninety minutes had given her insight into Jayson that she wasn't able to see through their online exchanges. He'd been patient, especially when she'd flubbed up the numbers, transposing them. Thankfully, he'd caught her mistake. Thoughtful, too. She hadn't said out loud that her neck ached and that she needed a break. He saw her rub her hand along her neck and recognized that she could use a few minutes to relax her shoulders.

With him gone, she glanced around the deserted office and noticed all the other areas were darkened. The office had never appeared so stark or bare. It hadn't felt like that when Jayson was by her side.

She took note of the time, and the thought went through her head that he needed to be home before nine so they could chat online, though she supposed he could use his work computer. There was plenty of time still. The irony didn't escape her. Jayson assumed she'd canceled or delayed her Friday-night date, not realizing, of course, that her date was with him.

Yes, against her better judgment, she'd decided to chat again with Jay that evening.

She'd regretted giving in at the time. Now she wasn't so sure, seeing this new side of him. He was much more her online Jay tonight than Jayson, her rude and sometimes dictatorial boss. The problem was how she would go about letting him know who she was. But not yet. It was still too early to make that decision, but if she believed they had a chance, she would.

This relationship was important to her. When she'd admitted that she'd missed their time together online, it hadn't been an exaggeration. She'd felt as if she'd been at loose ends all week, and if she was being honest, she'd been miserable. Even Patrick had noticed, which was what had prompted him to reach out to Jay without her approval.

Merry had found Patrick sitting at the computer, intently typing away. When he noticed her watching, the guilty look on his face was all she needed to guess what he'd been doing, and she'd confronted him. Her brother was as readable as a dinner menu.

Poor Patrick's face instantly went bright red, knowing he'd been caught. He'd immediately blurted out that he'd been chatting online with Jay.

"Why would you do that?" Merry demanded.

"You were so sad, and I knew Jay was sad, too, and so I had to tell him." Her brother lowered his head and Merry couldn't argue—her brother was right.

At first Merry had been upset. Not with Patrick but with Jay. When she'd realized he was still online, her fingers had pounded on the computer keys, unable to hide her irritation. Her anger hadn't lasted long, though. She'd missed him. So much.

And he'd missed her.

Then he'd typed that one word. The one that convinced her to continue.

Please.

She couldn't refuse him, couldn't refuse herself. Later that night, her emotions were mixed and she wavered back and forth, wondering if she'd done the right thing.

Footsteps echoed in the office and Merry stopped typing, alert now because she wasn't alone. A shadowy figure appeared. It didn't take her long to recognize that it was Jayson.

He'd come back.

He held two take-out drinks in his hand. Before she could say anything, he set one on her desk.

"I didn't know where you were," she blurted, and immediately regretted it.

He blinked, seeming surprised that she'd care. "Guess I should have left a note."

"It was creepy here by myself." That sounded better than admitting how keenly she'd felt his absence.

"Sorry, Mary, that was thoughtless of me. I assumed I'd be back in only a few minutes, but the line at Starbucks was long. Apparently, something's going on downtown tonight. I heard several people mention something having to do with Figgy Pudding, whatever that means."

He smiled and her heart melted. "Oh . . . it's a singing choral contest that benefits the local food banks," she blurted, the words spilling out of her.

"That explains it," he said, and then, looking down at the drink in his hand, he added, "I got you an eggnog latte. I thought you might need something to tide you over."

She blinked, surprised by his thoughtfulness, and she was grateful. "Ah . . . thanks."

"I hope you like eggnog."

"I do." It was her favorite for this time of year.

He grinned and all she could do was stare. Jayson Bright's entire face was transformed by a simple smile. His eyes brightened as their gazes connected. Fearing she was about to reveal herself, Merry made a determined effort to look away, although she immediately felt a sense of loss.

"You like Christmas, don't you?" he asked.

Merry sipped her latte and nodded. "It's my favorite time of year."

From their weeks of lengthy conversations, she knew Jayson's childhood had been less than nurturing. He'd told her about his parents' unhappy marriages and his life in East Coast boarding schools. There had been almost a complete lack of tenderness in his life.

What Jayson saw in her, the online Merry, what attracted him to her, she suspected, went back to his childhood. Whether he recognized it or not, Jayson was drawn to the warmth and love of family.

Her family.

That sense of belonging was the real draw. In terminating their relationship, claiming there was no hope for them, she'd taken that warmth and acceptance away from him. The stories she'd shared with him about their holiday traditions—decorating the tree, baking cookies, sending out Christmas cards—had been like a drug to someone who had never known what it meant to be part of a family. Little wonder he was willing to let go of his pride and plead to continue their online relationship.

Jayson cleared his throat, distracting her from her thoughts.

"You're staring at me."

"I am. Sorry," she murmured, embarrassed, looking away. Because she felt she needed to offer an excuse, she said, "It's just that I didn't expect the latte. Do I owe you anything?"

"No, Mary, I'm the one who owes you. You don't need to reimburse me."

She took the Starbucks cup and set it aside. "I started again and got quite a bit done," she said, eager to get back to inputting the data.

Jayson grabbed the chair and scooted next to her desk, papers in one hand and coffee in the other.

It was close to eight by the time they finished.

"I couldn't have done it without you, Mary."

"I was happy to help," she said, and she meant it.

"I'm thankful for your time," he said, moving back his chair.

She reached for her coat and purse and noticed he remained seated, reading over the last of the report.

"You're staying?" she asked, wondering how late he would remain at the office. As for herself, she needed to hurry if she was going to catch the eight-fifteen bus, otherwise she'd be late to chat with . . . him.

"No, I need to get home myself." He stood and headed

toward his office. "Give me a minute and I'll walk you out."

"Oh." That was another surprise. Jayson Bright was turning into a man she barely recognized. The two Jays were merging together in her mind and she wasn't sure that was a good thing. It would make keeping her true identity a secret that much more complicated.

Once he'd locked up the office, they walked to the elevator and stepped inside.

"Have you ever noticed," he asked, suppressing a smile, "how the reflection shows in the smooth surface of the elevator door?"

What an odd question. "Not really."

His mouth quirked again.

"What makes you ask?" As soon as she phrased the question, Merry knew the answer.

"If you're going to make faces at me behind my back, Mary, you might want to make certain that your reflection doesn't show on the doors."

She gasped and was convinced her face turned the color of an overripe tomato. Once she found her voice, she said, "It's a wonder you didn't fire me."

"The thought never entered my mind."

"I'm sorry; that wasn't professional of me."

"No worries. I was more amused than upset."

The elevator landed on the ground floor and they walked together toward the exit.

"Your Friday-night date—was he upset about you needing to cancel?"

"No, it worked out fine. We aren't getting together until later anyway," she assured him. What he didn't know was that her hot date was a conversation . . . later, at nine, with *him*.

He checked his watch. "What time is he picking you up?"

She didn't dare explain that there would be no "picking her up" for her date, who unknowingly stood by her side. "Nine."

She turned and rushed toward the bus terminal, walking at a clipped pace along the brightly lit avenue. The trees were strung with white lights, giving a festive air to the cold night. Merry was surprised when Jayson's steps caught up to hers.

"You don't have a car?" he asked.

"I ride the bus."

"In that case, I'll drive you."

He glanced at his watch. Merry knew with the Seattle traffic being what it was, he'd never return in time. If he did, he'd be late for their date. That he would offer to drive her home, knowing he would be late, was completely unexpected.

She wanted to talk to Jay; she'd been looking forward to it all day. "I appreciate the offer, but it's not necessary."

"I don't want you to be late for your date."

"I won't be. The bus is the most efficient way for me to get home."

He hesitated and she secretly wanted to tease him for being so willing to give up his "date" with her. Of course, he didn't know that.

"If you're sure."

"I'm sure."

He walked her to the bus stop, and they went their separate ways.

Merry was home, sitting in front of her computer, at nine. Jay didn't leave her waiting long.

Merry? Is this you, or is this Patrick again?

She didn't understand why he would ask her that, then remembered that she hadn't agreed to go online.

It's me, Merry.

If you could see me, you'd see a big smile. I wasn't sure you'd be online.

The truth is I couldn't stay away.

I couldn't, either. I want you to know I've given a lot of thought to what you said to me. You're right. I'm arrogant and annoying, but I'm trying not to be. I'm willing to change my ways if that means I can have a chance with you.

Merry had already seen the evidence of that, although she couldn't let Jayson know.

This evening I went out of my way to be nice to one of the office staff.

A woman? Should I be jealous?

Maybe.

Merry grinned. Little did he realize she was the employee he was referring to.

You better explain.

I asked her to stay late and she did.

I hope you paid her double time.

She's a temp, but yes, I'll be sure she's well compensated. Later I offered to drive her home.

This was the perfect opportunity to find out what Jayson thought of her. If they ever did meet, he might not take kindly to the underhanded method she'd used, but so be it. The temptation was too hard to resist.

Is she young? Single?

Yes, to both.

Hmm, interesting. Is she pretty?

Pretty enough.

Pretty enough! Merry was insulted. Fingers at the ready, she was about to tell him exactly what she thought of his assessment of her. Thankfully, she stopped before she gave herself away.

You're taking a long time to respond. You're jealous, aren't you?

A little. She decided to humor him.

No need. You're the one who fills my head. Besides, she's involved with someone else. Had a date she was hurrying home to meet. It's you, Merry. You. You're the one who has talons in my heart.

That sounds painful.

It is. If only you knew. Tell me you're willing to meet me. Let's put this silliness behind us.

She was tempted. Really tempted. Not yet.

If not now, when? He sounded frustrated with her.

I'm not sure. It'll happen when the time is right.

She could almost feel his frustration. All right, I'll prove I can be as patient as the next man. I'm grateful you're willing to talk to me again.

A full two hours passed with them exchanging messages. The time flew by, and when she was finished, a warm, happy feeling came over her. She didn't know how she was ever going to find the strength to let go of Jay.

This chatting isn't enough for me any longer. I want to get to know the flesh-and-blood Merry. Please reconsider.

His "please" got to her every time. It told Merry she

was as important to him as he was to her, and that denying him would be almost impossible.

Okay, I give in. We'll meet before this year ends.

Promise?

Promise.

Merry didn't know what would happen when he
learned who she was. One thing she did know was that she
couldn't bear it if he broke her heart, because he already
held it in the palm of his hand.

✳

CHAPTER TEN

Jayson

Jayson worked the entire weekend, finishing the report that he would present on Tuesday to the Boeing executives. He'd been analyzing the data for weeks but was only now able to draw a conclusion. He was pleased with the results and convinced his insights would save the company money without requiring layoffs. It felt good that he could offer a viable solution to their current needs.

The only breaks he took over the entire weekend had been to chat with Merry. Spending time with her, even if it was online, was like taking a summer stroll. It refreshed and invigorated him. After they talked, he felt ready to tackle the project again with renewed energy and insight. He didn't know what it was about her that inspired him. All he knew was how he felt. He wasn't a man driven by feelings. He'd never been comfortable with them. As a youth, he'd learned to suppress and hide his emotions. Merry had the ability to draw them out unlike anyone he'd ever met. The guard he kept between himself and others had disappeared behind the anonymity of the computer screen.

By Monday morning, he was both exhausted and exhilarated. He'd met his deadline and was eager to have his uncle read his conclusion. As he entered the building, his gaze instinctively went toward the data-entry department.

Mary had been instrumental in helping him with the final phase of the report. He saw that she was at her desk and decided to stop by and thank her once again. Merry had questioned him about Mary on one of their weekend chats, and he'd made light of his interest in her. He had strong, strange feelings for Merry, but she seemed to be secretive and wary, which raised questions in his mind.

What surprised Jayson was that he found himself attracted to Mary, too. Over the weekend, he'd found his thoughts drifting toward her and he had to forcibly turn his mind away from her. He wasn't sure what it was about her.

When Mary noticed him, she looked up and automatically smiled. Over the last few weeks he'd caught her frowning at him any number of times. Seeing her welcoming smile now caught him off guard. His steps slowed as he worried that he was flirting with temptation.

"Good morning," Mary said, her eyes bright and welcoming.

"Morning."

"Did you finish the report?"

He didn't remember mentioning it to her, but clearly he must have. "I did, and I wouldn't have been able to if you hadn't stayed on Friday."

"I was happy to do it."

"I wanted to be sure you knew how much I appreciated your help."

"You're welcome, Mr. Bright."

He grinned. "No need to be formal. My name is Jayson."

Her eyes twinkled when she asked, "Is that allowed in the employee handbook?"

Chuckling, he said, "It's all right to make an exception now and again."

"Good to know."

As he started toward his office, he noticed a couple people giving him odd looks, and he wondered if it had anything to do with the smile on his face.

Mary amused him. He found it interesting how one night of working late together could change their testy relationship. He wasn't sure what exactly had brought about the transition; whatever it was, it pleased him.

First on his agenda Wednesday morning was the meeting with his uncle, who praised him for getting the report finished ahead of schedule. Jayson accepted the praise. He'd been thankful for the opportunity to prove himself, and his uncle had given him the tools and confidence he'd needed.

If Matterson Consulting garnered more business from the Boeing Company, Jayson was certain that his uncle Matthew would hand the company reins over to him when he retired. That was what Jayson wanted, what he strived to accomplish, and this report went a long way toward making that desire a possibility.

As he entered his office, Jayson's cellphone rang. He reached inside his pocket and saw that it was Cooper.

"Hey," Jayson greeted, happy to connect with his best friend. "What's up?"

"Not much. Thinking about Christmas."

As far as Jayson was concerned, there wasn't much to think about. Christmas was like any other day to him. By choice, he ignored the holiday, seeing that it brought up nothing but unwelcome memories.

"You got plans for Christmas with that new girl of yours?" Cooper asked. He'd been on Jayson from the first about Merry, digging for information. For the most part, Jayson had been able to sidestep his questions.

Except one.

Like a dog after a bone, Cooper wanted to know about their meeting. The meeting that had never happened. Each time Jayson put him off, his cousin had grown more suspicious.

"Merry and I haven't made plans yet," he said, which was true.

"In case you haven't noticed, Christmas is only a few days away."

"I know." Looking to divert Cooper's questions, he asked, "What about you and Maddy?"

"I'll be with her family. You met Merry's family yet?"

"Not yet. How are the wedding plans coming along?"

Cooper exhaled a long, slow sigh. "I have to tell you, man, I had no idea a wedding would take this much planning. Far as I'm concerned, we could stand barefoot on a beach and be done with it. Maddy's got a completely different idea. There are flowers and musicians, and a catered dinner at this posh resort. Her mother is involved with the plans now, and I swear there was less involved in the construction of the Great Wall of China."

Jayson couldn't squelch his laughter. "Next thing I know you'll be wanting me to wear a tux by the pool."

"I have no idea what Maddy and her mother are going

to want. For now, I'm staying out of it. I'm on a need-to-know basis."

"Probably the best way to handle that."

"Now quit avoiding the subject. I want to know how it's going with your girl."

Jayson's smile slowly faded. "It's going great." And it was, except for that one blip. But they were communicating again, and that was what mattered to him.

"I want to hear what she's like in person."

Jayson sighed, which seemed to prompt more questions from his cousin.

"She was a disappointment, wasn't she?"

"No." Seeing that they'd never met face-to-face, he could say that in all honesty.

"Was she everything you expected?"

Jayson hesitated, considered lying, and then decided he needed to be honest. His shoulders sagged and he released a sigh. "I guess I might as well tell you. She didn't show."

His answer was followed by a heavy silence.

"She didn't show?" Cooper repeated.

"You heard me right." He bristled, irritated that his cousin could get him to confess what had happened.

"Why not?"

This was where it got tricky. "I'm not exactly sure. She said she knew me."

"So?"

"Well, it seems she'd already met me. I just have no idea when or where. Apparently, I didn't leave a good impression." Jayson had racked his brain to figure what could have happened. All he could think was that he'd had an especially bad day and overreacted to something, but if that was the case, he didn't remember it. "We set a time and place to meet. Merry took one look at me at our designated spot and had a change of heart, deciding it was best that we not get involved."

Cooper was outraged on his behalf. "What the—"

"I talked her into giving me another chance," Jayson said, cutting off his cousin before he went on a tangent.

"Hold on," Cooper said, his words coated with annoyance. "You talked to her?"

"Not talk talked. But online talked."

"Man, I have to tell you, I haven't met this girl, but I have serious doubts. You're a catch, and if she doesn't recognize that, then be done with her."

Cooper had always been his staunchest supporter.

"I briefly considered that," Jayson admitted. "I have to admit my ego took a direct hit, and like you, I thought, whatever. If that was what she wanted, then so be it, but as the days went by I found myself thinking about her more and more. Going online with her was and is the highlight of my day. I look forward to that time with her as much as I do my first cup of coffee in the morning. More so."

Cooper appeared to be weighing his words. "You like her that much?"

"I do."

"You don't think all this talk is an excuse on her part? She could be hiding something."

"I doubt it." This was something Jayson had considered himself. Of course, it was possible, but he didn't think it was true with Merry. "Everything I know about her tells me she's a straight shooter."

"I hope you're right," Cooper said in that thoughtful way of his. "You've always had good instincts, so if this girl is as special as you seem to think, then go for it."

Jayson grinned. "I appreciate the vote of confidence. The thing is, there's this other . . ." He hesitated, wondering if he should say anything about his unexpected attraction to Mary from data entry.

"Other what?" Cooper pressed.

Once again Jayson tried to avoid the subject. "I've been involved in putting together this report."

"Yeah, yeah, I know all about that. You've been working for weeks on that Boeing project."

"My hours have been crazy, and frankly there hasn't been time to date. Merry is busy at her job, too."

"Jayson, come on, man, give it up. What aren't you telling me?"

Cooper knew him far too well.

"Something about working all these hours. Spill, Jay."

"Okay, okay, there's this girl in the office that's been a big help to me and I sort of find her attractive." That was a gross understatement, but he didn't want to admit how attracted he was to her, even to himself.

"Then ask her out. It might bring Merry around if she knows she has competition."

The idea had started to take root long before Cooper's suggestion. It went without saying that this was problematic for several reasons. He didn't want to play one woman against the other. He'd seen far too much of this very thing from his parents and their various marriages. Lots of other reasons came to mind, too.

"I can't date her."

"Because she's an employee?" Cooper picked up on that right away.

"Well, that, too, although she's only a temp. But that isn't the only problem."

"Then what is?"

Jayson stared at the ceiling and exhaled slowly. "She's dating someone else."

"Have you two spent time together?"

"A little," he confessed.

"Is she interested in you?"

Jayson needed to mull this over before he answered, being as truthful with himself as he could be. "I think she is."

"Then make your move," Cooper advised. "If this other guy was important, she wouldn't be sending you vibes."

"Vibes? Mary's not sending me vibes."

"Wait. What did you say her name was?"

"Mary. M-a-r-y, not to be confused with M-e-r-r-y."

Cooper chuckled. "I am confused. You're attracted to two women, both of whom are named Mary, but spelled differently."

"Yup."

"How is it that you find more ways to complicate your life than anyone else I know?"

Jayson had to agree and then chuckled. "Yes. But I'll never have a problem confusing their names, now, will I?"

"That you won't," Cooper agreed. "Listen, keep me updated on what happens. Guess I'll tell Maddy you'll be bringing a date to the wedding, and most likely her name will be Mary."

Jayson grinned. All he had to do now was figure out which Mary it would be.

※

CHAPTER ELEVEN

Merry

Merry was just about to leave the office Friday night when she got word that Jayson Bright had asked to speak to her. He sent his assistant, Mrs. Bly, to fetch her. She was a middle-aged woman who was rumored to have been with Matterson Consulting since its infancy.

Merry was immediately suspicious that Jayson had somehow uncovered who she was—her real identity. He'd requested that she come directly to his office.

Perhaps she'd made a mistake with the data on Friday that had completely messed up the report. In which case he would be angry and he'd fire her on the spot. Would he do that? Especially now, when only a little more than a week remained in her contract?

"You in trouble with the boss again?" Lauren asked as soon as Mrs. Bly left.

Kylie shook her head at Merry. "Hey, think positive. Maybe he's giving you a bonus for staying late last Friday."

"I didn't do anything wrong. I swear." She hoped.

"Well, don't keep him waiting," Lauren said, shooing her away with both hands. "But keep us in the loop. If the company is handing out pink slips, I need to know about it."

With her heart bouncing up and down in her throat like it was on a pogo stick, Merry approached the executive area of the office.

Mrs. Bly had returned to her desk, and when she noticed Merry, she said, "You can go right in. Mr. Bright is waiting."

Merry knocked once and then slowly opened the door to his office. Jayson sat at his desk, leaning back in his chair with his hands on the back of his head. He appeared to be deep in thought and didn't notice her for a few awkward moments.

When he did, he looked at her and blinked, as if finding her standing in the doorway to his office was completely unexpected.

"You asked to see me?" she reminded him. Her hands felt clammy and she gripped them in front of her, literally holding on to herself. She felt as if she was in junior high and had been called to the principal's office.

"Yes, yes." He gestured for her to come inside. "Close the door, if you would."

She did as he asked and remained standing, moving closer to his desk.

"Please sit down. You might be a few minutes."

She sank into the chair, sitting on the edge of the seat. The high-back chair was made of buttery soft leather and vastly unlike her own uncomfortable desk chair.

As if to make her even more nervous, Jayson continued to stare at her as though looking straight through her. She swallowed hard, convinced now that he'd managed to guess the truth.

Waiting for him to speak was torture. Merry did her best to be patiently composed, although her nails dug into the tender part of her palms, leaving deep indentations. Her heart continued to pound, but this time hard enough to play drums in a rock band. If Jayson was going to explode, then it was important that she remain calm and serene, no matter what.

"I imagine you're wondering why I asked to speak to you."

Because her mouth had gone dry, she nodded rather than respond verbally.

"Don't worry, this has nothing to do with your job."

That didn't reassure her. She glanced at her watch, wondering if she would make her bus.

Noticing that she looked at the time, he said, "This might take awhile. Will that be a problem for you?"

"No, but I'd like to know how long I'll be."

He cocked his brow and asked with a grin, "Another date?"

"No. If I'm going to miss the bus, then I'll need to make a phone call."

"You share an apartment with friends? Not that it's any of my business, of course." He was showing more curiosity about her now than he had in all the time she'd worked for the company. Merry couldn't help wondering what that meant, if anything. "Never mind. If you miss the bus, then I'll be happy to drive you home."

"There'll be other buses I can catch, don't worry. And no, I don't mind telling you. I live in a house."

"Rent being what it is, I suppose you have roommates," he commented. His eyes widened and he raised his hand. "Sorry, I did it again. None of my business."

Merry smiled, enjoying his discomfort. She liked that he wanted to know more about her and then realized she was competing with herself. It seemed silly to be jealous of the other woman when *she was the other woman.*

"Do you need me to stay late again? I can."

"No, no, the project is completed."

He didn't seem to be in a hurry to get to the point. His scrutiny made her uncomfortable. All he seemed to want to do was intently look at her, to study her every feature. He seemed hesitant, as if unsure of himself, which was nothing like the Jayson Bright she knew.

"Is something wrong with my appearance?" Merry asked, looking down at her outfit. She wore a green-and-blue jacket and a pencil skirt with knee-high boots. She couldn't imagine he would find fault with that.

"Your appearance?" he repeated, shaking his head. "No. Not at all. You look great. More than great. Lovely."

He was complimenting her. This was strange and it worried her. If she sat any closer to the edge of the chair she was sure to slip off and land on her butt, which would be terribly embarrassing.

"I wanted to personally thank you for everything you did to help me finish the Boeing report," he said. "Having you enter the last bit of information made a big difference."

"I was happy to help."

"I understand that, and it's appreciated. I realize we've had our share of differences in the past, but you haven't let that affect your work."

"Thank you." His praise embarrassed her. Little did he know how happy she was to spend that time with him.

She'd seen more of the Jay she knew from her online chats with him than Jayson, her boss. He'd been grateful and considerate. A week or two ago she hadn't been able to see that side of him. That one evening showed her there was more to Jayson Bright than she'd realized.

"I understand you were hired short-term by an agency," Jayson continued, cutting into her thoughts.

"My contract was for a year." Even though she'd been with the company for nearly twelve months, he hadn't paid much attention to her until the last few weeks, when the deadline for the report was pressing.

"That long?" He arched his eyebrows with the question, as though taken by surprise.

She did her best to hide a smile.

"At any rate, I wanted you to know if you're looking for a permanent position, I'd welcome you on staff."

This was unexpected, and for a moment she struggled to find words. For him to offer her a position was more than she'd ever considered. Her big fear coming into his office was that he wanted to fire her before her contract was completed. She'd never even suspected that he'd been considering giving her a permanent position. "I . . . I hardly know what to say. Thank you. That you would make such an offer means a great deal. It's tempting. This is a good company and the benefits are certainly appealing, but I've already registered for college classes." She'd been saving as much money as she could, in hopes of pursuing her goal to become a special education teacher.

"I didn't realize you were a college student." He frowned, as though wondering when she found the time to squeeze classes in with a forty- or fifty-hour workweek.

Merry felt she should explain. "I took the year off from school to save up enough to finish my last year. If all goes according to plan, I should have my teaching certificate by this time next year."

He nodded approvingly, as though he could see her in front of a classroom. "You'll be a good teacher, Mary. You have the patience and the temperament."

"I enjoy children, and it seemed a natural choice for me." She didn't mention her interest in special education, for fear he would make the connection between her and Patrick.

"I imagine you're eager to head home."

"I'm in no rush." She had plenty of time to catch the next bus; in fact, she had time to kill.

Jayson stood and escorted her to the door. "I'll see you at the Christmas party, right?"

"Actually, no."

"No?"

"I have plans that evening. Of course, you'll be there."

"Yes, it's more or less mandatory." Jayson walked to the door and opened it for her. She noticed that Mrs. Bly had already left for the evening, as had nearly all the staff. After all these weeks of mandatory overtime, it seemed everyone was eager to leave the office as quickly as possible.

"When is your last day?" Jayson asked.

Seeing that she wouldn't be working between Christmas and New Year's, it was coming up quickly. "The twenty-third, the day of the Christmas party."

"It's coming right up, then?"

"Yes. It's been a good year."

He grinned, his gaze warm. "Yes, it has. It's been a very good year on several different levels. Have a good evening, Mary."

Merry returned to her desk, collected her coat and purse, and headed out of the building. Because she had nearly an hour to wait for the next bus, she decided to grab dinner. It was her turn to cook, and because she was going to be an hour late, she would bring the meal home rather than keep everyone waiting on their food.

The New York deli a few blocks over was said to have a great reputation. She could easily grab something to go and make it to the bus stop in plenty of time. Splurging on herself and her family would be a treat.

Walking to the deli, her mood was high following her conversation with Jayson. When she arrived at the deli, she could see that they did a robust business, if the long line of customers was any indication. Glancing at her watch, she decided she had the time to wait in line, and she started reading over the menu posted behind the counter. A familiar voice spoke from behind her.

Jayson Bright.

"We meet again," he said. "You come here often?"

"No, it's my first time. Lauren recommended it and I thought I'd give it a try. I've got time before the next bus." The line, however, didn't seem to be moving all that quickly. "I think I do anyway."

"It's a popular place."

"So I see. What about you? You come here often?"

He shrugged. "Often enough to be on a first-name basis."

The line moved forward one person. Merry kept her hands buried in her coat pockets.

"Listen," Jayson said. "Would you consider letting me take you to dinner? To thank you. No obligation, just dinner between friends."

The question hung in the air between them with the tension of a tightrope.

"If you're thinking it's against company policy to date an employee," he quickly added, "then you're right. But technically you're not an employee of the company, so I feel confident I'm not going against company rules. And it's not really a date anyway. Just friends, remember?"

Merry couldn't help it—she laughed out loud. "You really *are* a stickler for the rules, aren't you?"

"No, I simply wanted to assure you that you're under no obligation to accept. No harm, no foul."

"Then I'll gladly accept. I'll need to make a call first, though."

He grinned. "Then you're game?"

She nodded, her smile so big her mouth hurt. This was a night filled with surprises. She'd been afforded a different side of Jayson Bright, and now he was giving her another opportunity to know him on a completely different level. "Sure, why not? Dinner between friends."

"What's your favorite food?" he asked. "Steak? Italian? Greek? Mexican?"

Over the weeks, they'd had extensive conversations about their likes and dislikes. She knew Jayson was a meat-and-potatoes kind of man. "A steak dinner sounds wonderful."

His eyes revealed his pleasure in her choice. "You make your phone call and I'll see about reservations."

"Deal." Merry couldn't hide her joy. Wanting privacy, she said, "I'll meet you outside."

Jayson already had his phone out and had it pressed against his ear.

As soon as Merry was outside the deli, she called the house. Patrick answered. "Hey, Patrick, any chance you could take care of dinner tonight for you and Mom?" Their dad was on an overnight business trip to Yakima, in the center of the state.

"It's your turn to cook," he reminded her. Patrick was the one who made up the schedule.

"I know. This is special, though."

"What are you doing?" he asked suspiciously.

"I have a date," she told him. This whole craziness had started because Patrick and her mother didn't think she got out enough.

"A date?" her brother pried. "With who?"

Merry lowered her voice. "My boss."

She could feel her brother's disapproval radiate over the phone. "You shouldn't do that. Jay wouldn't like you dating someone else."

It would be too complicated to explain everything to her brother. "It's fine, Patrick. I promise you, Jay won't mind at all. Can you take care of you and Mom tonight?"

"Okay. I can make chili with chips. I like chili with chips."

Not her mother's favorite meal, but she would eat it gladly when Patrick told her why Merry wouldn't be home for dinner that evening. "Okay. Thanks."

Merry ended the call at about the same time she saw Jayson approach. "I couldn't get a reservation until seven. I hope you don't mind waiting."

Glancing at the time on her phone, she saw that they had sixty minutes to spare. A later dinner gave her even more time to spend with Jayson, allowing her to get to know him better without him suspecting she was Merry.

Dangerous game or not, she couldn't be more pleased or excited.

✳

CHAPTER TWELVE

Jayson

"The restaurant is only a few blocks away," Jayson mentioned. "I hope you don't mind walking." The weather was relatively clear, although chilly. He enjoyed the cold, clear weather. His favorite time of year was winter, when the sky was blue and the cold air was crisp. He'd grab them a cab if Mary deemed it necessary, but he'd prefer the walk.

"Yes, please. It would be fun to see all the Christmas displays. I haven't had much of a chance to do that yet this year."

"You mean because of all the overtime?" he said, half jokingly. He felt bad about that, but there'd been no other option if he intended to get that report in on time.

"That, and for other reasons, too. I love the lights, the street vendors selling their wares, and there's usually a few caroling groups around Pacific Place. Would you mind?"

How could he refuse in the face of such enthusiasm? He walked to and from the office every day and hadn't noticed a single thing Mary had mentioned. "I think we could manage that and still make it to the restaurant in time."

"Great." She rubbed her hands together eagerly.

They walked away from the deli, and Jayson placed his hand at the small of her back, guiding her. She glanced his way and smiled. Such a simple gesture from her, and yet it touched him and he found himself smiling back. Jayson wasn't one who smiled freely. It felt strange and he realized he hadn't done nearly enough of that in the last few weeks. The relief he felt getting that report into Boeing was a huge weight off his shoulders.

As they crossed the street, Jayson's thoughts drifted to Merry. They'd made no official plans to chat that evening, though they usually connected every night, with few exceptions, at around eight-thirty, nine at the latest. It would do him good to miss a night, to keep her guessing. He didn't owe her an explanation. As much as he wanted to believe what they shared was real, his cousin's doubts had left him questioning his judgment. He'd never been one ruled by emotion. He wanted to believe Merry was everything she'd said, and that left him vulnerable in ways that made him uncomfortable. Skipping a night might be exactly what was needed for her to agree to meet.

Being it was the holidays, Jayson found the streets crowded with last-minute Christmas shoppers. Someone bumped into Mary and she stumbled forward a step. Jayson steadied her and then wrapped her arm around his elbow, surprised by how much he enjoyed the sense of being linked with her. He placed his hand over hers, sorry he wore gloves, as he'd enjoy the feel of her hand in his.

"There doesn't seem to be much of that goodwill toward mankind left these days," he commented.

"Oh, but there is," she insisted, looking up at him. "You just have to look for it. I promise you it's there." She pointed toward the woman who stood in front of Nordstrom, ringing a bell to remind those rushing about on the street of those less fortunate. "There's a good example."

She was right. Another woman stood on the corner, handing out notices for a church that was holding a free dinner for anyone who cared to attend. Mary took the flyer and read it aloud to him. "See?" she asked.

"Okay, you win. All I need to do is open my eyes."

"Oh look," Mary cried, hurrying their steps as she steered them toward a street vendor.

"What's this?" Jayson asked. The man at the cart had a pot going and people had lined up, waiting their turn.

"Roasted chestnuts," Mary said excitedly. "Let's get some."

"This is a real thing? Roasted chestnuts sound like something out of a Dickens novel."

"It does, and yes, it's a real thing."

"I'm happy to buy you some, but they don't sound all that appetizing to me."

"Give it a chance. They actually taste quite good."

Jayson was game to give them a try. He'd passed this vendor any number of times on his walk to and from the office but hadn't bothered to investigate.

They joined the queue and Mary gave him a brief rundown on what to expect, flavor-wise. Jayson didn't pay much attention to what she said; all he seemed capable of hearing was the sweet joy that radiated from her. It touched him in a way he found difficult to ignore. The more time he spent with Mary, the less his thoughts drifted to Merry. He felt drawn to her, almost as if he'd known her far longer and better than their limited contact accounted for.

When it was their turn, Jayson bought the chestnuts and had his first sample. He bit into the warm crunch and raised his brows, noticing that he had Mary's attention. She was right, they weren't half bad.

"Well," she asked, studying him. "What do you think?"

He shrugged. "Like you said, they're tasty."

"For me, it's more the novelty of it," Mary told him. She removed her glove and dipped two fingers into the bag to help herself to a second one. "Thank you for this."

He brushed off her appreciation, slightly embarrassed by her gratitude for such a small thing. They continued their walk with Jayson holding the bag of warm chestnuts, munching as they headed down the street toward the restaurant.

As they neared the corner, a group of singers dressed in Victorian garb approached. The women wore long wool coats with fur collars and had their hands inside matching fur muffs. The men were dressed in dark wool coats with top hats. Their voices blended in perfect harmony as they strolled along singing, "God Rest Ye Merry Gentlemen."

Jayson steered Mary back as the singers moved past. He noticed a dreamy look come over her, as if their music was equal to that of the angels.

"Aren't they wonderful?" she asked, smiling, eyes clean and bright with happiness.

For the first few moments, he was mesmerized by her smile. Thankfully, the question was rhetorical and didn't require an answer. Experiencing the joy of the season with her brought a new appreciation of the holidays. Christmas was just another day to him. He'd never paid that much attention to many aspects of the holiday season. But then, he acknowledged he never really had celebrated it. Oh, there'd been gifts. His fractured family had always seen to giving him material goods. But it was the important things like time, attention, love, and any kind of nurturing that had been sadly absent. It was as if his parents didn't know what to do with a child. Their gifts meant nothing to him. He routinely gave them away. He viewed their gifts as attempts to assuage their guilt for abandoning him. His refusal to accept their presents was his way of letting them know he couldn't be bought.

It started to snow—light flakes that drifted down from the heavens like small feathers released from angel pillows. Mary was beside herself with joy, tilting her head toward the sky and letting the flakes fall on her face.

"I've always loved catching snow on my eyelashes."

"What?"

"The song 'My Favorite Things' from *The Sound of Music*. Surely you remember that?"

He had seen the movie, but that had been years and years ago. "Sure," he said, "I remember it."

"I'd so hoped it would snow. This is perfect, just perfect." She all but danced down the sidewalk, dragging him along with her.

He stared at her in disbelief. The woman was nuts. Snow complicated everything, and even a small accumulation had the potential to cripple the city, causing all kinds of problems. Seattle didn't deal well with snow. A few inches were enough to paralyze the city.

"I hope it doesn't stick," he muttered. He was willing to admit he enjoyed her enthusiasm. He was more practical, though.

"You're joking." Mary looked at him like he'd suddenly sprouted horns. "It's almost Christmas," she reminded him. "Who doesn't long for a white Christmas? This is perfect." She threw out her arms and twirled around like a child on the playground.

Jayson grinned, finding her enthusiasm infectious. "Okay, okay, you're right. Snow is . . . beautiful and the timing is perfect, especially for kids."

"Christmas is the most wonderful time of the year."

"For some," he whispered, thinking she wouldn't hear. She did.

"It's more than a season," she said, wrapping her arm around his elbow and leaning her head against his shoulder.

Her familiarity surprised him. With anyone else he would have been taken aback, but for reasons he had yet to explore, he felt completely at ease with Mary. He found nothing pretentious about her. She was real and genuine, unlike many of the women he'd dated in the past. Not that this was a date . . .

"Christmas is a condition of the heart," she continued, and as she spoke she planted a hand over her chest. "It's being open and sincere, generous and kind to those with less, or showing our love to those we cherish." She stopped talking abruptly and glanced at him with a guilty look. "Sorry, I didn't mean to get on a soap box."

He smiled down at her, enjoying her more than he ever expected he would. As they walked toward the restaurant, Mary made multiple stops to gaze into the shop windows, pointing out little things he didn't notice in the displays, or along their walk, like the shining star in the distance atop Macy's department store.

"You know if it'd been three wise *women* searching for the newborn babe, they would have asked for directions much sooner, found the stable, swept it out, and had a meal waiting by the time Mary and Joseph arrived."

Jayson chuckled and shook his head. "No comment."

They saw children behind a display window of Santa's Workshop, waiting in line to visit Santa. Parents stood with them as the children squirmed. Jayson couldn't imagine the nightmare of standing in line with a bunch of fussy kids. Mary, however, had exactly the opposite reaction.

"Aren't the children adorable?"

He looked again, and all he saw were little ones clinging to their parents. A few were asleep on their father's shoulders and others were holding on to a mother's leg, terrified of meeting the oddly dressed man with a white beard.

"I feel sorry for them."

"Sorry?" The look she gave him suggested he was a space alien.

"Look at those parents," he commented. "They're exhausted, the kids are fussy, and Santa looks like he's completely worn out."

"That's what you see?" she asked, sounding shocked.

"You mean you don't?"

"No!" She stopped in front of the window. "I see that little girl in the ballerina-style dress entertaining her little brother and telling him all about Santa and those two mothers chatting happily, sharing experiences and information. As for Santa, he's the best. When I was small, my mother brought me to have my photo taken with Santa. I was so excited I could barely stand still. She still has the photo of me on his lap. I'm looking up at him adoringly. I savored the candy cane I got from him, and licked on it for three days."

Jayson paused, trying to see it through Mary's eyes, and realized she was right. Yes, there were a couple disgruntled and cranky children. The majority, however, were excited and happy, patiently waiting their turn.

When they reached the restaurant, their timing was perfect and they were seated immediately. They were given an upholstered booth with poinsettias displayed along the wall behind them.

Mary glanced around at the lushly decorated interior with the gold wall sconces and original artwork.

"Oh my goodness," she whispered, looking over the top of the menu, her eyes widening more by the moment. "I just saw the mayor of Seattle."

Jayson grinned. "It's one of the better steakhouses in town."

Her eyes grew even bigger when she reviewed the menu. He speculated she was looking at the prices.

She pressed the glossy menu to her chest and elbowed him before she whispered, "The cost of one steak here would feed a family for a week."

Jayson was busy studying the list of steaks. "Order whatever you'd like."

"I can't let you spend this kind of money on me," she said, keeping her voice low, as if afraid someone might overhear.

Jayson ignored her protest.

When the server approached, Jayson ordered a bottle of Malbec, one of his favorites. He talked her into sampling a glass.

The meal was everything he knew it would be. They carried on a conversation over the wine, and as he had earlier, Jayson found himself enjoying her company more and more. He casually mentioned Merry, explaining she was someone he'd met online but had yet to meet personally. Mary asked a few questions about that relationship. He felt comfortable enough to ask her advice about meeting a stranger online, and she admitted to doing it herself recently.

As they chatted, he sensed his feelings drifting away from Merry and toward Mary. He was interested in learning what he could about her. She had a close forever friend, who she hadn't seen in several months, and Mary missed her terribly. She told him about Lauren and Kylie, the two women she worked with in data entry. He avoided asking her about the man she was dating. If the two were serious, then it was doubtful she would have agreed to dine with him.

When they'd finished eating dinner, Mary leaned back against the cushioned booth and placed her hands on her stomach. "Wow, that was amazing," she said, sighing the words.

The dinner was excellent, he'd agree, but the company was more so.

Jayson couldn't remember a meal he'd enjoyed more. The steak was cooked to perfection, and watching Mary eat was a delight. She savored every bite and cleaned her plate. He enjoyed the fact that she enjoyed her food and didn't stress over every calorie.

When it came time to order dessert, she declared, "I couldn't stuff down another bite."

"Would you like to take one home for later?" he asked.

"I can do that?"

From her reaction, one would think he'd offered her shares in a gold mine. "Of course."

She couldn't seem to decide between the cheesecake and the chocolate cake.

"She'll take both," Jayson instructed the waiter.

A few minutes later, the waiter delivered a take-out bag containing the two desserts, along with the bill.

Leaving the restaurant, Mary checked her watch. "I have ten minutes to the next bus."

"No, you don't," he stated calmly.

"But I do. The bus comes fifteen minutes past the hour, every hour."

"Mary, I am not letting you ride the bus home. I'm driving you."

Her eyes got as big as dinner plates. "You're willing to face the Seattle traffic on a Friday night?" she asked, as if he needed to seriously reconsider.

"I insist on driving you home, so your answer is yes."

"But . . ."

"No arguments." He took her hand and led her to the high-rise where he kept his vehicle. The homeless man who'd taken to sleeping on the corner remained there, sitting over the grate. He glanced up at them.

To Jayson's amazement, Mary stopped walking, pulled her hand free of Jayson's, and started a conversation with the man. Thankfully, the conversation was a short one. Then, before he could stop her, Mary removed the chocolate cake from the bag and handed it to him, along with the plastic spoon.

"Merry Christmas," she told the man, and then rejoined Jayson.

"You're only encouraging him," he muttered once they were out of earshot.

"Maybe," she agreed, "but my guess is he's never had any dessert that will taste nearly as good as that chocolate cake."

And likely one that hadn't cost that much, either. Jayson didn't begrudge the man the ultra-rich dessert. He was in for a treat.

The doorman greeted Jayson and looked mildly surprised to find him with a guest. Jayson led Mary into the garage and to his assigned parking spot.

After opening the car door for her, she stared at all the lights and features in the car. After giving him her home address, he entered it into his navigational system and exited the garage.

They shared a companionable silence on the ride home. He enjoyed the fact that Mary didn't feel the need to fill the quiet and that she was content to sit in the heavy flow of commuters and listen to the music playing on the radio. Rarely had he been more aware of a woman at his side.

Mary was completely unpretentious and unlike any woman he'd ever known. Jayson was willing to admit that driving her home had been an excuse to spend more time with her. Already he was thinking of excuses so he could see her again.

He parked in front of her house. One look at the three-story Victorian told Jayson that this was more than a house. It was a home. Brightly lit wreaths with big red bows hung from nearly every window. The porch was surrounded by cheerful lights.

Mary interrupted his thoughts, and he took his eyes off her home.

"I had the most wonderful evening," she was saying. "Thank you for everything."

"I did, too," he returned, and it was no exaggeration. Her dimple deepened as she looked at him. He couldn't take his eyes off it. He found her one dimple simply adorable.

He *should* climb out of the car and walk her to the door, he thought, but he couldn't make himself move.

Mary glanced his way and it looked for a moment as if she had something on her mind. All he could do was hope it was the same thing that was on his.

Leaning forward, he pressed his mouth to hers. The kiss was gentle, more a grazing of their lips. A testing. Her mouth was moist and soft, so incredibly soft. Right away he knew it wasn't near enough to satisfy him and he wanted more. Needed more. Tucking his hand along the base of her neck, he brought her closer, deepening the exchange. To his delight, she leaned in to him, opening herself to him and sighing with pleasure. On second thought, he might have been the one who breathed out his own need, his own pleasure.

As sensation filled him, Jayson felt as though a weight had been lifted from him, freeing him from the burdens of his youth. A heady rightness that was physical as well as emotional crept over him. He'd been kissing girls since he was thirteen, but he'd never felt anything even close to what he did with Mary. He slowly released her and sat back, wondering what this might mean.

Following the kiss, all that either of them was able to do was stare at each other in total amazement at what had just happened. Mary smiled and then he did, too, unsure if she felt anything even close to what he had.

She must have. How could she not?

He braced his forehead against hers and resisted the urge to kiss her again, afraid that if he did, he wouldn't be able to stop.

"I should go inside," she whispered, and then cleared her throat as if she found it difficult to get the words out.

"I'll see you Monday."

"Okay. It's my last day in the office."

"I know." To his way of thinking, that was good news. She wouldn't be working for him, which meant no one from the office need know they were seeing each other. He assumed they would continue dating. He couldn't imagine not seeing Mary again.

He walked her to the door and was strongly tempted to kiss her again but restrained himself. With her hand on the door handle, she hesitated. "Thank you again for everything."

"I appreciated the advice about online dating," he said, reminding her of their earlier discussion at the restaurant.

"Sure. Anytime."

"Listen," he said, stopping her by placing his hand on her forearm. All at once it became important to make sure this was only the beginning and not the end. "Would you like to go out again . . . sometime? When it's convenient for us both? I know you're seeing someone else, so if I'm stepping on anyone's toes, I apologize." If she was serious about the other man, then she'd let him know.

"I'd like that," she said without hesitation, her face alive with a smile, as though she wanted this as much as he did.

"And this guy you're seeing that you met online . . . ?" He left the question hanging, eager to hear her response.

"Aren't you involved with someone online as well?" she asked without answering him.

Merry.

Jayson wanted to slap his forehead, aghast that she had completely slipped his mind. "Yes, of course. I need to resolve that."

She smiled and then kissed his cheek. "I've got a relationship to resolve myself."

He waited for her to open the door and step inside before he returned to his car and headed back into the city.

Once back at his condo, Jayson decided to log on to his computer to see if Merry had left him a message.

He discovered she hadn't, but Patrick had.

Jayson, Merry isn't home from work yet. She won't be here when you want to talk to her. I thought you should know.

Dad got a jigsaw puzzle and we'll put that together Christmas Day. We do that every Christmas. It's fun, but I'm not good at finding the pieces. Merry helps me. Please don't be mad at Merry. And don't tell her I sent you a message, okay?

So while he was out on a date, Merry was working overtime. He felt a pang of guilt, not that he should. The guilt had to do with the fact that she had completely slipped his mind.

He grinned as he leaned back in his chair and stared at the computer screen. Like Cooper had said, only Jayson could become involved with two women with the same name. But Jayson was determined not to complicate his life. He had a decision to make and had a strong feeling about which way he leaned.

CHAPTER THIRTEEN

✻

Merry

Merry woke Saturday morning with the most delicious feelings. Her evening with Jayson had been above and beyond anything she could have expected.

His kisses lingered in her mind, warming her.

She had no idea she could feel so much in a simple kiss. Thinking about it made her want to wrap her arms around herself and hold on to the memory. Their time together had been wonderful in every way. She loved the walk to the restaurant, sharing the bag of roasted chestnuts, listening to the wandering Victorian singers, glancing in the display windows and looking over the Christmas decorations. Merry couldn't remember a time she'd enjoyed more, and it had nothing to do with the fancy dinner. It was him, all him.

While they were parked outside the house, she was tempted to tell him she was the Merry he'd met online. But then he'd kissed her and that was the end of that.

She really needed to get up and help her mother, but before she could convince herself to leave the luxury of her bed . . .

"Merry?" Her brother called from the other side of her bedroom door.

No time to dwell on Jayson any longer. "Yes, Patrick?"

"Can I come in?"

"Sure." She sat up in bed and drew the covers up tighter around her torso to avoid the chill.

Her brother cracked open the door and peeked inside. His eyes avoided hers, which was a sure sign he'd done something he thought would displease her.

"Patrick?"

"It's Saturday."

"I know." He kept his gaze down on the floor.

"Is there something you want to tell me?"

Adamantly shaking his head, Patrick looked away, but not before she saw his eyes widen, as if he feared she'd been able to read his mind.

"Then why won't you look at me?"

He shuffled his feet. "Because if I look at you then you'll know."

"Know what?"

His shoulders lifted with a huge sigh. "Okay, I'll tell you. Last night when you went out with the mean boss . . ."

"He isn't mean . . . I just didn't know him."

Not to be dissuaded, her brother continued. "Anyway, while you were out I logged on to Mix & Mingle and left a message for Jay."

This should be interesting. "Did you tell him I was on a date with another man?" she asked.

His eyes shot open and became as round as golf balls. "No, I wouldn't do that. It would hurt his feelings."

That was her brother, hyper-aware of doing anything unkind.

"I told him you weren't home from work yet and not to be upset with you," he said, and then quickly added, "but I didn't say *why* he should be upset. It was okay to say that, right?"

"It's fine."

"Oh, and I told him about Dad buying the jigsaw puzzle to work on Christmas Day and that I need help finding the pieces and that you help me put them in place so I don't feel bad. I might not have said all that exactly, but that was what I was thinking." He chanced a look her way, keeping his head lowered. "You're not mad, are you?"

"Of course not. Who could be mad at you?"

"Sophie is. She wanted me to kiss her at the Christmas dance and I didn't want to because people were looking and she got mad."

"Is she still upset with you?"

He shook his head and then grinned. "I kissed her later in the dark."

Mentioning his kiss with Sophie reminded Merry of kissing Jayson, and she expelled a sigh.

"Hey, would you like to bake cookies this morning?" she asked, knowing baking was one of Patrick's favorite activities.

His face lit up with a huge smile. "Can we make the ones where you put your thumb in the cookie?"

"Sure, thumbprint cookies it is."

Saturday passed in a blur. After baking cookies with her brother, they delivered baked goods to the neighbors who had been helpful with Patrick and her mother. It was a small thing to do and showed their gratitude.

Later, Merry did the grocery shopping at a strip mall for the week. As she pushed the shopping cart toward the family car, she passed the window of a dress shop. Uncertain what caught her attention, she glanced at the outfit in the display. The dress was made of red silk, hitting about mid-thigh, with full length sleeves and a touch of lace at the fingertips. It was simple, chic, and spelled the holidays.

Mesmerized, Merry nearly stumbled before she could stop herself. For one crazed moment, she saw herself in that dress, walking toward Jayson when she revealed her identity. Merry would casually stroll toward him, the silk dress moving seductively against her body.

Jayson would be eagerly waiting to meet her. It would happen at the company Christmas party scheduled for Monday evening. There'd be music and champagne and magic in the air. Their eyes would meet and Jayson would be unable to look away from her. As she approached, his gaze would flare with appreciation, and he would be blinded by surprise that he had known her all along but hadn't realized the online woman was the very one he'd held and kissed. Then, unable to resist, he would hurry to meet her halfway. Naturally, he'd gently take her in his arms, and like the scene from one of her favorite romantic movies, *You've Got Mail*, he'd whisper in her ear, "I'd hoped it was you."

Well, she could dream, couldn't she?

It was silly, unrealistic, and about as far-fetched as Santa scooting down the chimney to deliver gifts. Nevertheless, the fantasy lingered in her mind.

Still, the lure of that dress was strong. Before she could give in to the temptation to go in and try it on, she pushed the shopping cart into the parking lot and unloaded the groceries and headed home.

Saturday evening Merry logged on at eight-thirty, their normal time. Sure enough, Jay was waiting for her.

Hey, she wrote.

Hey! Missed talking to you last night. Don't tell me that boss you're always complaining about made you stay late again.

Didn't realize I complained that much about my boss.

All the time, but you haven't so much lately.

Yes, well, I've had a change of heart about him.

Oh?

He's not half bad. I've come to like him quite a bit, actually.

I've always pictured him as old and cranky. He's not?

Nope. Young, your age, and good-looking, too.

There was a pause before Jay responded.

Are you trying to make me jealous?

Not really. I think we all need to have a more generous attitude toward others, especially this time of year.

Ah, Christmas. What is it with women and Christmas?

She read the message twice, unsure of his tone. It almost seemed that he was dismissing her Christmas spirit. Merry chose not to look at it that way.

I do love Christmas.

Speaking of which, I'm anxious for us to meet.

Oh?

It's time.

Yes, I suppose it is.

Past time. I don't want to be put off again.

I understand.

Good.

Tell me when and where and I'll be there.

His answer showed up almost immediately. The company where I work is in the downtown area, which I assume is relatively close for you. We have a Christmas party scheduled Monday evening. You should come.

He listed the address and told her the time.

I'll be there.

I'll look forward to meeting you at last.

Me, too.

They chatted for a bit longer until Patrick told her he needed the computer. He wanted to email Sophie. She explained to Jayson that the family had only the one computer. Merry would like nothing better than to get her brother his own; with only one laptop in the house, they were all forced to share. Merry so often controlled it in the evenings now that she felt obligated to get off when asked.

—

175

Sunday morning, the family was up early for church. Because this was the last Sunday before Christmas, the choir was going to perform the cantata. Patrick was excited, and his enthusiasm rubbed off on Merry.

She'd spent a restless night, planning how best to reveal herself to Jayson the following evening at the company Christmas party. She wanted it to be a welcome surprise and not one that would upset or embarrass him. As she pondered what was best, regrets crowded her mind. Not revealing herself to Jayson had gone on far longer than she'd ever intended. Everything hinged now on Jayson's reaction to her true identity.

She pictured him holding out his arms, smiling at her. Then he'd tell her that he'd guessed it was her from the very beginning.

That was the best scenario and the one least likely.

Her mind reviewed another. In this one, his eyes were cold, his mouth pinched, all the while glaring at her and accusing her of playing him for a fool.

Always the optimist, Merry went for option number one. Not that she was completely convinced once he learned the truth he would be pleased. Delighted, even. Well, a girl could hope.

Following church, Merry had lunch with her family when the house phone rang.

Her mother answered. "Yes, hold on a minute, she's here," she said and handed the cordless receiver to Merry.

"Who is it?" she mouthed.

Robin shrugged but had a gleam in her eye. "*He* didn't say."

He? Now Merry was all the more curious. "Hello," she said tentatively.

"Hey."

Her heart leaped into her throat. It was Jayson. "Hi," she whispered, feeling giddy inside, a bit like she did in junior high when Mason Dunlap, a boy she'd liked, had phoned her.

"I hope you don't mind. I asked HR for your phone number earlier in case I needed any more help over the weekend. And I wanted you to know I've arranged to meet Merry."

"Merry?"

"Yes, the online woman I mentioned."

"Oh." Her heart started a drumroll beat, as if playing out taps before a firing squad.

"You were right to suggest we each resolve our other relationships," he said. "I gave her a time and place to meet."

"Didn't you mention at dinner that she'd left you hanging once? Rather rude of her, if you don't mind my saying so. Do you think she'll show this time?" she asked, her heart in her throat. She could almost feel her pulse hammering away on the side of her neck.

"I can't say."

"I bet she will." Merry did her best to hide her nervousness.

"It's her decision. If she doesn't, then I guess I'll know that it wasn't ever meant to be."

"From what you said Friday evening, you enjoyed your online chats and getting to know her."

"True," he agreed, albeit reluctantly, and then abruptly changed the subject. "I was calling to see how things are going with you."

In other words, he was asking if she'd followed through. "I . . . I haven't had a chance yet . . . you know. It's only been a couple days and . . ." She didn't know what more to say.

What she needed to do was tell Jayson, right then and there, that Mary was Merry, but it seemed wrong to blurt it out over the phone.

"I understand."

She was convinced she heard disappointment in his voice.

"Have you had a good weekend so far?"

"I have. You?"

He sighed softly. "I enjoyed getting to know you, Mary, and wish you the very best."

Lowering her voice, she whispered, "I enjoyed our time together, too."

Merry started to fill him in on her weekend activities when the phone beeped with an incoming call. "I should probably get that," she said, reluctant to let him go.

Beep.

"Are you sure you won't reconsider coming to the Christmas party Monday night?" he asked in a rush.

"No, sorry." She would be coming to the party, but as Merry, the woman he'd met online, not Mary, the temp.

"I'll see you at the office on Monday, then."

Beep.

"Good-bye, Jayson."

"Till Monday."

He disconnected, and Merry answered the call, which was from a friend of her mother's. Merry delivered the phone to her mother and then returned to the kitchen for dinner preparations.

As she worked, her mind sped ahead to the Christmas party. All she could do was hope for the best.

✳

CHAPTER FOURTEEN

Jayson

For a good part of Monday, Jayson was on edge, anticipating meeting Merry, especially considering his growing
attraction to Mary. This was technically her last day in the
office. When he walked past the data-entry area earlier
that morning, he noticed that her coworkers had brought
in a small cake to celebrate the end of her contract.

Over dinner on Friday they'd talked about her future
and her goals, and he'd mentioned a few of his own, surprised with the ease he felt discussing his life with her. She
hadn't made a big deal out of it, but it was understood
that money was tight with her family. When she spoke of
her family it was with genuine love and affection. They
were everything to her. Jayson had never felt that love or

acceptance. She would create that same environment for her own husband and children one day. The man who married her would be fortunate.

From Mary, his thoughts automatically drifted to Merry. He was anxious to meet her in person. If she didn't show, he would delete his name from Mix & Mingle and scratch off the entire experiment as a learning experience.

He liked Merry. Genuinely liked her.

The thing was, he liked Mary, too. Ever since Friday, he hadn't been able to stop thinking about her.

He felt conflicted between the two women. His memories of all the nights he'd chatted online with Merry proved that she was more than a passing fancy. He'd spent more time getting to know her than any other woman he'd ever dated.

Dated.

That was the crazy part. They'd *never* dated. Never met. And yet he felt like he knew her.

Then there was Mary, whose eyes always snapped at him with irritation. Well, almost always. Things had changed between them. He barely knew her, and yet his feelings were strong. He was comfortable with her, at ease with no need to be anyone other than himself.

Either way, this was the day Jayson was convinced he would get clarity. In situations like this, the one person he felt comfortable talking to was his cousin.

He reached for his phone and punched the button that would connect him with Cooper.

"Merry Christmas," his cousin greeted.

"Back atcha," Jayson said, leaning back in his chair, relaxing.

"I bet I know why you're calling. You've finally met your dream girl."

"No."

"No you haven't met, or no that's not the reason you're phoning."

"Both, actually."

Cooper seemed to find his answer amusing. "What's going on?"

"I'm scheduled to meet Merry tonight," Jayson started off explaining. He wasn't sure what he expected Cooper to say. He'd never been one to openly share confidences, not the way his cousin did. Most everything that went on in his life was held close to his chest. Now there were two women, and he was confused and uncertain about what to do and how to handle these rare emotions. His focus had always been on his career and not on the nuances of women.

"It's about time," Cooper said. "You think she'll show?"

Who knew? Jayson pinched the bridge of his nose. "Don't know, and the truth is I'm of two minds."

His cousin took a moment to ponder his words. "What do you mean by that?"

Jayson wasn't sure he welcomed his cousin's counsel, but he trusted Cooper. He'd always had his back, and vice versa. It was how they'd managed to survive boarding school.

"I had a dinner date Friday night," Jayson admitted.

"The one you mentioned earlier? The other Mary?"

"Yeah." The image of Mary smiling up at him, reveling in the falling snow, trying to catch snowflakes on her eyelashes, brought a smile to his face. Every time he thought of their evening together, a warm, mushy, foreign sensation came over him. He'd enjoyed every minute with her, and selfishly, he wanted more. Lots more.

"What is it about her that attracts you—well, other than her name?"

"Funny," Jayson muttered. "First off, she's bright and funny, and she's about as real as they come. Her work is impeccable, she's dedicated and hardworking and . . ."

"Hey, I'm not looking to hire her. What does she look like?"

"Cooper, there's more to a woman than looks." He might have sounded righteous, but he wasn't backing down. This was the lesson he'd learned with his online match. He didn't have a clue what Merry looked like physically. And to him it no longer mattered. It might have at one time, but he'd come to know her as a person. That was what had attracted him, kept his attention, kept him coming back to talk to her night after night. He'd enjoyed the opportunity to lower his guard and be himself behind the anonymity of the keyboard. Merry had absolutely no idea he would one day inherit a company, what he looked like, or how much money he had, which was an impressive amount, actually.

"I know, brother, I get that, but if she's beautiful, it can't hurt."

"What attracted you to Maddy?" Jayson asked. He remembered her as having frizzy, unmanageable auburn hair, braces, and thick glasses. Not exactly the classic beauty.

"Well, she's changed since we were in school together. A lot. The braces are long gone and so are the eyeglasses. She's beautiful," he said and laughed. "She's still got that crazy hair, sticking out in every which direction. It would be easier to tame a rattlesnake. But that crazy red hair is part of Maddy, and she's the one I love. She's the one I choose to spend the rest of my life with and I mean that with every fiber of my being. I'm not making the same mistake my parents made. This woman is it for me, man. One woman for the rest of my life."

Jayson pictured two or three children in his cousin's future with big, bright smiles and frizzy red hair. The image made him smile so big, his mouth ached.

"I get it," Jayson said, and he did. He realized he felt the same. Over the years, he hadn't given a lot of thought to marriage and a family. He'd seen the effects of divorce and wasn't willing to risk his heart. It surprised him that Cooper was willing to take the leap and trust the future. He loved Maddy enough to give it his all. That impressed Jayson more than he was willing to admit. It set him to thinking that a wife and family might be possible for him, too.

"Okay, tell me more about this other Mary."

"She's about five-five, maybe five-six, slender. Brown hair and eyes, and she has the cutest dimple on one side of her mouth. Only one. It shows itself when she smiles and sometimes when she's irritated. I swear I can't take my eyes off her . . . I mean . . . the dimple."

"The dimple," Cooper repeated. "Listen, Jay, it sounds like you're hooked on this girl from the office."

"I am." He wasn't going to lie. Ever since they'd kissed, he had trouble remembering Merry, and then he'd go on-line and get involved in a conversation with Merry and be sucked into all those feelings. It reminded him of the din-ghy he and his cousin would ride on the Puget Sound, when it became choppy. The swells would carry them up and down and up and down.

His heart wanted Mary.

And then it wanted Merry.

"So, tonight's the big night. Where are you meeting the online Merry?"

"Company Christmas party."

"You think that's a good idea? How's she going to know who you are with all those people floating around? And won't the other Mary be there as well?"

"You've forgotten that she's seen me before, Cooper, remember? And, no, the other Mary won't be there, which is a good thing. She said she had other plans."

"I'll be curious to see what happens and what you decide."

"Decide?"

"Yes, between Merry and Mary. You'll keep me updated, right?"

"Sure." He was grateful for Cooper helping him sort things out.

They ended the conversation. When Jayson looked at the clock, he was surprised to find it was time to head over to the Christmas party. The company had rented hotel space and the event planners had handled all the details, including decorations, music, food, and everything else. It was meant to be an elaborate affair. His uncle went all out with this party. This was the last full day of work before two paid holidays, Christmas Eve and Christmas Day, so everyone would be coming to the party directly from work in their business attire.

When Jayson walked into the Four Seasons, the room was filled with employees and their significant others.

He was greeted by a server with a tray of filled champagne glasses. He took one, sipped it, and smiled. Although it was a medium-priced label, the champagne wasn't bad. He'd looked over the food and wine budget and knew exactly the brand of sparkly that had been ordered.

Servers circulated the crowd with trays of appetizers. He was offered a variety of tasty hors d'oeuvres, all of which he refused. He wasn't in the mood for food. Wanting to get his official duties out of the way first, he greeted staff and made polite conversation with the executives and other colleagues. Once he was done making the rounds, he parked himself in the corner of the room and sipped his champagne.

He recognized most every employee but was unfamiliar with all their names. His gaze wandered over the room, seeking an unfamiliar face.

"Merry Christmas."

Mary joined him in his corner space, her eyes warm and her smile wide.

He frowned, distinctly remembering that she'd said she would be unable to attend the company Christmas party.

Her dimple was on full display, and he had a hard time looking away. "Merry Christmas," he returned. "I thought you couldn't make the party."

"I had a change in plans."

"That's great. I hope you enjoy yourself. Did you get a glass of champagne?" It took him a moment to realize he needed to pay more attention to the crowd in order not to miss identifying Merry.

"Not yet. By the way, I brought you a small gift."

Jayson took his gaze away from the crowd and turned to look at Mary. "Oh?"

"I baked you cookies. I stopped by the office and left them with Mrs. Bly. You'd already left for the party. I wanted you to know so you could bring them home."

"That wasn't necessary, but thanks."

"I told you I would, you know."

Jayson didn't remember that, but apparently, she had. He must not have been paying attention. He wouldn't make that same mistake now. He had an eagle eye out, scanning those attending the party, most of whom he recognized. Everyone was familiar, and he was beginning to grow discouraged.

"Merry's here, somewhere," he commented. "Or so I hope."

"She might be right before your eyes," Mary told him.

He doubted it. "Possible, but I don't think so. I'd recognize her if she was. I recognize everyone here so far."

"You think you'd recognize her?" she asked with a soft laugh that got his attention.

"I've never seen her, but I should be able to pick out an unfamiliar face."

"Perhaps she is familiar," Mary said.

"She implied as much; she said she knew me, which indicates that I'd know her." He'd spent countless hours wondering about that very thing and couldn't imagine how he knew her.

"Did you know HR misspelled my first name on the nameplate that was on my desk?" she asked him.

He blinked, finding it odd that she would mention this on her last day in the office.

"Did you tell HR?"

"Three times, but they didn't feel it was worth going to the trouble when I was a temp."

"I'm sorry. If you'd mentioned it earlier I would have made sure it was corrected." It was too late now, though.

"There's a reason I'm telling you this, Jayson. There's something you need to know . . ."

"I see her." Jayson exhaled quickly when he spotted the woman who came into the ballroom area. It had to be Merry, and she was gorgeous. His breath caught in his lungs. It *had* to be her. He knew every employee, and she was alone and walking purposefully toward him.

She was stunning. Stop-traffic gorgeous. She wore a red silk dress and heels, and the dress clung to her body in all the right places. And her body . . . wow, she was perfection. Her gaze zeroed in on him, and a small smile widened her mouth.

Automatically he stepped forward and held out his arm to her, welcoming her.

"Jayson," Mary said, touching his arm. "That can't be her."

Unable to take his eyes away from the beautiful woman walking directly toward him, Jayson didn't hear a word Mary said.

Merry was only a few feet away from him now. The closer she got, the more enraptured he became. She was a vision; her beauty took his breath away. Merry was far and away more than he'd ever anticipated or expected. What shocked him was that he didn't recognize her. He quickly scanned his thoughts, wondering where and when he might have seen her before, because she definitely wasn't someone he would forget.

"She's wearing my dress," Mary gulped.

That caught Jayson's attention. "What?"

Merry's brows rose to a perfect arch. "My dear, I can assure you that this is *my* dress."

Mary's face filled with a color that would rival Santa's suit. "I know, I apologize, it's just that I saw it in the store window and wanted it so badly." She snapped her mouth closed and then shot Jayson a mournful look. "She's beautiful. . . . I'll leave you two to become acquainted."

"Thank you," Merry said, smiling cordially at Mary.

"Here," Mary said, and handed Jayson a card. "Merry Christmas . . . I meant to leave this with the cookies, but I think it's best I didn't."

He took the card and Mary walked away.

As soon as Mary was out of sight, he turned to Merry and took her hand in both of his. "Merry. We meet at last."

"Merry?" she returned, smiling at him with perfectly white, even teeth. "My name isn't Merry. It's Sylvia. Sylvia De La Rosa. I'm the event planner you hired. I believe you're Jayson Bright, am I correct?"

"Your name isn't Merry?" He was too flustered to think clearly.

"No," she reiterated. "It's Sylvia. I thought I should introduce myself and ask if everything was to your satisfaction."

It took him an awkward moment before he could answer. "Yes, yes, it's perfectly fine."

"Good. We appreciate your business and hope that you'll consider using our company for other events."

"Of course," he said, doing his best to disguise his disappointment and embarrassment.

They shook hands and Sylvia left him to oversee the servers.

Once again, his eyes scanned the room. He couldn't find Merry anywhere.

Then it hit him, what Mary had said, and his head felt like it would explode.

It seemed out of context at the time, and he hadn't understood the significance of what she was trying to tell him. Human Resources had misspelled her first name. Why in the name of heaven would she mention that to him now, at this party? Really, how many ways could you spell . . . his chest tightened.

Mary.

Merry.

Closing his eyes, his shoulders slumped forward as he groaned at his own stupidity.

Merry . . . *his* Merry had been right in front of him and he was too blind to see her. He fought back the urge to slap his forehead. He couldn't have been any denser.

She'd tried repeatedly to tell him and he hadn't heard her. A sick feeling attacked the pit of his stomach. Then Sylvia had appeared and he'd mistakenly assumed she was the woman he'd spent all those nights with chatting online. He couldn't imagine what Merry/Mary was thinking about him now. His groan grew louder. This was a worse disaster than even he could imagine. He'd been swayed by a pretty face and ignored the beauty standing right next to him.

It all made sense now. Merry/Mary arrived at Starbucks and recognized him immediately. She didn't want anything to do with him. Prior to that, every time they had contact in the office it had been confrontational.

Still, there had been ample opportunity to explain who she was—that Mary and Merry were one and the same. And she hadn't done that. Instead, she'd strung him along. He was sorry for the way he'd acted, but she wasn't completely innocent in all of this. Furthermore, she owed him an explanation.

Jayson felt his breath freeze in his lungs, wanting to wipe out the entire night and start over. Good luck with that.

Without realizing what was happening, he'd set himself up as the poster child for fool of the year.

But Mary/Merry also had to carry part of the blame. She should have told him who she was long ago; many opportunities had presented themselves.

Looking around, he didn't see her anywhere.

He started working his way through the crowd, weaving around couples until he saw a familiar face from the data-entry department.

"Kelly," he said, gripping the young woman by her shoulders.

"It's Kylie," she said.

"Kylie," he repeated. "Have you seen Merry?"

"Merry Knight?"

"Yes," he returned impatiently. "Merry Smith. Mary Knight. Whatever her name might be."

"She left."

*

CHAPTER FIFTEEN

Merry

The entire evening couldn't have gone worse. Merry had all but told Jayson who she was and his focus had been on the woman in red who was gorgeous, tall, and graceful. She could have been a supermodel with the perfect body and perfect hair and makeup.

Perfect everything.

And Merry wasn't. No way could she compete against that. Furthermore, she wasn't going to try. If that model was the kind of woman Jayson wanted, the kind he was most attracted to, then this wasn't meant to be. That just wasn't her. Nor did she ever want to be.

Walking at a clipped pace out of the hotel, Merry couldn't get away from the party fast enough. The cold air hit her as she made her way down the street, her hands buried deep in her pockets.

Gradually, disappointment slowed her steps and she caught her breath. She bit into her lower lip, struggling to hold back the disappointment. She'd wanted this night to turn out so much better than it had.

Tears blurred her eyes and she quickly blinked them back. No way was she going to cry over him. She might not be competition for this supermodel, but she had nothing to be ashamed about.

"Merry."

She heard her name and recognized Jayson's voice. Choosing to ignore him, she picked up her pace and walked faster until she was practically trotting.

"Merry," he said again, his voice strong and unrelenting.

He sounded breathless, as if he'd jogged the entire way from the hotel. If he knew her better, he'd know it was best to leave her alone until she was ready to talk, and she was no way near ready.

Within a matter of seconds, he raced up alongside her. "We need to talk this out."

"Now isn't a good time."

"It's as good as any," he argued. "I want to know why you didn't tell me who you were earlier." His tight features demanded an explanation.

She didn't answer, which only seemed to frustrate him further.

"You had the perfect opportunity any number of times."

Her mouth remained closed and tight. She refused to look at him, staring down at the sidewalk instead.

"You played me."

That was too much. "I played *you*?" she cried. "It was circumstances, not something I planned deliberately. Think what you want, but you're completely off base. How could I have possibly known it was you until . . . never mind. It isn't important. Like I said, believe what you want."

"You're the one who refused to meet me."

She glared at him, unable to hold back any longer. "And you wonder why? You came across as arrogant and rude at work. I tried to cut ties, but you wouldn't let me. You were the one who said *please*."

"*Please?*" he demanded. "When did I say that?"

"You didn't say it. You typed it and . . . and then I gave in. My bad. Isn't that what you said? I knew then, and I should have listened to my gut because it would hurt a whole lot less now if I had."

"Did your coworkers know you were playing me for an idiot? Was the entire company aware of your game?"

"Oh right. I told everyone," she said sarcastically. "I

blabbed it to anyone who was willing to listen. Couldn't wait to make you a laughingstock. That's so like me."

His gaze narrowed into thin slits. "Did you, Merry? Did you purposely try to embarrass me?"

She could tell by his look that he wasn't sure if he should believe her or not.

She didn't want him to think she had set out to humiliate him. Hanging her head, she briefly closed her eyes. "No . . . no one knew."

He exhaled a harsh breath. "Thank you for that."

The fight left her as quickly as the anger came. "I'm sorry, Jay, sorrier than you know. I'm not the woman you want." If he'd been looking for someone like that beauty queen, then it would never be her. "I think it would be best if we forget about this whole fiasco."

He exhaled a deep breath, glanced toward the sky, and then slowly nodded.

Her heart felt like it was going to break in half. She had no one to blame but herself. She'd known the moment she saw him sitting in Starbucks holding that bouquet of daisies that they were all wrong for each other.

"I guess there's nothing more to say, then," she murmured.

He nodded. "I am curious about one thing."

She looked up at him, struggling to hide the pain pounding in her chest. "What?"

"This." He caught her by her shoulders and brought his mouth down to hers. His lips were cold against her own. Catching her by surprise, she wasn't sure what was happening and why he would want to kiss her, especially now that she was ready to walk away entirely and be done with this entire mess.

Once the shock left her, she found herself opening to him. Rising on the tips of her toes, her arms circled his neck and she gave herself over to this kiss. He tasted wonderful, a mixture of champagne and desire. His kiss was everything she remembered.

And so much more.

She wasn't sure how long they continued to kiss. Not until someone shouted a catcall in their direction did they stop. He pushed her away and stared at her for several seconds. Neither of them seemed capable of speech.

Merry raised her fingertips to her lips while keeping his gaze, holding on to the wonder of his kiss, although that was impossible. "Do you have your answer?"

He nodded.

And with that, he turned his back to her and walked away.

CHAPTER SIXTEEN

✳

Jayson

Jayson couldn't get away fast enough. As he headed down the street, he mused that it would have been far better if he hadn't kissed Merry again. But he had and now his head and his heart were filled with the taste of her. All it had done was create a craving for more.

Her contract had ended, so he wouldn't see her at the office again, which was good, as that would have been awkward. For all intents and purposes, she was out of his life. It was better that way.

Instead of returning to the Christmas party, Jayson headed home, discouraged and depressed. He'd had high hopes for Merry and him. High hopes that had come crashing down with the speed of a misfired rocket.

The doorman greeted him with a smile, which quickly

faded when he saw the look on Jayson's face. Not wanting to ruin anyone else's evening, Jayson raised his hand, acknowledging the other man. It was then that he noticed the homeless man sitting at the corner.

The doorman's gaze followed Jayson's. "I've notified the authorities and he leaves, but then the next day he's back."

Jayson walked over to the man, who looked up at him with determination. "I ain't moving. You can call the cops if you want, but this is a public sidewalk."

Jayson didn't argue. "You have a name?"

"What do you want to know for?"

"I'm Jayson."

"You were with that girl who gave me the chocolate cake?"

Jayson nodded. "That's me." Reaching inside his three-quarter-length raincoat, he pulled out his wallet and removed a hundred-dollar bill. "Merry Christmas," he said.

The homeless man looked at him like he was dreaming. "You sure you want me to have that?"

"I'm sure."

"Name's Billy."

"Merry Christmas, Billy." He headed into the building where it was warm and beautifully decorated for the holidays with lights and a large Christmas tree. Merry and bright.

"Merry Christmas, Jayson," Billy called after him.

Peter, the doorman, stared at him like he didn't recognize Jayson, but he didn't say anything.

Jayson rode the elevator to his condo. The inside was cold and dark by contrast. He had no decorations. No holiday display of any kind. It felt stark and bare. His life felt the same.

As was his habit, he walked over to the wine rack and poured himself a glass of wine. He left the lights off and sagged down onto his sofa, staring into the night with the festive lights below. It'd started to snow and he glanced at his wrist, checking the time. Thirty-five minutes after the hour. Merry would be on the bus. He could see her sitting by the window, looking out at the falling snow. He wondered what her thoughts were or if she was as disheartened and disappointed as he was.

What a major debacle their relationship had turned out to be. To think he'd known Merry all along. He should have figured it out. How unbelievably dense he'd been. She'd practically told him outright who she was. The comment about the woman he was looking to meet being right in front of him, and later how HR had misspelled her first name. What a dunce!

Reaching for his phone, he pushed the button that would connect him with Cooper. His cousin answered on the second ring, and Jayson could hear festive music in the background.

"Hey, did your long-lost love finally show?"

"Yeah."

The teasing quality immediately left Cooper's voice. "What happened?"

"Where are you?" Jayson asked instead.

"Doesn't matter."

"Cooper!"

"I'm with Maddy and her family. Now tell me what happened, and it doesn't sound like it was good, if what I'm hearing in your voice is any indication."

Jayson had no intention of denying it. "Remember how I told you she said she knew me?"

"Yeah, so?"

"So, to make a long story short, Merry is Mary."

"Say that again."

Jayson had hoped his cousin would catch on right away. "M-A-R-Y and M-E-R-R-Y are one and the same."

"Merry and Mary are the same person?" Cooper exhaled as he took in the significance of what Jayson had said. "Wow, bet that was a shocker."

"It was. I should have guessed sooner. I blew it, Cooper. Blew it big-time. Saw someone else and thought it was her. It wasn't. Mary was trying to tell me she was M-E-R-R-Y but I was distracted by someone else who I *thought* was Merry. When I realized what she'd been trying to tell me, I got angry, thinking she played me for a fool."

"Did she?"

"Don't know. In retrospect, I doubt that she did."

"You like her? Both Merry and Mary?"

He wasn't sure how to answer. "I don't know what to think. Thought it was best to end it, walk away. She suggested it and I agreed, but I did something utterly stupid."

"What?"

"I kissed her."

His words were met with silence and then, "How was it?"

"On a scale of one to ten, it was about a hundred."

Jayson knew the minute he'd walked away how badly he wanted Merry. The background music faded slightly, which told Jayson his cousin had walked out of the room. He didn't want to disrupt his cousin's holiday celebration. "Listen, Cooper, you're in the middle of a party. I'll catch up with you later."

"Don't be a fool, Jay. If you care about this woman, then do something about it."

"Right." The problem was he didn't know where to start. Merry wanted nothing more to do with him. The entire situation was a disaster. His initial reaction was to end it all, but the choice had been hers. At this point, he could only do so much, and he felt like he had to abide by her wishes.

Cooper continued talking, offering Jayson friendly advice, most of which faded into silence, lost on him. When he didn't respond, his cousin suggested Jayson sleep on it and call him in the morning and they'd talk some more.

Jayson agreed but suspected there would be no sleep on his part. It felt like a lead weight had landed on his chest, paralyzing him.

After a second glass of wine, Jayson grew sleepy. He rarely drank more than two glasses. It was only nine-thirty, too early to go to bed. Leaning his head back against the couch, he closed his eyes. That was a mistake, because the minute he did, Merry's image took shape in his mind, her fingertips pressed to her lips, looking up at him with eyes that made him want to do nothing more than kiss her again and again.

He couldn't have bungled the situation any worse. How could he have mistaken the event planner for Merry when the beautiful woman he'd fallen in love with stood right in front of him? His initial reaction was to assume Merry had played him for a fool. He was a fool, all right, one of his own making.

Thinking she might have had a change of heart, he felt a surge of energy and stepped into his home office and logged on to his computer. His heart swelled when he saw there was a message from her. He immediately clicked on it.

You hurt my sister.

Patrick.

I don't like you anymore, and neither does she.

Reading this was only torturing himself. Anyone with half a brain would disconnect and leave matters as they were. Not Jayson. He was looking for punishment and so he continued to read.

Merry is in her room and she won't talk to me or my mom and dad.

After spilling his guts to his cousin, he wasn't in the mood to talk much, either.

You ruined my sister's Christmas, and she's a good person. Why would you do that? Why would you hurt her feelings? I liked you and Mom liked you, too, and even my dad liked you. We were all happy that she was going to meet you and then she came home and wouldn't talk to anyone. What did you do? What did you say? Tell me, because Merry won't say anything.

His heart sank as he struggled with how to make this right and realized it wasn't possible. The best he could do was wait until after the holidays and find a way to build a bridge.

This is going to be the worst Christmas ever. Merry is sad and now Mom thinks we did the wrong thing and it's all your fault. I hope you have a crummy Christmas. Patrick.

Jayson could guarantee that he was going to have a miserable Christmas. It had never bothered him before. Christmas had no real meaning for him. It never had. The best he could do was have dinner with his uncle and they would discuss business. A restaurant meal.

Heaving a sigh, he closed his laptop and headed into his room for a shower. It felt as if he carried the weight of the world on his shoulders.

Merry Christmas. His would be without the Merry for sure.

CHAPTER SEVENTEEN

✳

Merry

Merry spent a sleepless night. When she emerged from her bedroom on the morning of Christmas Eve, she saw the worried look her parents sent her way. Patrick, too.

"Are you ready to tell us what happened when you finally met Jayson?" her mother asked, her face tender and concerned.

Pouring herself a cup of coffee, Merry debated how much to say. After her first sip, she managed to offer those she loved most a reassuring smile. "The meeting between Jay and me didn't go as well as I'd hoped." That said it all and so much more. She'd rather not go into lengthy explanations. As much as possible, she wanted to put last evening out of her mind.

"From your reaction when you arrived home last night,

that was pretty much our assumption," her mother surmised.

Merry realized she would need to explain a bit more. "Jayson . . . was upset and thought I'd played him for a fool."

"Oh Merry," her mother whispered sympathetically. "Surely you told him that was never the case."

"I tried, but I don't think he believed me."

"Did you give Jayson the cookies we baked?" Patrick asked and reached for his hot cocoa.

She nodded. "I left them on his desk at the office."

"Take them back."

"Patrick," their mother chastised, "they were a gift. We'd never take them back." She returned her attention to Merry. "Now tell us about your last day at the office."

"It was great. Lauren and Kylie brought in a cake and we celebrated together. I'm going to miss them."

"If you're not working for Jayson, it will make all this easier," her mother commented.

"I thought of that, too. It would be agony to see him every day." It went without saying that Jayson would have no desire to see her.

"I hate to see you upset," her mother said. "I know this meeting was a big disappointment. I feel bad. Your brother and I were the ones who involved you in all this. I hope you know our intentions were good."

"Mom, please." Merry walked over to where her mother sat at the kitchen table and wrapped her arms around Robin's shoulders and kissed her temple. "I wouldn't have missed this for the world. Jay will always hold a tender spot in my heart. I don't have a single regret."

"You don't hate him?" Patrick demanded.

"I could never hate Jay," she said, and remembered the beautiful kiss they'd shared. She would always remember his kisses.

"But he hurt your feelings," Patrick said, interrupting her thoughts.

"I'm disappointed, yes, but I think Jay was genuinely disappointed, too. It happens that way sometimes. I should have known better than to involve my heart, but like I said, I don't regret a single minute. I'm grateful because Jay helped me to appreciate how blessed I am with all of you." Jay had never known the love of a close-knit family the way she had; he'd never experienced a real Christmas.

"Do you think he liked you, too?" Patrick asked next.

That question required some thought. After all the nights spent online, opening their lives and their hearts to each other, she had to believe that he did hold some tender feelings for her. He couldn't have faked that. Nor could she. "In his own way, I believe he liked Merry. It was the other woman who confuses him."

"What other woman?" Patrick wanted to know, cocking his head to one side to understand.

"The Mary who worked in his office."

"But that's you." Patrick shook his head as if that would help him understand.

"I know. It's rather confusing."

"Is Jay confused?" Patrick asked.

"I don't think Jay is, but Jayson definitely is."

Patrick looked at her long and hard and she could almost see the wheels in his mind spinning. "But isn't Jay Jayson?"

She nodded rather than go into a lengthy explanation. "Like I said, it's a big muddled mess to him, to me, and to just about everyone else."

"It's Christmas Eve," her mother reminded them all. "No sad faces are allowed. I have a turkey in the refrigerator and we're going to stuff that bird and cook him into the finest Christmas dinner we've ever had."

"You bought a turkey?" Patrick was thrilled. "I like turkey."

"You like everything," Merry reminded him, kissing him on the top of the head. "What can I do to help, Mom?" she asked, determined not to let her hurting heart dampen the family's Christmas spirit.

Her mother locked eyes with Merry, seemingly aware of her daughter's effort to make the best of the situation.

"I'd like to get as much of the food preparation done today so we won't be spending all our time in the kitchen tomorrow."

"Good idea." The busier Merry was, the less time she'd have to think about Jayson and the mess she'd made. She'd put off thoughts of him until later, when she felt better prepared to deal with the myriad of emotions that churned inside of her.

Well, she could try.

Her mother had a list of tasks that kept Merry busy until mid-morning. Her father was out and about, and it wasn't until noon before she realized her brother had been quiet all morning. He almost always enjoyed helping in the kitchen, too.

"Where's Patrick?" Merry asked, her suspicions rising.

Her mother was busy at the kitchen table, peeling potatoes, and glanced up. "The last time I saw him he was playing computer games."

That made sense, seeing that Merry had dominated the family computer for weeks now. The only time Patrick had to play his computer games was right after school.

"Lunch is ready. I'll get him."

Merry sought out her brother and found him sitting on his bed with the computer on his lap. "Patrick?"

He glanced up and his eyes widened with a look of surprise and guilt.

Merry knew that look all too well. "What are you doing, Patrick?" she asked, stepping farther into his bedroom.

He closed the computer and shook his head adamantly. "Nothing."

"It doesn't look like nothing to me." A sickening feeling attacked her stomach. "Were you online with Jay?"

Her brother's eyes bulged and again he adamantly shook his head. "I promised not to tell."

"Patrick." She groaned and sank onto the bed next to her brother. "What did you do?"

"He made me promise not to tell."

"What did you tell him?" she pleaded. "Please, Patrick, I need to know."

He stared at her for a long time. "You promise not to be mad at me?"

She wasn't sure she could swear to it. "I'll do my best."

"I told him you were sad. I was mad at him, too, and told him I wanted him to have a crummy Christmas, but then I felt bad and told him I changed my mind and he could have a good Christmas and I was sorry I said all those things to him."

Merry sat down on the bed next to her brother. "I'm glad you apologized."

"I . . . I told him what you said," he added evasively.

"Which was what? Remember, I said a lot of things."

The guilty look returned and he avoided eye contact. "Just that you had no regrets and that you couldn't be angry with him. You said that, right?"

Her chest tightened before she nodded. These were words she'd prefer he hadn't shared. Rather than berate her brother who only meant well, she reminded him it was time for lunch.

"Did you make toasted cheese sandwiches?" Patrick asked. Those were his favorite, along with peanut butter and jelly.

"I believe I did," she said, hugging her brother. She wasn't entirely sure what Patrick had said to Jayson. "Will you do me a favor?" she asked as she looped an arm over his shoulder. "Don't write to Jay again, okay?"

Her brother sighed expressively. "Never?"

"Please," she whispered, her throat tight and raw.

"I'll do my best," he said, repeating her own promise to him earlier.

Her mother tired out easily and laid down to rest following lunch. Merry was cleaning the kitchen when the doorbell rang. Bogie barked and raced across the living room, while Patrick leaped from the kitchen table and rushed to the front door. Bogie raced to the door with him, tail wagging.

With a dish towel slung over her shoulder, Merry followed her brother.

Patrick opened the door and Jayson walked into the house. Bogie barked furiously, slapping his tail against his legs in eagerness to greet him. Jayson petted him, which Bogie loved, and then Bogie dutifully returned to his bed.

Merry gasped, sucking in a deep breath.

His gaze instantly locked with hers. "Merry Christmas."

"What . . ." She fumbled with words, hardly knowing where to start. She meant to ask him what he was doing. Instead, she stood looking at him, her mouth hanging open and her voice completely lost.

He looked good, as if he'd slept like a baby, while she'd spent a miserable night staring up at the ceiling, wondering what she could have done, should have done, differently. She wanted to ask him that very question. Instead, she stood rooted to the floor, hardly able to breathe, just looking at him.

Her mother was in the recliner and woke, opening her eyes. She blinked a couple times and then smiled. "You must be Jayson Bright."

"I am." Jay stepped forward and gently took her mother's hand.

"I believe you're here for my daughter," her father said, standing to greet him.

"I am," he answered, his gaze wavering briefly away from Merry.

"He's here for me, too," Patrick insisted. "I invited him. Mom said I could."

"Mom?" Merry asked, unable to hide her surprise.

"I believe we should give Merry and Mr. Bright a few minutes alone," her mother told Patrick. "You okay with that?"

Patrick nodded, but Merry sensed his reluctance.

She retreated into the kitchen and Jayson followed her. She stood with her back against the counter, fearing her heart was in her eyes for him to read. He simply took her breath away and so she waited for him to speak first.

"You feel any different this morning?" he asked.

She swallowed against the lump in her throat. "Different about us, you mean?"

He shrugged. "I'm here to ask if you're willing to give us a shot? I want to apologize for the things I said yesterday. I wasn't thinking clearly. Here you were standing right in front me, doing your best to tell me who you were. Instead of listening, I had my eye on another woman, certain she was the one I'd been longing to meet."

"She was beautiful, and sophisticated and graceful—"

"But she wasn't you," he said, cutting her off. "You're the woman I want, Merry, and you're beautiful, both inside and out. That event planner might have been attractive, but she isn't you, and you . . . you mean the world to me."

Merry's eyes welled, but she refused to let the tears come.

"You are the most amazing woman I've ever known, Merry Knight, and I'm crazy about you and that dimple of yours."

"My dimple."

"Fell in love with it the first time I saw it."

"Oh. And when was that?"

He grinned. "I saw you eating lunch at your desk, which is . . ."

". . . against company policy," she finished for him.

"I stared you down and you didn't flinch, but that dimple appeared. Ever since that day I've wanted to kiss it in the worst way."

"That's not true."

"Maybe not then, but it is now." His grin widened. "It's out in full force right now."

She raised her hand to her cheek as if to confirm what he said.

He exhaled slowly. "After I left you at the bus stop last night, I went home to an empty, cold condo and realized something important."

"Oh."

"It was dark there even with the lamp on. Even with the

city below in full holiday display. You're the light in my life, Merry. You have my heart. When my cousin told me he was marrying Maddy, a girl we'd both known years ago, he told me he just knew that she was the one for him. He wasn't going to take a chance on losing her. At the time, I had trouble not rolling my eyes.

"I understand what he meant now. You're the one for me, Merry. I know if I let pride stand between us that it could possibly be the biggest mistake of my life, and I'm not willing to risk that. So," he said, and breathed deeply, "I'm asking if you're willing to give me another chance."

Her heart melted at his words, and despite what he said, she had trouble believing it was really her he wanted. "But . . . you saw the woman in red and you wanted her . . ."

"Wanted her? No way. I was a fool not to recognize what was right in front of my eyes. I'm so sorry about that, Merry. My name might be Bright, but until I met you I was lost in a black void. You were the one who showed me the way out of the dark. You're the one who showed me I was *in* the dark."

He stepped toward her and she met him halfway. He pulled Merry into his arms and hugged her close, as if she were the most precious gift he'd ever received. "I knew the minute I held you we were meant to be together. And those kisses we shared. Tell me you felt it, too?"

She nodded, because she, too, had experienced that sense of rightness. She felt at home in his arms.

"I knew it," he whispered and kissed her again, his mouth warm and eager over hers. Merry wrapped herself around him, holding on to him as if she never wanted to let him go.

"Mom, Mom," Patrick cried out from the hallway. "They're kissing. That's a good sign, right?"

"A very good sign," Merry heard her mother reply. "I'd say the future looks merry and bright," she said, calling out from the kitchen.

"That's funny, Mom," Patrick said, laughing.

Jayson Bright broke off the kiss and Merry smiled up at him. Leaning up on her tiptoes, she pressed her forehead against his.

"I'll never look at Christmas the same way again," he whispered close to her ear. "Not as long as I've got you in my life."

Patrick stuck his head around the corner and whispered back to his mother, "They're kissing again."

"Patrick, please," Merry warned. "Jay and I would like some privacy."

Her brother cast his gaze to the floor. "I wanted to know that Mom and I did the right thing."

"You did," she assured him, smiling up at Jayson. "You couldn't have chosen better."

"I'm the lucky one," Jayson insisted, wrapping his arms around Merry, holding her close. He kissed her again and then broke away and looked at her brother.

"Say, Patrick, could you give me a hand."

Ever eager to help, Patrick leaped up and followed Jayson outside to where he'd parked his car. Together the two of them carted in beautifully wrapped gifts to set under the tree, and then Jayson returned for a second load while Merry looked on, unable to believe her eyes.

Merry and her parents watched in stunned disbelief when Jay returned with a large box, which he set on the kitchen counter. Merry glanced inside and noticed a prime rib roast.

"I was going to invite myself to dinner," Jayson explained when she cast a curious look in his direction. "It seemed rude not to make a contribution toward the meal."

Sorting through the contents of the box, Merry noticed he'd provided an entire four-course dinner fit for royalty. "We were going to order pizza tonight . . ."

"Prime rib," her father broke in. "Merry, we're having prime rib. I think we can forgo the pizza."

"The roast is cooked and ready to eat. All that's needed is for everything to be heated."

"Jayson, oh my," Robin whispered, seemingly overwhelmed, her hands close to her mouth. "This is too much."

"I wanted to thank you and Patrick for signing Merry up on Mix & Mingle, and Bogie, too—"

"Mom, Dad, look," Patrick cried out, interrupting Jayson. Her brother sat next to the Christmas tree, crumpled Christmas wrap at his feet, holding a laptop computer. "Jayson got me my own laptop."

"Patrick, you're supposed to wait until Christmas," his father chastised.

"I know, I know, but it was a big package and it had my name on it."

"Oh Jayson," Merry whispered, her eyes clouding with tears. She knew how badly her brother wanted his own computer. "That's perfect."

He wrapped his arm around her waist as though being separated from her longer than a few minutes was too long. "The only thing that feels perfect is being with you and your family," he whispered.

"We don't need gifts as long as I've got you."

"You've got me," Jayson said. "My cousin told me I'd know when I'd found the right woman, and I do."

"I know, too," she whispered back. And she did.

THE END

Stay friends with Debbie Macomber

Join Debbie and your fellow fans online to chat and swap stories

 /DebbieMacomberWorld

@debbiemacomber

@debbiemacomber

/debbiemacombervideos

Check out Debbie's website and sign up to her newsletter for all the latest news on her books, giveaways, recipes and much more.

www.debbiemacomber.com

Did you love *Merry and Bright*?

Fancy a bit more festive fiction?

Read on for the first few chapters of Debbie's

bestselling Christmas novel

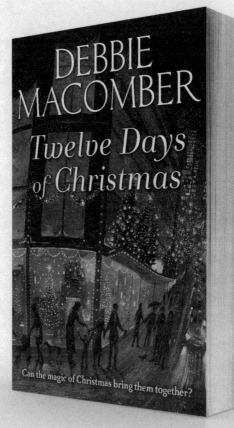

CHAPTER ONE

*

Cain Maddox stepped into the elevator, and then just as the doors were about to close he heard a woman call out.

"Hold that for me."

Cain thrust out his arm to keep the doors from sliding shut. He inwardly groaned when he saw the woman who lived across the hall come racing toward him. He kept his eyes trained straight ahead, not inviting conversation. He'd run into this particular woman several times in the last few months since he'd moved into the building. She'd stopped several times to pet Schroeder, his Irish setter. The one he'd inherited from his grandfather when Bernie had moved into the assisted-living complex. She'd chattered away, lavishing affection on the dog. Not the talkative type, Cain responded minimally to her questions. He liked her all right, but she was a bit much, over the top with that cutesy smile. Okay, he'd admit it. He found her attractive. He wasn't sure what it was about her, because usually the chirpy, happy ones didn't appeal to him. Regardless, nothing would come of it, and that suited him. He knew better. Yet every time he saw her a yellow light started flashing in his head. *Warning, warning. Danger ahead*. Cain could feel this woman was trouble the first moment he saw her and heard her exuberant "good morning." Even her name was cheerful: Julia. Looking at her, it was easy to envision the opening scene from *The Sound of Music*, with Julie Andrews twirling around, arms extended, singing, joyful, excited. Even the thought was enough to make Cain cringe. He could do happy, just not first thing in the morning.

To put it simply, he found little good about mornings, and second, he'd learned a long time ago not to trust women, especially the types who were enthusiastic and friendly. Experience had taught him well, and, having been burned once, he wasn't eager to repeat the experience.

"Thanks," she said a bit breathlessly as she floated into the elevator. Yes, floated. Her coat swirled around her as she came to stand beside him. On her coat's lapel she wore a pretty Christmas-tree pin that sparkled with jewel-tone stones. "I'm running late this morning."

Pushing the button to close the door, Cain ignored her. He didn't mean to be rude, but he wasn't up for conversation.

"Didn't I see you walking Schroeder in the dog park the other day?" she asked.

"No." He hadn't seen her. Maybe he had, but he wasn't willing to admit it.

"Really? I'm pretty sure I saw you."

He let her comment fall into empty space. Could this elevator move any slower?

Fortunately, the elevator arrived at the foyer before she could continue the conversation.

"You aren't much of a morning person, are you?" she asked as he collected his newspaper, tucked it under his arm, and headed for the door.

Julia reached for her own and followed him. Would he never shake this woman? They were welcomed by the Seattle drizzle that was part of the winter norm for the Pacific Northwest. Cain's office at the insurance company where he worked as an actuary was within easy walking distance. Julia matched her steps with his until she reached the bus stop outside the Starbucks, where, thankfully, she stopped.

"Have a good day," she called after him.

Cain would, especially now that he was free of Ms. Sunshine.

———

"Excuse me?" Julia Padden stood in the foyer of her apartment building the following morning, astonished that her neighbor would steal her newspaper while she stood directly in front of him. She braced her fist against her hip and raised both her finely shaped eyebrows at him.

Showing his displeasure, Cain Maddox turned to face her, newspaper in hand. He had to be the most unpleasant human being she'd ever met. She'd tried the friendly route and got the message. Even his dog had better manners than he did.

"I believe that newspaper is mine." Her apartment number had been clearly written with a bold Sharpie over the plastic wrapper. This was no innocent mistake. For whatever reason, Cain had taken a disliking to her. Well, fine, she could deal with that, but she wasn't about to let him walk all over her, and she wasn't going to stand idly by and let him steal from her, either.

At the sound of her voice, Cain looked up.

Irritated and more than a little annoyed, Julia thrust out her hand, palm up. "My newspaper, please."

To her astonishment, he hesitated. Oh puleese! She'd caught him red-handed in the act and he had the nerve to look irritated *at her.* How typical. Not only was he reluctant to return it, but he didn't have the common decency to look the least bit guilty. She'd say one thing about him . . . the man had nerve.

"Someone took mine," he explained, as if that gave him the right to steal hers. "Take someone else's. It doesn't matter if it's technically yours or not."

"It most certainly does; it matters to me." To prove her point, she jerked her hand at him a second time. "I am not taking someone else's newspaper and you most certainly aren't taking mine. Now give it to me."

"Okay, fine." He slapped the newspaper into her open palm, then reached over and snagged some other unsuspecting apartment owner's.

Julia's jaw sagged open. "I can't believe you did that."

He rolled his eyes, tucked the newspaper under his arm, and headed toward the revolving door, briefcase in hand.

This wasn't the first time her morning paper had mysteriously disappeared, either, and now she knew who was responsible. Not only was Cain Maddox unfriendly, he was a thief. Briefly she wondered what else he might be responsible for taking. And this close to Christmas, too, the season of goodwill and charity. Of course theft was wrong at any time of the year, but resorting to it during the holidays made it downright immoral. Apparently, her grumpy neighbor hadn't taken the spirit of Christmas to heart.

That shouldn't surprise her.

Cain and Julia often left for work close to the same time in the morning. Three times this week they'd inadvertently met at the elevator. Being a morning person and naturally cheerful, Julia always greeted him with a sunny smile and a warm "good morning." The most response she'd gotten out of him was a terse nod. Mostly he ignored her, as if he hadn't heard her speak.

Julia waited until she was on the bus before she called her best friend, Cammie Nightingale, who now lived outside of Denver. They'd attended college together. Cammie had graduated ahead of her when Julia's finances had dried up and she'd been forced to take night classes and work full-time. After seeing so many of her friends struggling to pay off student loans, Julia had opted to avoid the financial struggles. Yes, it took her longer to get her degree in communications, and no, she hadn't found the job of her dreams, but she was close, so close. Furthermore, she was debt-free. Currently she worked at Macy's department store, where she'd been employed for the last seven years.

"You won't believe what happened this morning," she said as soon as Cammie picked up. Her friend was married and had a two-year-old and a newborn.

"Hold on a minute," Cammie said.

In her irritation, Julia hadn't asked if Cammie could

talk. She waited a couple minutes before her friend picked up again.

"What's going on?"

"My disagreeable neighbor, the one I told you about, is a thief. He tried to steal my newspaper."

"He didn't?"

"I caught him red-handed, and when I confronted him and demanded he give it back he took someone else's."

"What? You're kidding me."

"No joke. Not only that, he was rude *again*." Come to think of it, he'd never been anything but unfriendly. It was men like him who put a damper on Christmas. Julia refused to let him or anyone else spoil her holidays.

"Are you talking about the guy who lives across the hall from you?"

"The very one." The more Julia thought about what he'd done, the more upset she got. Okay, so he wasn't a morning person. She could deal with that. But to steal her newspaper? That was low.

"What do you know about him?" Cammie asked.

"Nothing . . . well, other than he has a gorgeous Irish setter that he walks every morning." She'd tried being neighborly, but Cain had let it be known he wasn't interested. She'd started more than one conversation only to be subtly and not so subtly informed he took exception to small talk. After several such attempts, she got the message.

"Maybe he's shy."

Cammie possessed a generous spirit, but this time she was wrong. Anyone who'd take her newspaper without a shred of guilt wasn't shy. "I doubt it. Trust me on this. Cain Maddox isn't shy, and furthermore, he's not to be trusted."

"You don't know that."

"You're wrong. I have this gift, a sixth sense about men. This one is sinister."

Cammie's laughter filled the phone. "Sinister? Come on, Julia."

"I'm serious," she insisted. "Just what kind of man steals a newspaper? I don't know what I ever did to offend him, but he's made it more than clear he would rather kiss a snake than have anything to do with me." That bothered Julia more than she was comfortable admitting. He was kinda cute, too, in a stiff sort of way. He was tall, a good six or seven inches above her own five-foot-five frame.

His hair was dark and cut in a way that said he was a professional. The shape of his jaw indicated he had a stubborn bent, but that could be conjecture on her part, based on what she knew about him. And as best she could tell, he didn't possess a single laugh line, although he did have beautiful, clear dark chocolate eyes.

The only time she'd seen him in anything but a suit was when he was at the dog park. He wore a jacket with the name of an insurance company and logo, which she assumed he was connected to in some way, and jeans. Even then he didn't look relaxed, and he held himself away from others.

"Are you attracted to him?" Cammie asked.

"You've got to be kidding me. No way!"

"I have a feeling this is why you're thirty-one and not in a serious relationship. How long are you going to hold on to Dylan, Julia?"

"That again?" Julia didn't have time for relationships and she for sure wasn't going to drag Dylan into the conversation. She was over him and had been for a long time. The problem was she had no time to date, between working and volunteering at church and for the Boys and Girls Club. Cammie knew that.

Besides, she had more important matters on her mind. The blog. The challenge.

She'd gone through two intense interviews at Harvestware, a major software company, and the list had been narrowed down to two people. Because the job was in social media, the company had suggested a competition between the two candidates in the form of a blog. The one who could generate the largest following in the month of December would be awarded the job.

Julia had gladly accepted the challenge. Unfortunately, she hadn't had a lot of success so far; her following was minimal at best. This was her chance to prove herself.

"Maybe your neighbor is the man of your dreams."

"Cain Maddox? He's cold, Cammie. You haven't seen him. I have. Trust me—he's not the kind of man you'd want to meet in a dark alley."

The more Julia thought about it, the more convinced she became that her neighbor was some disreputable character. A chill went down her spine just thinking about the cold look in his eyes.

Cammie laughed out loud. "Your creative imagination is getting away from you, my friend."

"Maybe, but I doubt it."

"Julia," her friend said in that calm way of hers that suggested Julia was overreacting. "He took your newspaper; he didn't threaten to bury you in concrete."

"It's the look in his eyes, like he sees straight through people."

"You've noticed his eyes?"

"Yes, they're brown and dark. Really dark and distant." Okay, Cammie was probably right. To see him in criminal terms was a bit of a stretch, but Julia wasn't exactly having warm, cozy feelings toward her neighbor.

"If that's the case, then I think you should kill him," Cammie suggested.

Julia gasped. She couldn't believe her bestie would even hint at such a thing.

"Kill him with kindness," Cammie elaborated.

"This guy needs a whole lot more than kindness." Leave it to her tenderhearted friend to suggest something sweet and good.

"It's twelve days until Christmas," she added after a moment, sounding excited.

"Yes. So?"

"This is it, Julia. You've been wanting an idea that would generate interest in your blog. Your neighbor is the perfect subject." Cammie seemed to be growing more enthused by the second. "Weren't you saying just the other day how you were desperate for an over-the-top idea?"

"Well, yes, but . . ."

"This is perfect," Cammie continued. "Kill him with kindness on your blog and report your progress for the next twelve days."

Julia wasn't keen on this. The less exposure to Cain Maddox she had, the better. "I don't know . . ."

"The countdown is sure to attract attention to your blog. All you need to do is to be kind to him. You're naturally friendly and funny. This guy won't know what hit him. And then you can document what happens on your blog. Mark my words, readers will love this."

"Did you even hear what I said?" Julia reminded her friend. "I can tell you right now kindness isn't going to affect him one way or the other."

"You won't know until you try."

Julia bit down on her lower lip as visions of winning that highly paid position swirled in her head. Maybe Cammie was right. Maybe this idea would be just what she needed to generate a following that would show off her communication and writing skills.

"I think people are responding to my blog about Christmas decorations."

"Julia, do you have any idea how many people blog about making homemade tree ornaments? You're no Martha Stewart. You need something fresh and fun. A subject that will pique interest, something different—and frankly, wreathmaking isn't it."

Surely there was a better way to tackle this challenge. Showing kindness to someone she disliked wouldn't be easy. In addition, she sincerely doubted it would make any difference. The man was annoying, disagreeable, and stubborn.

"You aren't saying anything," Cammie said, interrupting her thoughts. "Which, from experience, I know is a good sign. You're actually considering doing this, aren't you?"

Bouncing her index finger against her mouth, Julia said, "I suppose killing him with kindness is worth a try."

"It totally is. And you can title your blog 'Twelve Days of Christmas.' "

Truthfully, Julia wasn't convinced this would work.

Cammie had no reservations, though. "It could inspire an entire movement."

"I'll give it some thought."

"Good. Gotta scoot. Scottie's eating the cat's food again."

Julia smiled as she disconnected, picturing the toddler eagerly stuffing cat food into his mouth while his mother was sidetracked on the phone. Cammie was a great ideas person, and Julia appreciated her friend's insight.

Bottom line: Julia didn't know how much longer she could hold out working in menswear at Macy's. The holidays were the most challenging. Her hours were long and she was required to work in the wee hours of the morning on Black Friday, which meant she hadn't been able to fly home for Thanksgiving.

Spending time with her family over Christmas looked to be a bust, too. Her parents would have been happy to pay for her airfare, but at thirty-one, Julia didn't feel she should rely on them to pick up the expense. Besides, she had commitments.

As her church's pianist, she was needed to accompany the choir. The talented singing group had scheduled a few special appearances, the last of which was coming up this weekend. She was grateful her boss had agreed to let her schedule her hours around those obligations. In addition,

Julia was a volunteer for the holiday program at the Boys and Girls Club.

The bus continued to plug along as her thoughts spun with ideas. Julia gazed out the window, admiring the lights and the window displays along the short route that would take her to the very heart of downtown Seattle. She really did love the holidays. It was a special time of year.

Maybe she could treat Cain Maddox's surly mood with extra doses of nice. It would be an interesting test of the power of kindness. As a bonus, she wouldn't need to stress about content for her blog. She would simply be reporting the results. Easy-peasy.

But being impulsive had gotten her into trouble before, and so Julia decided to mull it over before making a final decision.

By the time she returned to her apartment that evening, it was dark and miserable, with drizzling rain and heavy traffic. Her feet hurt and she was exhausted. These long holiday hours at the store were killers.

Killers. Hmm . . . her mind automatically went to her neighbor. Killing him with kindness. It was a shame that Cain Maddox was such a killjoy.

Not wanting to fuss with dinner, she heated a can of soup and ate it with her feet propped up in front of the television. She caught the last of the local news broadcast. The weatherman forecasted more drizzle.

In the mood for something to lift her spirits, she turned off the television and reached for her phone. A little music was sure to do that. Besides, it would be good to familiarize herself with the songs for the performance coming up this weekend. Scrolling down her playlist, she chose a few classic Christmas carols, the ones the senior citizens seemed to enjoy the most at the choir's last performance at an assisted-living complex.

Julia sang along with the music as she washed the few dishes she'd dirtied and tidied her apartment. Music had always soothed her. She sang loudly through her personal favorites: "Silent Night." "O Little Town of Bethlehem." "It Came upon a Midnight Clear."

She was just about to belt out "Joy to the World" when someone pounded against her door. The knock was sharp and impatient. Determined.

Oh dear. Julia hoped her singing hadn't disturbed anyone.

She opened the door wearing an apologetic smile and was confronted by her nemesis from across the hall. Cain Maddox. She should have known.

His eyes snapped with irritation.

"What can I do for you?" she asked, doing her best to remain pleasant.

He continued to glare at her, his scowl darkening his already shady eyes. It was a shame, too—he was an attractive man, or he could be if he wasn't constantly frowning. She noticed he had a high forehead above a shapely mouth. Her father claimed a high forehead was a sign of intelligence, which was ridiculous. The only reason he said that was because his forehead was high. The thought caused her to smile.

"Is anyone dying in here? Because that's what it sounds like."

Holding her temper was a challenge. "Are you referring to my singing?"

"Tone. It. Down."

Not please, not thank you, just a demand.

With one hand still on her apartment door, Julia met his stare. "It's music. Christmas music, to be precise."

"I know what it is," he said with a groan, and briefly slammed his eyes shut.

"Would I be wrong to suggest that a kind, gentle soul such as yourself objects to a few classic Christmas carols?" she asked, ever so sweetly. Her words flowed like warm honey.

He glared at her as if she'd spoken in a foreign language. "All I ask is that you cut the racket."

"Please," she supplied.

"Please what?"

"Please cut the noise," she said with the warmest of smiles, fake as it was.

"Whatever." Cain shook his head as if he found her both irritating and ridiculous. She searched for a witty retort but couldn't think of anything cutting enough to put him in his place.

Before she could respond, Cain returned to his own apartment and slammed the door.

"Well, well," Julia muttered under her breath as she closed her own door. Perhaps Cammie was right. This man desperately needed help, and she was just the woman to see to it.

She'd kill him with kindness if it was the last thing she ever did.

Inspired now, she took out her laptop and sat down on the sofa. Making herself comfortable, she stretched out her legs, crossing her ankles. Booting up her computer, she went to her blog and saw that only fifty people had logged in to read her latest post. So far her efforts weren't going to impress anyone. Most of those who read her blog were family and friends. The solitary comment had come from her mother.

Julia's fingers settled over the keyboard, and she typed away.

Julia's Blog

December 14

Meet Ebenezer

I'm wondering if anyone else has encountered a genuine curmudgeon this Christmas season? The reason I ask is because I believe Ebenezer Scrooge lives in my apartment building. To be fair, he hasn't shared his views on Christmas with me personally. One look and I can tell this guy doesn't possess a single ounce of holiday spirit. He just so happens to live directly across the hallway from me, so I've run into him on more than one occasion. To put it mildly, he's not a happy man.

Just this morning I discovered he was something else:

A thief.

I caught him pilfering my newspaper. Really, does it get much lower than that? Well, as a matter of fact, it does. This evening, not more than a few minutes ago, I was confronted by said neighbor demanding that I turn down the Christmas "racket." I happened to be singing. He claimed it sounded like someone was dying.

When I complained about him to a friend—and, okay, I'll admit I was pretty ticked off at the time—it came to me that this coldhearted "neighbor" is a living, breathing Scrooge.

My friend, who is near and dear to my heart, suggested *I kill him with kindness.*

So, my friends, I hope you'll join me in this little experiment. I fully intend to kill my surly neighbor with the love, joy, and fun of Christmas. Naturally, I will keep his identity confidential, referring to him only as Ebenezer.

I'm not exactly sure where to start. If you have thoughts or suggestions, please share them below. I'll be updating this blog every day until Christmas. Hopefully, by then, this Grinch's heart will have grown a few sizes.

My expectations are low.

I'm not convinced kindness can change a person.

We'll find out together.

I welcome your comments and ideas . . .

To be continued . . .

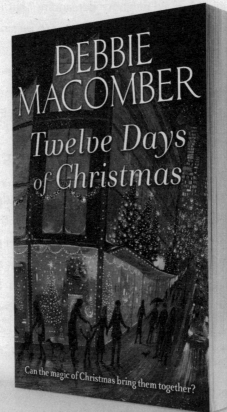

THE BRAND NEW NOVEL

Any Dream Will Do

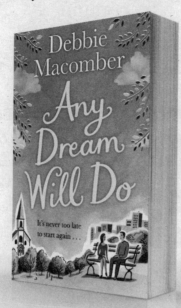

Shay Benson adored her younger brother. She tried to keep Caden on the straight and narrow, but one day her best intentions got her into the worst trouble of her life.

Drew Douglas adored his wife. But, since losing Katie, all he could do was focus on their two beautiful children; everything else came a distant second.

Shay and Drew are each in need of a fresh start, and when they meet by chance it's an unexpected blessing for them both. Drew helps Shay get back on her feet, and she reignites his sense of purpose.

But, when a devastating secret is uncovered, Shay and Drew's new lives are threatened. It will take all of their strength, faith and trust to protect the bright future they dream of.

Available to buy in paperback and ebook

A best friend is there for you

Spring

Spring is full of Blossom Street and New Beginnings

Winter

Curl up with a Christmas classic

Discover your next Debbie Macomber

through all the seasons

Summer

Spend the summer a world away . . .

ROSE HARBOR

The Inn at Rose Harbor
Rose Harbor in Bloom
Love Letters
Silver Linings
Sweet Tomorrows

A ONE OFF

Any Dream Will Do

Autumn

These Rose Harbor ebook short stories
are the perfect mini break

When First They Met
Lost and Found in Cedar Cove
Falling for Her

———————————————

Meet friends you'll call family

Dashing Through the Snow

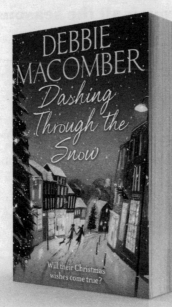

— This Christmas will be full of surprises…

All that **Ashley** wants for Christmas is to get home to surprise her widowed mother. But all the flights are booked and there's only one car left to hire.

Dash is in a hurry. Newly demobbed from the army, he has an interview to attend, and he's determined to get the job. If getting there means sharing a car with the extremely talkative Ashley, then that's what he'll have to do.

The last thing either of them expected was that they may begin to like each other…

Available to buy in paperback and ebook

Mr. Miracle

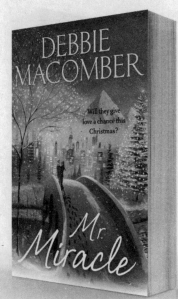

Harry Mills is a guardian angel on a mission: help **Addie Folsom** to get her life back on track – and help her find love.

Creating a happy ending for Addie and her neighbour Erich doesn't seem like much of a challenge. But soon after arriving in the town of Tocoma, Harry realises he might need some guidance. Addie and Erich can't stand each other: growing up he was popular and outgoing, while she was rebellious and headstrong. Addie would now rather avoid Erich entirely, especially at Christmas.

Harry is going to need all the help he can get, and a bit of divine inspiration, to help Addie and Erich find their Christmas miracle.

Available to buy in paperback and ebook

Starry Night

Carrie Slayton, a big-city society- page columnist, longs to write more serious news stories. So her editor hands her a challenge first: Carrie must score the paper for an interview with **Finn Dalton**, the notoriously reclusive author.

Living in the Alaskan wilderness, Finn has written a bestselling book about surviving in the wild. But he declines to speak to anyone, and no one knows exactly where he lives. With her career at stake, Carrie sacrifices her family celebrations and flies out to snowy Alaska.

When she finally finds Finn, she discovers a man both more charismatic and more stubborn than she expected. And soon Carrie is torn between pursuing a story of a lifetime and following her heart.

Available to buy in paperback and ebook

Starting Now

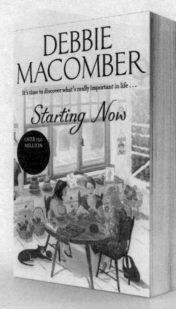

Libby Morgan has sacrificed everything for her career as a lawyer – friends, marriage, her chance of a family. Until, after years of hard work, the unthinkable happens, and suddenly Libby must rebuild her life … starting now.

With no job in sight, Libby spends her afternoons at A Good Yarn, the local knitting store. There she forms a close bond with the sweet-natured shop owner; and with **Ava**, a shy and troubled teenager who needs her in ways Libby could not have expected. She even finds time for romance with a handsome doctor.

But just as her life is coming together, Libby risks losing everything she holds most dear.

Available to buy in paperback and ebook

Blossom Street Brides

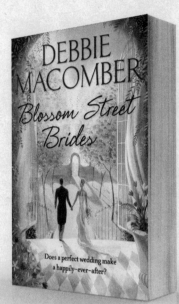

Lydia is blissfully happy in her marriage, but worrying about her adoptive daughter and the future of her business.

Bethanne is still madly in love with her husband, but their long-distance relationship is becoming difficult, and her ex-husband is determined to win her back.

Lauren has always yearned for marriage and a family, but her long-term boyfriend just won't commit. Could a whirlwind romance with an unlikely stranger lead to the happily-ever-after she's always dreamed of?

These three women meet in their local knitting store, and as their lives intersect in unexpected ways, they realise that the best surprises in life and love still lie ahead.

Available to buy in paperback and ebook

Last One Home

Twelve years ago, **Cassie Carter** chose the wrong man, and one fateful event drove three sisters apart. Now, hoping to leave her past behind, Cassie has returned to Washington with her daughter. Though her sisters don't live too far away, she doesn't expect to see them.

Karen, the oldest, is a busy wife and mother, balancing her career with raising two children. And **Nichole**, the youngest, is a stay-at-home mum whose husband indulges her every whim. But one day, Cassie receives a letter from Karen, offering the hope of reconciliation.

As Cassie opens herself up to new possibilities – making amends with her sisters, finding love once more – she realises the power of compassion, and the promise of a fresh start.

Available to buy in paperback and ebook

A Girl's Guide to Moving On

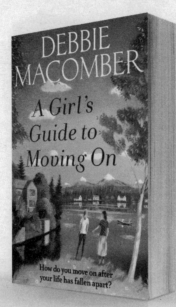

When **Leanne** and her daughter-in-law **Nichole** went through divorces at the same time, they compiled a list to help them move on from the heartbreak.

Now, two years on, these unlikely best friends have managed to pick up the pieces, and love is on the cards for them both.

Leanne's friendship with Nikolai, one of her language students, has deepened into something more meaningful. And Nichole has finally allowed herself to trust a man again. Rocco is the complete opposite of her ex-husband, and though he's a little rough around the edges, he has a heart of gold.

But just when it seems they've figured it all out, life throws up more challenges, putting their hard-won contentment at risk . . .

Available to buy in paperback and ebook

If Not For You

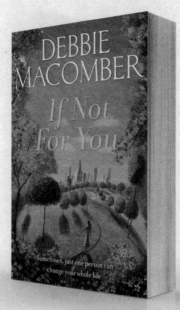

If not for her loving but controlling parents, **Beth** might never have taken charge of her life.

If not for her friend **Nichole**, Beth would never have met Sam Carney – a tattooed mechanic who is her conservative parents' worst nightmare.

And if not for **Sam** – who witnessed a terrible accident and rushed to her aid – Beth might never have survived and fallen in love.

Yet there are skeletons in Sam's closet that prevent him from ever trusting a woman again. Will he be able to overcome his past and fight for love?

Available to buy in paperback and ebook

The Inn at Rose Harbor

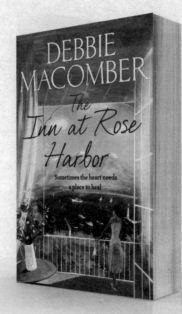

The Rose Harbor Inn welcomes you to Cedar Cove…

From the minute she sees Rose Harbor Inn, **Jo Marie** knows that this is the place that will help her find the peace she craves. And if the inn can comfort her, surely it can offer the same refuge to her first two guests.

Joshua has come home to care for his ailing stepfather. The two have never seen eye to eye, but a long- lost acquaintance proves to him that forgiveness is not out of reach and love can bloom in the unlikeliest places.

Abby left Cedar Cove twenty years ago after a devastating accident. But as she reconnects with family and old friends, she realises that she needs to let the past go if she is to embrace her future.

Available to buy in paperback and ebook

Rose Harbor in Bloom

Jo Marie has started to feel at home running the Rose Harbor Inn. And while she still seeks a sense of closure after losing her beloved husband, she welcomes her latest guests . . .

Annie arrives in town to organise her grandparents' fiftieth wedding anniversary celebration. But she's struggling to move on from her broken engagement.

Mary has achieved success in business, but illness has led her to face her sole regret in life. Almost nineteen years ago, she ended her relationship with her true love, George, and now she has returned to Cedar Cove to make amends.

Together, the women discover that sometimes you have to travel far from home to find the place where you really belong.

Available to buy in paperback and ebook

Love Letters

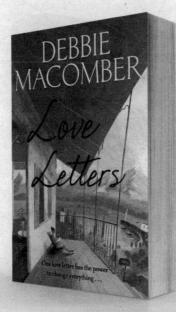

Ellie travels to Rose Harbor to meet a man she's been writing to, but he reveals a secret that makes her question their relationship.

Maggie and her husband have grown apart. Can a love letter from long ago help them to find the spark they have lost?

And **Jo Marie** finds the courage to revisit the last letter her husband sent her before he was killed in Afghanistan, and for the first time is able to see the future ahead of her.

Once again, the Rose Harbor Inn proves to be a place of comfort and healing as the women find that these letters could change the course of their lives forever.

Available to buy in paperback and ebook

Silver Linings

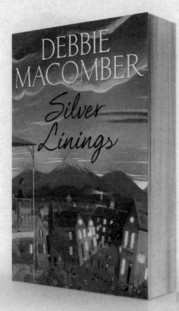

Even the darkest cloud has a silver lining…

Since opening the Rose Harbor Inn, **Jo Marie Rose** and handyman **Mark Taylor** are becoming more than just friends, yet he still won't reveal anything about his past. Then he tells her he's moving out of town.

Coco and **Katie** have returned to Cedar Cove for their high school reunion. Coco wants to confront the boy who broke her heart, while Katie wants to reconnect with her old boyfriend – the one who got away.

As Katie hopes for a second chance, Coco starts to believe that people can change – and that the future might hold exciting possibilities for them both.

Available to buy in paperback and ebook

Sweet Tomorrows

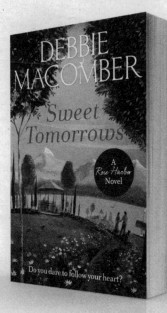

Jo Marie thought that Mark was the one – but now he's left Rose Harbor. The Rose Harbor Inn doesn't seem the same without him, but Jo Marie knows she has to move on with her life.

Emily has suffered heartbreak and is hoping that a long stay at the inn will be exactly what she needs to get her life on track again. She has no idea she is about to meet a neighbour and form an unexpected bond. The last thing she was looking for was a relationship, but is she willing to take a chance?

The Rose Harbor Inn has always been a special place of healing. Can it work its magic one more time?

Available to buy in paperback and ebook